PLAYING SPACES IN EARLY WOMEN'S DRAMA

ALISON FINDLAY

CAMBRIDGE UNIVERSITY PRESS
Cambridge, New York, Melbourne, Madrid, Cape Town, Singapore, São Paulo, Delhi

Cambridge University Press
The Edinburgh Building, Cambridge CB2 8RU, UK

Published in the United States of America by Cambridge University Press, New York

www.cambridge.org
Information on this title: www.cambridge.org/9780521105293

First published 2006
This digitally printed version 2009

A catalogue record for this publication is available from the British Library

ISBN 978-0-521-83956-3 hardback
ISBN 978-0-521-10529-3 paperback

For David,
who makes the best playing spaces

Contents

Illustrations

Acknowledgements

This book has turned into a much bigger project than I originally intended and has taken me to some unfamiliar places so there are many people I need to thank. My sincere gratitude goes to the Arts and Humanities Research Board and Lancaster University who funded research leave over 2003–4. The staff of Lancaster University Library have supported me magnificently by responding to my varied requests. In particular, I wish to thank David Barron, Jenny Brine and Ken Harrison. My individual research is founded on a bedrock of support and inspiration from colleagues in the Department of English and Creative Writing, so heartfelt thanks are due here. Richard Dutton helped me to formulate ideas for the book during his final year in the Department. Hilary Hinds has gone above and beyond the call of duty in reading through drafts and encouraging me to strengthen the arguments of the chapters. I offer her warm thanks for being such a great scholar and friend throughout the writing process. In chapter 4, my study of convent drama led me to 'strange / Unknown ways and paths to tread', as Climeana says in *Love's Victory*. I thank Meg Twycross, Professor Emeritus at Lancaster for her judicious guidance as I ventured into the world of liturgical drama. My thanks extend to medieval scholars beyond Lancaster, namely Jocelyn Wogan-Brown, Roberta Gilchrist, and Margaret Pappano, who responded enthusiastically to the queries of a novice in the field. I owe a special debt of gratitude to Elissa B. Weaver who corrected some errors of translation in Antonia Pulci's plays for me. I thank her and look forward to her forthcoming translation with pleasure. I also thank Peter Davidson and Julie Sanders for sharing their work on the Tixall family papers, and Margaret Hannay and Naomi J. Miller for commenting wisely on chapter drafts of my material. I wish to acknowledge and thank all those who aided my archival research. The staff of the Kent Archive Office were unfailingly helpful, and Mr Stuart Bligh of the Dean and Chapter of Canterbury Cathedral produced excellent digital photographs. Special thanks are due to Viscount De L'Isle for kindly agreeing to let me reproduce the *Survey of Penshurst* in his private collection and to Sir Reresby Sitwell for granting me permission to reproduce the sketch of Bolsover Abbey's fountain garden. For generously sharing their work on Apethorpe Hall and the Cavendish Houses, I thank Emily Cole and Lucy Worsley of English Heritage. Staff at the National Monuments Record and James Mitchell at the National Library of Scotland kindly helped me locate images for reproduction. Finally, I offer humble thanks to my children, Robert and Eleanor and, most of all, to my husband David. They have made space for me to research and write, even though this has meant the loss of playing spaces. No one could ask more of a family.

Introduction

Henri Lefebvre, probably the most enigmatic and intriguing analyst of spatial practice, argues that 'space is at once result and cause, product and producer; it is also a *stake*, the locus of projects and actions deployed as part of specific strategies, and hence also the object of *wagers* on the future – wagers which are articulated, if never completely'.[1] Lefebvre's model for reading space identifies it as a liminal zone between past and future, hence temporal as well as topographical. It is Janus-faced: constituted as an expression of existing power structures and simultaneously constituting the potential for challenging those structures. At any specific moment, space is the product or result of given cultural practice, the means by which one is assigned a place. The interests of particular groups are represented in such spatial configurations while the interests of others are disadvantaged. Space is the grid that commands bodies, prescribes and proscribes movements and gestures. At the same time, and in contrast, space is a producer of change, the vehicle through which alternative futures can be explored. It is a movement from one's given place, a field where strategic investment in a different spatial and cultural practice can be enacted. Space is therefore a gamble: the investment of agency is staked or risked in order to produce a future that will re-place the individual to his or her advantage.

The playing spaces of early women's drama, which I explore in this book, exemplify the paradox of restriction and possibility identified by Lefebvre. The venues where women composed and performed drama can be read in terms of the grid of spatial practices that framed their minds and bodies according to a set of values that privileged their male counterparts. The title page of Brathwait's *English Gentlewoman* (1631) (Figure 1), shows how the virtuous woman was ideologically and physically produced in a series of clearly bounded arenas. Decency, for example, 'accommodates her selfe to the *place* wherein she lives'.[2] Female script-writers and actors likewise worked from the prescriptions and

Figure 1. Title page of Richard Brathwait's *The English Gentlewoman* (1631), 4° B.25. Art. [*By permission of The Bodleian Library, University of Oxford*].

proscriptions of the various sites in which they were placed by patriarchal society. Their drama was given concrete boundaries, both physical and cultural, by the venues in which it was created. Nevertheless, drama superimposes a fictional setting onto the venue of one's given place. Setting, the second type of playing space I explore, is not limited in the same way as venue. Imaginative and physical freedom offers opportunities for playing with space. Settings can therefore be read in relation to new modes of spatial practice enacted by female playwrights and performers to critically re-mobilise the existing structures of which they were a product.

To engage actively as producers of spatial practice was, as Lefebvre recognises, a strategic investment and a risk. For women playwrights and performers, drama was a wager of their intellectual and physical endeavour that usually involved risks to their reputations. By producing plays they entered a space that was 'at once result and cause, product and producer'. The relationship between venues and settings is thus a crucial nexus for the study of women's agency. The deployment of space in early women's drama both before and after the Restoration was strategic; it was, in Lefebvre's terms, a stake on which wagers for the futures of characters, authors, and womankind more generally, could be articulated. Women who chose this genre knew both the risks and the rewards. A sense of place is often a significant dimension of early modern women's writing, in the settings of poems, scenes in romances, or the real and imaginative sites evoked in religious meditations for example. However, in scripts, venue and setting are absolutely crucial determinants of meaning. Women who composed plays in preference to prose or poetry, and in spite of having no immediate public venue in which to perform before 1660, did so with a keen awareness that drama constitutes a more immediate expression of spatial practice than any other form of literature. It is a genre designed to generate, or to be exploited within, a spatial practice. As such, it provided the best expression of their ideas about woman's place, both physically and culturally. It was a vehicle through which their own spatial experiences could be translated into play, and through which they could lament, reject, criticise, celebrate and, most importantly, renegotiate their place in the world. Drama constituted a route for transforming place into space.

DRAMA, PLACE AND SPACE

Critical negotiations of the terms 'place' and 'space' are notoriously complex, sometimes even contradictory. Like a dramatic performance, any conceptual distinction between them is a matter of contested interpretation rather than straightforwardly referential. Such elasticity does, however, lend itself well to the analysis of multiple levels of signification in dramatic practice. De Certeau's definition of space '*as a practiced place*' is useful for reading drama. He distinguishes between 'place', a static location governed by the rule of the 'proper' which situates each element in a distinct position, and 'space' as the effect of active operations that intersect within a place to actualise it or mobilise it in a range of different ways. To illustrate, he offers the examples of a street designed by urban planning as a place that is transformed into a space by the practice of walkers, and the example of a written text transformed into space by the practice of reading.[3] Drama draws on both these types of practice to produce a multi-layered interaction between place and space. Its written script is a practised place, in that it spatialises (mobilises and interprets) the places of everyday life in its representations of actions within defined settings. An early modern woman who chooses to write a play is thus already *practising* place, mobilising and perhaps challenging the 'proper' positions allotted to her in a given social and physical order, through her writing. Even if the script is not produced, it remains a form of spatial practice.

At the same time, the written script is a place: it fixes boundaries around the action by allotting each element a 'proper' position, spatially and temporally, in the play, giving each a local habitation and a name. In the case of women's drama, the local habitation is, of course, a place created or authored by a woman. As such it can be radically different from its everyday equivalent, a place where the constituent elements 'emerging from their stability, transform the place where they lay motionless into the foreignness of their own space', to use De Certeau's words (p. 118). The static, given dimension of the script can be likened to his term 'region': the space determined by a particular interaction, in this case the inter-action or interlocution between the female author and the place(s) she chooses to set her play.

Performance mobilises the script in a second round of spatial practices that overlay those of the author. The presence of actors and objects on the fixed place of the stage puts all the elements of the script into polyphonic play within the ludic arena created by performance. Early modern drama thus charts the environment differently from either the story or the map. Unlike the story, it appears to limit interpretation by the choice of actors, costumes, movements, but the stage's own theatrical self-consciousness (which reminds spectators that this is a fictional performance), inevitably makes those interpretations provisional. The provisional nature of a play's interpretation of place allows it to incorporate a historical contingency or sense of 'process' that De Certeau argues is eliminated in early modern maps. He sees maps as 'a totalising stage on which elements of diverse origin are brought together to form the tableau of a "state" of knowledge', but complains that they are guilty of pushing offstage the operations of which they are the result or necessary condition 'as if into the wings' (p. 121). Early drama by women works differently. Like the map, it combines elements from a received tradition (place) and those produced by the observations of all those involved in the production, but not on 'a totalising stage' which simply presents a product. Instead, performance physically enacts the play's journey or narrative through space and time. Its spatial processes are the essence of dramatic action. Drawing attention to the operations of spatial practice can raise critical consciousness about the status quo, even if the play does not create a better alternative.

Far from converting space into place, then, early women's drama reconverts set place into active space. Its characteristic *jouissance* subverts the rules of the same by overthrowing ideas about appropriateness, reintroducing sensuality (the language of the body, the physical present). The abundant, creative playing arena offers a fluid, dynamic field with which spectators engage in the making of meanings. In particular, it transgresses boundaries. Early women's drama frequently sets out to activate flexible relationships between venues and settings, a process that raises scepticism about existing structures (physical and cultural, material and psychological).

VENUE AND SETTING

My book's concentration on venue and setting distinguishes between physical movement through space and the action of interpreting spatial orientation. I explore the venues of composition and performance as sites of physical movement through space, while the dramatic scripts are spatial interpretations of place. Fictional settings, the *mise-en-scène,* creatively interpret the sites on which they are based. The interaction between venue and setting in drama thus produces an active reproduction of space in a heightened, self-conscious way. For early modern women, the venues of composition and potential performance were the sites of lived spatial practice. Like Brathwait's English Gentlewoman, their subjectivities and dramatic outputs were constructed within the given frames of the rooms, buildings and outside arenas that they occupied. Philosophers Henri Bergson and Gaston Bachelard have argued that space is fundamental to psychological and emotional existence, that the very structure of our mind is tied to locality.[4] *Playing Spaces* takes that idea as a starting point to treat venue in a broad sense as the place of literary and imagined production. In so doing, I argue that the places where the dramatists lived and wrote are embedded in the texts and that the plays often draw on those surroundings for dramatic effect. The power of memory and its topophilic manifestation, as theorised by Bachelard, is used to read Margaret Cavendish's play *The Religious*, for example. Brief information about architecture, furnishings, location is presented as a context for reading the plays. Thus, the gardens at Nonsuch and its banqueting house are explored as venues that, almost invisibly, become the settings for Jane Lumley's translation of *Iphigenia*. I argue that Jane Cavendish and Elizabeth Brackley's *Pastorall*, discussed in chapter 2, makes active use of Bolsover Castle, one of the family estates, for its effects.

I believe it is important to think of early women's plays as coterie dramas, texts that are specifically 'placed' in that they depend on a particular venue and community of spectators for their effects. Theatre is a social event where spectators and actors are participants, so I draw attention to the relationships between them in cases like royal entertainments, where information is easily recoverable and is obviously a vital element of the theatrical occasion. In addition, I endeavour to construct some potential 'audiences' for communal readings or household performances by examining the social circles within which the writers moved, such as in my analysis of Mary Sidney Herbert's *Tragedie of Antonie* and the literary circle which made up part of her extended household. It is important to remember that reading could be a communal, social activity as well as a solitary one.[5] Lady Mary Wroth's *Urania* describes a room in which Princess Dalina has been reading aloud to her gentlewomen while they sew, while Margaret Cavendish reported her husband's and Ben Jonson's skill in play reading.[6]

Considering the effects of performance in such venues is an important way to restore a spatial dimension to the plays. In many cases, the venues are the dramatists' aristocratic households; the chapters on 'Homes' and 'Gardens' argue my conviction that the plays have been written with those specific venues in mind. In the case of female performances in court theatricals, venues are much easier to establish. The effects generated by the architecture of buildings like Hampton Court and the Stuart Banqueting Houses or the country estates of Kenilworth or Cowdray are considered in chapter 3. The social meanings of those venues as households or theatres belonging to the King, Queen or courtier, also exert a significant influence on the dramatic effects produced there. Similarly, the architectural and cultural significance of enclosed venues such as abbeys, convents and churches is an important factor in the construction of female-centred drama, as chapter 4 examines. In the case of most post-1660 scripted drama (though significantly not the work of Margaret Cavendish), venues can be identified, and the specific construction and location of the theatres factored in as part of theatrical effects generated by women's plays.

Lines spoken or sung, movement and dance all acquire meaning through their relationships with material venues. Discussion considers how venues positioned the female performers and writers, and the ways in which those women inserted themselves into existing structures or manipulated them in their own interests. By looking at how and where drama takes place, this book also examines the appropriation of traditionally male spaces by women. In a production, a fictional text literally 'takes' place and remakes it through performance. In the process of superimposing a fictional setting onto a space demarcated for performance, it puts assumptions on trial, in the manner imagined by Lefebvre: 'Trial by space invariably reaches a dramatic moment, that moment when whatever is being tried – philosophy or religion, ideology or established knowledge, capitalism or socialism, state or community – is put radically into question' (p. 417).

The setting of a play is the other vital component in its spatial configuration. Luckily, this is much easier to establish than venue, and all early women dramatists, I would argue, are acutely sensitive to the resonances of place in their choices of setting. Hanna Scolnicov's book *Woman's Theatrical Space* argues that the changing spatial conventions in drama, such as indoor and outside scenes, doorways and window scenes are 'faithful expressions of the growing awareness of the specificity of gender differences and the changing attitudes to woman and her sexuality'.[7] Her study is mainly confined to male-authored drama but provides some excellent starting points for analysing early plays by women. Here, we have evidence that the overarching fictional worlds, the scenic division of space into specific locations by means of inclusion and exclusion, and the physical dimension of pivotal moments in the drama are carefully constructed through the scripts. Settings are often intrinsically linked to genre, so the discussion of, for example, rural scenes in the drama of Rachel Fane or Cavendish and Brackley involves an examination of their use of pastoral. Similarly, the city dramas of Elizabeth Polwhele, Aphra Behn and Mary Pix are particular engagements with the conventions of Restoration comedy, although detailed examinations of genre are beyond my scope here.

PERFORMANCE AND SPATIAL PRACTICE

My book's aim to explore the spatial dimension of early women's drama is, like that drama, characterised by strategic risk. Although space is the most crucial dimension of theatre, its deployment by early women has received relatively little attention.[8] Important work on masques and post-Restoration drama, where we are lucky to have material traces of performance, has been undertaken. Designs, eye-witness accounts, and records of the buildings used as venues allow us partially to reconstruct the ephemeral theatrical occasions fashioned by women. Clare McManus's *Women on the Renaissance Stage* and many of the fine essays in *Women and Culture at the Court of the Stuart Queens* have successfully identified examples of female agency in the construction of court entertainments. Paula Backscheider's *Spectacular Politics* deftly analyses the theatrical quality of the Restoration court and its relationship to professional drama to which women contributed, while studies of Aphra Behn use evidence about playhouses and performers to reveal her expertise as a theatrical craftswoman.[9]

It is much more difficult to construct theatre histories for other entertainments penned or performed by female hands, bodies and voices from the medieval period to the Restoration. All the information about any possible production is contained within the texts themselves. The lack of substantial external evidence for contemporary performance has led critics to envisage different kinds of dramatic production, from the extremes of private composition and solitary, silent reading to fully realised household theatricals. Katherine Acheson has argued that women's closet drama exhibits a resistance to performance, an 'anti-theatricality' shared by female protagonists who refuse to perform or do so only reluctantly.[10] Karen Raber's comparative study of plays by men and women reads closet drama as the writerly product of a literary elite that comments on theatrical practice rather than enacting it. Closet drama is, she argues, 'drama that does *not* function as theater'. Her carefully nuanced analysis of the relationships between class, gender and genre sees 'this classical style of nontheatrical drama' as a site in which women could examine what it means to have a voice in Renaissance English culture. Raber links closet drama to the printed dialogue and recitation of pastoral verse in eclogues, arguing that the different dramatic personae in these forms allowed women to 'represent the self' through heightened or consciously produced modes of speech in opposition to the multi-vocality of theatre.[11]

Marta Straznicky's *Privacy, Playreading and Women's Closet Drama* focuses differently on the practices of reading and the mediums of manuscript circulation and print, to propose that women's dramatic writing moves strategically between so-called public and private realms, frequently engaging with a public arena while apparently retreating from it. Women's decision to write closet drama is not, she argues, a symptom of their exclusion from a privileged, public stage, but a tactical manoeuvre that licensed particular forms of engagement with the social and economic politics of the public arena.[12] In this sense, the closet is both a closed and a subversively open space; anything produced there (written, spoken or acted) is beyond the censorship of the Revels and therefore uncontainable. The illusion is easily maintained in cases where scripts remain in manuscript copies, as in the case of Lady Mary Wroth's *Love's Victory* for example. When copies of a woman's play appeared in print, however, as with Lady Mary Sidney's translation of Garnier's *Tragedy of Antonie* or Elizabeth Cary's *Tragedy of Mariam,* its author could avoid public censure only by insisting that her play was not performed on the public stage.

Straznicky usefully points out that a culture of private dramatic production does not necessarily oppose performance, since play reading and courtly or academic stages are all venues belonging to an elite, private culture. Even silent reading invokes imaginative constructions of performance, including spatial practice.[13] A preface to Margaret Cavendish's 1662 collection of *Playes*, for example, tells her readers that 'they must not read a Scene as they would read a Chapter; for Scenes must be read as if they were spoke or Acted'. When read skilfully, 'the very sound of the Voice that enters through the Ears, doth present the Actions to the Eyes of the Fancy as lively as if it were really Acted'.[14] Here, stage space is constructed imaginatively by any reader to establish a perspective from which s/he can view the fictional world represented and simultaneously assess its relationship to his/her own world. Closet plays are not opposed to theatricality *per se.* That they *can* be performed has certainly been established through practice in the case of several scripts.[15] The Women and Dramatic Production project that I co-directed with Stephanie Hodgson-Wright and Gweno Williams demonstrated the multi-dimensional quality of early dramas penned by women. The idea that such texts were never intended for performance has now been rendered questionable.

We have thus reached a new critical frontier. To argue the performability of early women's drama is insufficient, but to move ahead and try to put such plays in their place as theatre, we must enter unknown territory. We cannot access material traces of any original productions so, inevitably, any attempt to construct or reconstruct theatrical realisations of these plays is highly speculative. Crossing that frontier is, like Lefebvre's definition of space itself, a gamble, a wager to create a place from which to develop new critical understandings of early women's drama. This book's study of venues and settings constitutes a strategic attempt to fill the spaces of performance that are in some cases blank and in others sketched in through scraps of material evidence. By focusing particularly on the relationship between venues and settings I hope to open up the playing spaces *for* women's drama as determinants of meaning and to show how women played *with* space in scripts and performances as a form of political intervention.

The interaction between setting and venue is the crucible in which dramatic spatial practice is forged. What different effects are created when a prison scene is played in an aristocratic household (as in Cary's *The Tragedy of Mariam*), and on the stage of a professional theatre (as in Polwhele's *The Frolicks*), for example? How does the representation of supernatural deities change when they move from a purpose-built Banqueting House to the hallway of an aristocratic household? To answer questions like these that preoccupy my book throughout, we need an analysis of theatre space that accounts for its complex, multi-layered quality. Lefebvre's categorisation of space includes, alongside 'spatial practice', two other modes that are appropriate to reading the interactions between lived, perceived and conceived space in theatre.

First, he defines 'Representations of space' as the abstract codes and signs which are conceived to impose an 'order' on space. These are the models of planners and social engineers, intellectually formulated through systems of signs, that dominate our perceptions of the world around us. Second, he defines 'Representational' or symbolic space, which is sometimes coded, sometimes not, as 'space as directly *lived* through its associated images and symbols'. Closely connected to the realm of art, and taking its source from individual and communal histories, 'it overlays physical space, making symbolic use of its objects'.[16] Representational spaces are those local anchors for our psychological and emotional being, such as bedrooms, dwellings, houses, tunnels, holes, passages, labyrinths, churches. They are the places fetishised in order to fill the spaces of lack. Using Lefebvre's terms, I will argue that a performance space is both a representation of space (a critical, creative intervention into spatial texture which imposes an order) and a representational space, lived through its associations and images. It is, moreover, a space that is produced to be read and lived, at least temporarily, by the spectators and the actors. Participants read the stage with a dual consciousness; theatre is both truth (live bodies in a real place) and fiction, so they can appreciate a performance on two levels: spectators live it passively and critique it actively; actors live more actively and read more passively. Although he never discusses theatre in any detail, Lefebvre does appreciate that it is composed of 'an interplay between fictions and real counterparts' and an 'interaction between gazes and mirages in which actor, audience, "characters", text and author all come together but never become one'. This space is neither simply 'a representation of space or a representational space' but both.[17] By investigating the rich inter-textuality of spatial practices invoked in selected scripts this book aims to deepen our understanding of early women's drama.

Bakhtin's work on the chronotope, although it relates to the novel, can be usefully adapted to develop the interaction between fictional and real counterparts in theatrical space identified by Lefebvre, particularly as these occur through time. Having established the chronotope as the 'primary means for materializing time in space,' Bakhtin goes on to explain a complex exchange between the 'real, unitary' world of readers, performers and listeners (those united in the venue), and the '*represented* world in the text' (conjured by the settings). The shared world of a group of women united behind the walls of a convent or a Queen's court, for example, is a very distinctive real and unitary place of performance. Such venues interact with the given settings in the represented world of a play in complex ways. Bakhtin begins by arguing that although the active engagement of the former chronotope (the venue) with the latter (the setting) is necessary to create the latter and endow it with meaning, these chronotopes coexist in dialogical fashion without disturbing the relationships contained within each. However, he goes on to admit that the line between the represented world and the actual world is permeable. Each enters the other as part of a process of mutual renewal. This leads him to identify a 'special *creative* chronotope' in which the exchange happens, 'which constitutes the distinctive life of the work'. The theatrical occasion is the dramatic version of Bakhtin's creative chronotope, a distinctive, unique space of play in which setting and venue mutually inform and re-form each other.[18]

Anne Ubersfeld has written eloquently about the relationship between fictional and social space in theatre, pointing out that presentation of place on stage necessarily incorporates into the fictional space a transposition of the image held by any particular group of spectators of social and spatial relationships in the society in which they live.[19] In effect, the arrangement of a performance space in a production (for example, a tomb), constitutes a commentary on the nature of the place (for example, a household), as experienced by a group (for example, seventeenth-century aristocratic women). This includes sensitivity to the cultural history of a place: for example, the household converted from a former abbey. As the following chapters show, the relationship between venue and setting in women's drama frequently builds on the interaction of layers of perceptions to create striking dramatic effects. Theatre's peculiar ability to encompass different, even contradictory, elements gives it a liminal quality. As Gay McAuley astutely observes, the stage is, like the fetish, a place of 'thirdness' suspended between binary oppositions, like reality and illusion, absence and presence, and constantly undermining them. This makes it an intrinsically subversive place. Like the fool's cap and bauble, however, its ludic nature always masks its disturbing truths in the form of play, thus 'allowing the spectator to access normally suppressed levels of consciousness'.[20] This has obvious advantages for early modern women, writing at a time in which the position and patterns of behaviour assigned to each gender were sanctioned from scripture as well as secular tradition and law.

Within the safe boundaries of theatrical play, dramatic text allowed women to cross conventional boundaries, enacting those transgressions in imagination or in practice, and, thus, enabling them to supersede the limitations of their own signifying practices through action. The constitution of a dramatic selfhood, as character, performer or author, was a way in which a new wholeness, or subjectivity, could be created. Lefebvre asks for a holistic history of space that 'must account for both representational spaces and representations of space, but above all for their interrelationships and their links with social practice'.[21] *Playing Spaces* endeavours to construct such a history of early women's drama. The chapters are arranged thematically, devoted to five key spaces, but there is a logical chronological development through each and in the overall structure, with the first four chapters addressing drama before 1660 and the final one considering plays written for professional stages in the city.

The opening chapter, 'Homes', considers how noblewomen's plays use spatial effects to demonstrate their alienation from aspects of the patriarchal household, and to remake it as a place to call home. Translations and original plays by Mary Sidney Herbert, Elizabeth Cary and Rachel Fane are discussed here as spatial rather than verbal critiques of women's place in the household, an approach that differs from previous studies. The relationship between the great house and the State was often analogical so the interrogation of a household hierarchy in these plays frequently commented on the gendered divisions of private and public space. Women's managerial roles, including their artistic control of domestic settings, can be read as political interventions into the public arena. Changes in the meaning of the country house, from feudal community to fashionable commodity, and social changes wrought by the English Civil War opened new opportunities to women writing or producing plays at home, as I explore in discussion of entertainments by the women of the Cavendish family.

The following chapter moves outwards to consider different religious and social meanings of the garden, exploring the extent to which natural settings offer more freedom to female characters and writers. With reference to the writers' country estates, it suggests how open-air stagings of their entertainments could have contributed to that liberty. Readings of Mary Sidney's pastoral dialogue, Elizabeth Russell's entertainment for Queen Elizabeth, and Lady Rachel Fane's 'Christmas Entertainment' in relation to her home Apethorpe Hall, demonstrate how drama can politically renegotiate the relationship between the country house and surrounding garden, and woman's position within that geographical and cultural landscape. The pastoral setting of Lady Mary Wroth's *Love's Victory* is read in relation to both interior and exterior locations at Penshurst to examine its feminist rewriting of arcadian retreat. The garden took on extra significance during the Civil War as a green sanctuary, or lost paradise for royalists. Lady Jane Cavendish and Lady Elizabeth Brackley's *Pastorall* (1645) combines the political dimension with religious and personal resonances, and is discussed as a peripatetic entertainment which draws specifically on the enclosed gardens at Bolsover to achieve its effects.

Chapter 3 takes a new approach to court performances via the buildings occupied by the royal households. It discusses the ways in which these palaces offered women powerful stages for the production of dramatic writing and performances. By way of introduction, it contrasts the Scottish and English courts and the dramatic activities of Mary Stuart and Elizabeth I, including her scrap of translation of Seneca's *Hercules Oetaeus*. Since masque performances have already been the subject of considerable critical analyses, this shorter chapter focuses on selected examples to argue that the theatrical production of space was a means whereby the Stuart queens negotiated their positions as consorts. The chapter discusses female performers appropriating male-created spaces such as the Great Hall at Hampton Court (*Vision of the Twelve Goddesses*) and the Banqueting Houses at Whitehall (the masques of *Blackness, Beauty, Tethys Festival* and *Chloridia,* for example). It examines how fragile but spectacular manifestations of female subjectivity could be produced in such venues.

It also asks how much control women exercised over artistic space by positioning themselves in relation to the monarch through costumes and extravagant settings that seemed to offer a panoramic landscape for the participants. Somerset House is read as an alternative, female-centred playing space; a venue of innovation, especially under Henrietta Maria's control. The Queen's palace was an important theatre through which the consorts established their courts as distinctive, feminine commonwealths.

A more complete spatial withdrawal is examined in chapter 4, 'Sororities', which focuses on how female communities provide alternative spaces for the development of performance. It discusses the appeal of dramatic representations of female 'companies': company as a source of shared experience, education and visions, and playing companies of female performers. It argues that the convent is an important trope of female community, reading it as a real but lost place in Britain. Unlike the rest of the book, this chapter looks further back to the past in order to recover the tradition of female performance in convents, arguing for the importance of tracing continuities between medieval and early modern women's drama. It discusses the Easter liturgical dramas of Wilton Abbey and Barking Abbey in which the nuns were key participants, the development of convent theatre on the continent after its disappearance from post-Reformation Britain, and briefly analyses the adept spatial practice of the Italian dramatist, Adriana Pulci. The legacy of convent sororal culture is then traced in the establishment of substitute female sororities in England. The dramatic representations of convents and female academies, and the threats they posed, are discussed in entertainments from the courts of Catholic Queens Anna and Henrietta Maria, and in the plays of Margaret Cavendish. The educational dimension of the sorority is examined in analyses of *Cupid's Banishment* (1617) presented by pupils from the Ladies Hall Deptford to Queen Anna, through to Margaret Cavendish's *The Female Academy.* Henrietta Maria's promotion of a religious Catholic sodality is, I argue, refracted through the spatial dynamics of her masques and entertainments. Cavendish's *Youth's Pleasure and Death's Banquet* and *The Convent of Pleasure* are both read as troubled rewritings of the cloister as woman-centred utopia.

The final chapter discusses the placing of women's drama in the city from 1660 to 1705, using a selection of plays by Polwhele, Behn, Pix, and Centlivre and those presented under the pseudonyms 'Marcelia' and 'Ariadne'. There is, comparatively speaking, a wealth of drama by women in this period including texts with classical, rural, exotic and palatial settings, written for a range of venues.[22] Writers such as Anne Wharton and Anne Finch distanced their plays very publicly from the commercial stages. Restoration court drama involving the Queen, princesses and prominent members of the aristocracy continued to flourish. The final chapter of *Playing Spaces* takes a very selective approach. It begins by considering the expansion of court influence into the Town (a fashionable area between the City Walls and the palaces of Westminster) in post-Restoration London, and the development of theatre architecture from perspective scenery used in court entertainments. This context is used to open up the dramatisation of a new relationship between the court and the city in the court settings of early female-authored drama. Thereafter, the chapter discusses plays with city settings composed for the professional theatres owned by Duke's Company and King's Company. This selection of women's scripts does, admittedly, threaten to perpetuate limited perceptions of Restoration drama as city comedy. However, in line with the book's overarching aim, the plays have been chosen to provide the richest source of material for studying constructions of the city by early women dramatists.

London after the Great Fire was a paradoxical space both old and new, bounded by intensely patriarchal structures and yet porous to individual practices which deconstructed them. The theatres and their location in fashionable areas of the Town were part of this paradox. Commercial theatre, with its self-selecting audience, was a completely new type of venue for women writers and performers and the plays register the pressures and opportunities offered here. The chapter does not attempt a detailed analysis of the work of professional actresses such as Nell Gwyn or Mrs Betterton, or a re-analysis of the actress's significance following from the fine work of Elizabeth Howe. Instead, examples of scenes from plays across the period show how women dramatists became increasingly confident in playing with the stage space and the power of the actress to control the audience and critically re-evaluate woman as commodity.

The paradoxical nature of the city as prison and opportunity is amply exploited in the detailed urban geography of women's plays. Behn's *Sir Patient Fancy,* for example, sets up a deliberate opposition between enclosed household scenes and the open space of the city. Female characters who traverse the streets are read using De Certeau's model, as rewriting the city by participating in its busy commercial and cultural exchanges. The many opportunities created by the carnivalesque metropolis are reflected in exotic city settings as in Behn's *The Rover.* The settings of parks and taverns as places of exchange demonstrate that these places can allow women cultural as well as physical movement. Cavendish's

The Sociable Companions explores how women can use performance to penetrate even the male body of London's civic institutions. The dangers of being consumed by the city's commercial values are played out in Susannah Centlivre's plays. Consideration of *The Basset-Table* and *The Gamester* reminds us of the limitations to women's physical and cultural movement within the city.

The chapters that follow therefore represent my endeavour to reconstruct five different types of playing space, and to interrogate the particular opportunities and limitations of each for women who produced drama. To demonstrate the meanings generated by setting and venue I offer a brief examination of the cultural significance of each place, and how this links to its theatrical potential, before moving on to readings of the scripts. Most plays are discussed in just one chapter although references across draw comparisons of likeness as well as difference. Because the meanings of each place are distinctive and produce special effects of their own, the chapters can be read as self-contained units. However, the richness of spatial signification deepens when understood in the context of other settings and venues: the routes not taken. I hope that by journeying from homes to gardens, courts, sororities and cities, the reader will be able to build up a sense of early women writers composing scripts as sophisticated forms of spatial practice. By appreciating their production of theatrical space we can begin to understand their work as drama. We can sketch in some plausible theatre histories onto what is currently a blank space; politicially, we can recognise settings and venues as crucial sites for re-negotiating woman's place.

CHAPTER I

Homes

Dod and Cleaver's *Godly Form of Household Government* says the virtuous wife is 'a good *home-keeper*', whose loving husband 'cannot so well like the sight of any tapestry as to see his wife in his house'.[1] In addition to objectifying woman as furniture, the text's definition of wifely virtue in terms of home-keeping demarcates space in typically gendered terms: men abroad, women within walls. Luce Irigaray has argued that the domestic sphere is not 'home' for woman at all, but a male attempt to recreate his foetal dwelling place:

From the depths of earth to the vast expanse of heaven, time and time again he robs femininity of the tissue or texture of her spatiality. In exchange, though it never is one, he buys her a house, shuts her up in it, and places limits on her that are the counterpart of the place without limits where he unwittingly leaves her. He envelops her within these walls while he envelops himself and his things in her flesh.[2]

Irigaray's view that woman has no place of her own in the patriarchal household offers an appropriate, if controversial, starting point for testing the proxemics at work in early women's plays. The aristocratic household offered a privileged space for a small elite of noblewomen with wealth, leisure and education, to compose drama.[3] The great house is the venue where their scripts were conceived and written, and it is the most likely space for performance, although whether these texts were realised in production at their time of writing remains, in the majority of cases, a matter for speculation. Even in the absence of any concrete evidence for a performance, it is logical to suppose that the scripts of figures such as Mary Sidney Herbert, Elizabeth Cary, Jane Cavendish and Elizabeth Brackley were informed by the spatial practices of their family estates. An examination of relationships between the domestic venue and the ludic space created by a fictional performance raises questions about Irigaray's proposal that woman is robbed of the 'tissue or texture of her spatiality' in the home. The walls of the household necessarily impose limits on any performance, but do the material substances and spatial practices within those walls operate solely for the benefit of their male owner? To what extent does the fictional zone created by the script re-appropriate domestic space in the interests of women? Can we read drama as a reclaiming of their material environments, their own substance, texture, or 'flesh'?

Unsurprisingly, the great house frequently features as a setting in plays by aristocratic women writers. Here, architecture and architecture as scenography are even more closely interwoven than in the case of professional drama in companies like Shakespeare's. In private theatricals, the house becomes a stage on which actors perform in a fictional setting, but the venue is simultaneously a social space in which authors and actors live. With no access to stages at the Globe or the Blackfriars, women's plays appropriate the household usually assigned to the sex and recreate it dramatically to offer critical commentary on that arena. Early drama by women may be initially confined to the household but it frequently enacts what Martin and Mohanty define as a move from 'being home', where one lives within familiar, safe boundaries, to 'not being home' which 'is a matter of realizing that home was an illusion of coherence and safety based on the exclusion of specific histories of oppression and resistance, the repression of differences even within oneself'.[4] Women's drama frequently enacts such a move in consciousness, reaching beyond the familiar and familial to ask searching questions about woman's place. In this sense, plays located in the home have the ability to move beyond the walls, questioning the limits and boundaries they impose. Plays offer a more positive version of Irigaray's view of home as 'the counterpart of the place without limits where he unwittingly leaves her'.

The great household, however solid its walls, was poised on foundations of ambiguity. Many great houses, such as Wilton, home of Mary Sidney Herbert, were created after the Dissolution of the monasteries. On the one hand, they looked back to monastic traditions of hospitality and nurture. The royal patent granting Wilton and its neighbouring farms to the first Earl of Pembroke in 1543 insisted that the scholars and Provost of King's College Cambridge should continue to enjoy rights to grazing and supplies of wood, crops, fruit and cheese that they held under the Abbess before the Dissolution.[5] On the other hand, the building of country houses from monastic wealth marked a shift away from spiritual community towards secular individual ownership. Joseph Hall's poem *Virgidemiarum* (*c.* 1599) satirises the death of good housekeeping at Clarendon Park, blaming the second Earl of Pembroke and Mary Sidney

Herbert for daring to raise a house which 'Strives for a Court and for a College name'. While the monastery had granted tithes to King's College, this new elitist academy is unwelcoming. The chimneys 'which should be / The wind-pipes of good hospitality' are full of swallows' nests and the house is haunted by images of hunger while the landlord revels in the city.[6] Hall's satire conjures up a sense of emptiness but private ownership did not take the great household out of the public arena. Paradoxically, in spite of being a family residence, including enclosed apartments, it was still a comparatively public space occupied by many more people than the owner's immediate kinfolk. Its metaphorical configuration as a microcosm of the State gave it another public dimension. Kari Boyd McBride has pointed out that the country estate constituted an ideal hierarchical community presided over by the paternal landlord and working co-operatively to promote comfortable self-sufficiency. Country house discourse 'provided the script, set and cast for the performance of legitimacy'.[7] Thus, although the aristocratic lords bowed to the absolute authority of the monarch, that monarch's authority relied absolutely on the hierarchical structures of the great house. Thomas Bilson called the private family 'both a part and pattern of the commonwealth', while Thomas Smith's 1589 book *The Commonwealth of England* noted that 'the house or family is the first and most natural (but private) appearance of one of the best kinds of a commonwealth, that is called *Aristocratia*, where a few, and the best, do govern'.[8] The great household is a classic example of Lefebvre's notion of social space as both a product and a means of production. Its fixed hierarchy, in which all occupy a proper place, is intrinsically linked to its use value as a means to reproduce and sustain the State and superstructures of society.[9] The household was a physical manifestation of legitimacy through its exact disposition of people and objects.

Woman's position was governed by the same paradoxical dynamic that operated between lords and governor. The husband ruled with absolute authority within the home but relied absolutely on the reproductive work of his lady, in terms of biological reproduction of children, the material production of necessities (food and drink) that she managed, and the ideological reproduction of social values in the education of those in her care. Each new generation learned their place through their incorporation within the household. The noble lady's responsibility for the estate was, of course, particularly visible during the frequent absences of her husband. As well as attending Court, he might be called upon to manage matters of State, as in the case of Pembroke who was Lord President of the Council of the Marches of Wales. He might travel on the continent to develop a public persona, as did Sir Henry Cary, leaving his Berkhamstead estate and young wife Elizabeth in the care of his mother. In the extreme circumstances of the English Civil War women such as Jane Cavendish were left to manage and defend the houses of their menfolk. As men ranged abroad to establish their identity in the emergent capitalist world, the household became an increasingly female space towards the end of the sixteenth century and beyond.[10] This had consequences for both sexes. The potential for isolation and insecurity on the part of ladies living on country estates was obviously exacerbated by the difficulties of travel and communication. For men, the need to distance oneself from the home created insecurities about the household space: what had been nurturing became potentially suffocating.

Dramatic representations produced from within the household are invariably loaded with the tensions produced by this social context. In addition, as 'home' the household site is charged with a range of deep, often conflicting, personal emotions. It can be a safe haven and a place of imprisonment, a memory, a utopian longing and a site of violence. 'Home' is supposedly a place of origin and a point of return, a place of belonging, comfort and permanence, a destination to which one is guided by instinct. Of the places examined in this book, the household is the most overdetermined by psychological needs and conflicts. Elizabeth Grosz's work on women, *chora* and dwelling is therefore useful to gain insight into the emotional resonances of women's plays set or produced within the household. Drawing on the concept of *chora* proposed by Plato's *Timaeus,* and its interpretation by Kristeva and Derrida, Grosz defines *chora* as the 'space where place is made possible', a site whose attributes carry feminine associations with pregnancy and maternity. Although the *chora* has been understood in relation to the foundation and annihilation of the individualised speaking subject, Grosz seeks to re-evaluate it in spatial terms, using Irigaray's work to focus on the need to establish a viable 'dwelling' space and time, a home, for women.[11]

Irigaray's critique of Western philosophy argues that masculine modes of thought have suppressed the *chora's* connection with maternal space and female corporeality, the home from which all subjects emerge. The result is a gendered divide whereby women become 'the living represen-tatives of corporeality, of domesticity, of the natural order that men have had to expel from their own self-representations', in order to become self-determining subjects.[12] The women left as receptacles for the materiality discarded by men do not experience their own bodies or households as home: 'I was your house. And, when you leave, abandoning this dwelling place, I do not know what to do with these walls of mine', Irigaray's female speaker complains. Women have become psychologically exiled from the places they inhabit, trapped in an endless cycle of domestic production and reproduction in which the self is erased in favour of the affirmation of others: 'How can I find my way back? There are no doors, no windows in this shell of air. I am there, and yet in exile. I have become your exile.'[13]

Although the *chora* is distinct from the material world, I want to argue that dramatic space, as invoked by a script or realised in a performance, can revivify the household by returning it to a fuller maternal, corporeal presence which looks back to the *chora*. Drama thus has the potential to re-establish the household, albeit temporarily, as a viable home for women. Through domestic settings or performance a woman's play can recreate an indeterminate, ludic space like the *chora*:

It is the space that engenders without possessing, that nurtures without require-
ments of its own, that receives without giving, and that gives without receiving,
a space that evades all characterizations including the disconcerting logic of
identity, of hierarchy, of being, the regulation of order.[14]

The play text, and the fictive world invoked by any reading or performance are protective boundaries that create a free space for the nurturance of ideas and actions that have their origin in female creativity. Rules are suspended and licence to experiment is given freely. The carnivalesque quality of play-ing space dissolves social boundaries. Drama is, like the *chora*, an incubator in which new worldly forms, new places and identities for women can be engendered, brought into material existence, however briefly. It is a safe space to remake the household as home.

The creation of safe space to compose and perform is not just a female activity. The elite noblewomen who produced closet drama did so within households where paternal and fraternal encouragement was just as im-portant as the models of creativity presented by female relatives. The male relatives of Jane Lumley, Mary Sidney Herbert and Mary Wroth, Elizabeth Cary, Rachel Fane, Jane Cavendish, Elizabeth Brackley and Margaret Cavendish were all instrumental in constructing protective cultural and material frameworks around their households to nurture female creativity. Following on from Margaret Ezell's essay re-contextualising the woman writer as part of a familial network of literary collaboration, Marion Wynne-Davies's work establishes a crucial link between the provision of 'safe houses' and the development of female authorship across the sixteenth and seventeenth centuries.[15] The enduring example of humanist education in the extended family of Thomas More can be traced through to the Lumley, Sidney and Cavendish households. William Cavendish's encouragement of all his children to 'write but what you think' suggests that his daughters Jane and Elizabeth were brought up to think of themselves as domestic wits rather than exclusively as housewives.[16] The heroine Luceny in their play *The Concealed Fancies* (c. 1645) confidently proclaims 'We have been brought up in the creation of good languages, which will make us ever ourselves.'[17]

Doreen Massey reminds us that 'the identity of any place, including that place called home, is in one sense for ever open to contestation' and that 'that lack of fixity has always been so'.[18] Early modern women's closet drama frequently puts the household into play. Re-framing the domestic environment in fictional space, either by representing it in a household setting, or imposing a different setting onto a household venue, allows the plays to comment self-consciously on woman's contradictory position there. Such self-reflexivity likens it to Lefebvre's concept of abstract space which, by underpinning production and reproduction through successive recasting of social space, appears to generate false consciousness (and acceptance of a dominant homogeneity), but simultaneously can 'give rise, by virtue of a critical moment, to a clearer consciousness' which contradicts the establishment of a dominated space.[19] Critical consciousness is frequently evoked by these early texts by unsettling assumptions about the ownership of space.

TRAGIC DEMARCATION: *THE TRAGEDIE OF ANTONIE*

Mary Sidney Herbert's translation *The Tragedie of Antonie* (1591) displays the paradoxes of the household as both public and private, woman's position as both mistress and prisoner, and the tragic consequences of a gendered demarcation of space as described by Irigaray.[20] Its faithful translation of Robert Garnier's *Marc-Antonie* appears to be the iteration of a patriarchal perspective on woman, yet it also has the capacity to create a 'critical moment' in which a contradictory, subversive consciousness about woman's position can be realised. Indeed, the printed texts of 1592 and 1595 are 'publications' of Mary Sidney Herbert that transgress the domestic boundaries for women's activities. Her translation is also an intervention into national politics since it implicitly advises Queen Elizabeth to defend the Protestant spirit of her kingdom, in whose cause Philip Sidney had died.[21] Alongside the printed texts' public dimension, the translation is simultaneously marked by its particular moment and place of production. The local context of any translation shapes its meaning as Trill points out.[22] By endeavouring to reconstruct the social and material context of the Pembroke household we can explore how Mary Sidney Herbert translated a male-authored text into a woman's place.

How the play was realised in a private or communal reading or in a household performance is unknown. It is notable, however, that the script cites performance as a mode of celebration and mourning. Caesar says of Cleopatra's household 'Their time they pass'd in nought but loves and plaies' (1401). After Antonie's death, Cleopatra should build a tomb 'And yearly plaies to his praise institute' to 'Honor his memorie' (621–2). Mary Ellen Lamb has argued persuasively that *Antonie* may have been part of Mary's mourning process for her brother Philip and her mother.[23] Katherine Acheson has criticised the play's lack of stage 'depth', its 'neglect of three-dimensional space', and certainly much of *Antonie's* dramatic energy derives from its verbal power: the variation of sound and rhythm in long speeches by the protagonists, punctuated by heated exchanges with their servants or companions.[24]

Nevertheless, evidence of a tradition of reading and performance in the Pembroke household offers a suggestive framework on which to construct a new analysis of *Antonie* that acknowledges its powerful spatial effects. Margaret Hannay draws attention to the Sidney and Pembroke families' longstanding patronage of stageable drama, and her objection that a stageable *Antonie* 'would have taxed the resources of the Wilton Household' can be answered if we imagine a small coterie production drawing on clothes and objects from the household itself.[25] A rehearsed reading of the play at Hoghton Tower began to explore the possibilities of primarily oral performance.[26] Abraham Fraunce's *The Arcadian Rhetoricke* (1588), dedicated to Mary Sidney Herbert, may have provided a model for a production of *Antonie*. Fraunce recommends the learning of speeches from the *Arcadia* to demonstrate the use of voice and gesture, pointing out that 'the practise and exercise is all in all . . . oftentimes use to pronounce the same in such order and with as great a head as if thou wert in some great assemblie'.[27] Since he frequently selects the speeches of female characters (Gynecia as an example of 'furious voyce' (H4v) or Philoclea as modest gesture in 'the holding downe of the head and casting downe of the eyes' (J4)), we can assume that these directions are for female speakers as much as male. In *Antonie* Cleopatra seems to follow Fraunce's recommendations on rhetoric and manual gesture. Her expertise in 'training speache' to 'consorte' with fingers allows her to debate on equal terms with sceptered kings and ambassadors (728–32).

Even if we exclude the possibility of movement, a communal reading in one of the Countess of Pembroke's houses would provide a three-dimensional quality to the play. Most strikingly, its emotional power in Act 5 seems to rely on the physical presence of Cleopatra's children. Although they only speak four words, their silence is eloquent, evoking Cleopatra's agonised conflict until they exit with their tutor Euphron (1895). The household community, including the Countess's gentle-women, her children, and Hugh Sanford or possibly Daniel as their tutor, would have made an ideal group of readers for the play.

Works dedicated to the Countess suggest a culture of shared storytelling rooted firmly on the Pembroke estate. At the end of Part II of Fraunce's *The Countess of Pembroke's Ivychurch* (1591), for example, *Pembrokiana* (the Countess) commands her nymphs and shepherds to meet in mourning for Amyntas's death and tell stories in his memory (L1v–L2). This 'probably had a basis in a real gathering', as Lamb suggests, Ivychurch being Mary's favourite family house.[28] The *Third Part of the Countess of Pembroke's Ivychurch* (1592) and Moffett's *The Silkworms and their Flies* (1599) construct an educated coterie, accustomed, as readers or listeners, to the classical allusions in *Antonie*. Instead of the myth of a dramatic circle patronised by the Countess, we should think of a more intimate circle composed of the ladies who moved with Mary from Wilton to the properties at Ivychurch and Ramsbury (where *Antonie* was completed); members of the household like Gervase Babington, the family chaplain, and Moffett, the physician; and select guests, such as the lawyer Abraham Fraunce, a protégé of Sir Philip Sidney. Attending to the social composition of the household and the architectural places of literary production reveals the translation's capacity to realise a series of 'critical moments' where the play's conventional pronouncements about gender are disrupted.

The Tragedy of Antonie follows gender norms in the rigid distinction of male and female realms. Its definition of masculine achievement, as articulated by the Romans, is predicated on a public world of action. Caesar boasts he is 'Equall to Jove' (1380), the lord of fortune: 'As Monarch I both world and *Rome* commaund; / Do all, can all' (377–8). Absolute individualism and military dominance are the measure of male success. In a reading or performance at Wilton, the play's superficial celebration of the force of arms would be silently reinforced by the venue since military glory was literally engraved into the household. Aubrey notes that there was an impressive armoury at Wilton, and that the Earl of Pembroke, who was fascinated by heraldry, 'did set up all the painted glasse scutchions about the house. Many a brave souldier, no doubt, was here obliged by his Lordship.'[29]

Running counter to this aggressive Protestant militarism are textual observations translated from Garnier, and a non-verbal, domestic subtext through which Mary Sidney Herbert weaves in her own critical perspective on the masculine ideal. More than a Protestant intervention into the public arena, *Antonie* constitutes a radical critique of a way of life which privileges public, masculine competition over feminine values of nurture and community. Agrippa cautions the boastful Caesar that a Prince who fosters the love of the people makes for stronger government. Here the text seems to promote more feminine rule, based on nurture. This is entirely appropriate to a household drama since it reminds Queen Elizabeth that her power rests on a network of support including the legitimising authority of the aristocratic country house.[30]

Even the victorious Roman soldiers are ashamed of a conquest where 'madd Impietie' impelled them to attack 'the place us bredd', the places of nurture which should be home (1741–6). The self-destructive tendency implicit in a Protestant military ideal would have been powerfully resonant in any performance of the lines in rooms once frequented by Philip Sidney. As if speaking out against the stained-glass windows, the Egyptian Chorus seriously question the permanence of masculine achievements, imagining that time will 'to humble ashes turne / Thy proud wealth' and 'those guilt roofes' and turrets (845). (In fact, Wilton was ruined by fire in 1647.) In contrast to the architecture, the Chorus voice a living emotional legacy of loss, complaining that 'Warre and warres bitter cheare / Now long time with us staie' (231–2). This echoes the grief of the bereaved women in Mary's translation of Psalm 78. It is possible that the Choruses in *Antonie*, with their distinctive verse form, were designed to be chanted or sung like the Psalms.

Written from and for a domestic arena, *Antonie* enacts the breakup of the household at the end of the sixteenth century, in which the husband is forced abroad and the wife becomes mistress in his absence. Antonie and Cleopatra are both sacrificed to the gendered divide observed by Irigaray, where women embody the rejected domesticity, materiality and natural order that men have had to exorcise from their own self-representations in order to construct themselves as self-determining subjects. The destructive psychological effects of the division are the tragedies of the hero and heroine, who occupy separate spheres throughout the play. They never speak directly to each other, and are only physically together after Antonie's death in Act 5, so the text reproduces their enforced separation in spatial and verbal terms.

Antonie's tragedy dramatises the husband's separation from the home, showing how emotional needs are thwarted by an overwhelming sense of shame. His fear of betrayal by Cleopatra masks a deeper sense of self-betrayal, a loss of masculine selfhood in the domestic space. Antonie's military 'glory' is 'gone in smoke' (65), to be replaced by a fear of confinement. He sees himself 'Cag'd'; 'scarce maister of thy selfe / Late maister of so many nations' (129–31). Antonie's disgust at having 'Falne from a souldior to a Chamberer / Careles of vertue, careles of all praise' (1163–4), seems to devalue the household space. Pleasure, in the sensual comforts of home, is a recipe for disaster: loss of reason, military command, reputation and identity (1168). The hearth and the oven, 'a circular, closed and fixed space', returns masculine identity to the terrifying site of womb and tomb to be annihilated by primary comfort.[31]

As a chamberer – a courtier – in Cleopatra's palace, Antonie has realised the mythical history of his ancestor Hercules who became part of a female community of carding and spinning. Antony's loyal friend Lucillius ruefully recalls Hercules' shameful effeminisation:

> Spinning at distaffe, and, with sinewy hand
> Winding on spindles threde, in maid's attire.
> He conqu'ring clubbe at rest on wal did hang;
> His bow unstringd he bent not as he us'de;
> Upon his shafts the weaving spiders spunne;
> And his hard cloak the fretting moths did pierce.
> The monsters, free and fearless all the time,
> Throughout the world the people did torment,
> And more and more increasing daie by day
> Scorn'd his weake heart, become a mistress' play. (358–68)

In spite of such judgements, Mary Sidney Herbert's *Antonie* does not present the feminine domain as a devalued dwelling place that women cannot identify with. In the context of a household performance, these lines take on extra resonance. As well as imitating his ancestor, Antonie the character has literally become a mistress's play – part of a mistress's text – in Mary's translation and any possible performance at Ramsbury or Wilton. The mighty soldier of public action is enclosed within the feminine space, the *chora* of a mistress's play.

The three-dimensional context of the Countess's household materialises the subversive gender reversal by presenting a busy feminine industry in the production of textiles and, of course, texts. Accounts for the Pembroke estate include items for spinning and weaving and the Countess would have supervised her women's 'work' – the production, decoration and maintenance of fabrics.[32] Many writings by Mary and those in her circle link textiles and texts. Her dedication of the *Psalms* to Queen Elizabeth describes Philip and herself weaving the translation: 'But he did warp, I weaved this web to end; / The stuff not ours, our work no curious thing.'[33] John Taylor's *The Needles Excellency* (1634) praised the Countess's skill in making hangings for the walls at Wilton, which Aubrey described as 'admirable workes in Arras framed'.[34] They were probably produced corporately with her ladies, while they were entertained by reading or singing. Mary's niece, Lady Mary Wroth, depicts a typical scene of aristocratic female creativity in the *Urania*, where Parselius finds Princess Dalina and her ladies 'at worke'. Having passed through a 'brave roome richly hang'd with hangings of Needle-worke', he passes into a smaller presence chamber:

Her Ladies who attended her, were a little distant from her in a faire compasse Window, where also stood a Chaire, wherein it seemed she had been sitting . . . In that Chaire lay a Booke, the Ladies were all at worke; so as it shewed, she read while they wrought.[35]

If we consider the possibility that Mary Sidney's 'work' *Antonie* was read or performed to accompany her women's needlework, the play's material context significantly affects the status of its hero. Antonie's passivity, the emptiness of his boasting about foreign victories, and his view that in Cleopatra's palace time is 'abus'd' (1251) are made more ironic. When the Countess laid down the needle to take up the pen and weave her own meanings into Garnier's text, translation functioned like a pattern in embroidery, allowing her to work a new sense into the material.[36] She translated the male text into the female household whose setting and venue enact the gender reversal described in the history of Hercules. Male values (in the men's lines) are overborne by a hive of female activities: sewing, reading, writing.[37]

Cleopatra is mistress of the domestic space. Even though Caesar's forces invade Egypt, she remains a powerful, self-controlling figure. Members of her household point out her responsibilities to others – her servants, her children, her ancestors, the Egyptian population – and the play stages her amongst these living dependants. Their demands echo the Countess's own responsibilities: for smooth running of the Pembroke estates; to her two sons and her daughter Anne; and to the Sidney family's literary heritage in the preparation of her brother's writings for publication.

Nevertheless, domestic production offers only a limited arena to women. The manuscript of Mary's translation of Psalm 68 acknowledges this (its unorthodox viewpoint probably explains why she altered it for publication). In verse 12, her dislike of a gendered division between public and private spaces finds expression in the lines 'Wee house-confinèd maids with distaffs share the spoyle / Whose hew though long at home the chimneys glosse did foyle.'[38] Women are confined to the hearth and discoloured by domestic drudgery. As Hannay remarks, the translation asks to be read as a plea for an enlarged space for women.[39] In the play, domestic confinement fosters emotional insecurities for Cleopatra, manifested as jealousy of Octavia, Antonie's wife. Mary's original *Argument* to the play makes it clear that Octavia is wronged (14–15), yet maintains sympathy for Cleopatra, who is cast in a wifely role.

The translation opens a window to examine the problems faced by aristocratic ladies confined in the country while their husbands experienced the busy social life of the Court. *Antonie* demonstrates that it is a no-win situation for women: their physical restriction destines them to suffer personal insecurities and jealousies in competitive opposition to other women. By celebrating Cleopatra's unfailing loyalty, as Lamb has argued, the play provides women with a model to 'acknowledge the heroism of their ordinary lives' in a culture that endorsed double standards on sexual infidelity.[40] Indeed, *Antonie* seems to have initiated further literary representations of female heroism. Samuel Brandon's closet drama *The Vertuous Octavia* (1598), accompanied by a series of letters between Octavia and Antonie, and Samuel Daniel's 'A Letter from Octavia to Marcus Antonius', both elaborate on the plight of deserted wives and both were dedicated to women with immediate experience of marital unhappiness.[41]

The play further complicates the issue of female heroism by showing that Cleopatra's dedication to Antonie cannot be reconciled with her duties to her family, dynasty and kingdom:

> *Ch.* Our first affection to our selfe is due.
> *Cl.* He is my selfe. *Ch.* Next it extendes unto
> Our children, frends, and to our countrie soile.
> And you for some respect of wivelie love,
> (Albee scarce wivelie) loose your native land,
> Your children, frends, and (which is more) your life. (594–9)

Cleopatra must choose death to prove her constancy, but Charmian's critique exposes the illogicality, tragedy and the expensive consequences of female self-sacrifice. Cleopatra's controlling power over her family, community and country makes the tragedy of her death social rather than individual: loss of security for the next generation and the kingdom. The children become sacrifices, signifying the death of the community's future. Under a system which privileges deadly masculine competition above the nurturing qualities of the home, they can only live a diminished life within the household, no matter what their gender. Instead of sceptres they must 'learne t'endure' a future where they bear 'crooked shepehookes' or 'needles or forkes, to guide the carte or plough' (1883–6). These lines would have had a chilling frisson, spoken in the presence of Mary's children William (aged 10), Anne (aged 7) and Philip (aged 6) within the walls of the manor house at Ramsbury, where Mary Sidney dated the manuscript.

Ramsbury was a smaller residence than Wilton (for Elizabeth I's proposed visit in August 1599 a series of tents were planned to accommodate the Court), so if the play was shared with an audience or readership here, its imagery of confinement would have been striking. This comes to a climax in the death scenes. Here, Mary Sidney Herbert's translation of Garnier's text creates a playing space to transcend the negative effects of a gendered division which leaves women with a hollow sense of misbelonging in the empty shells of their own bodies or households. Her translation replaces the abandoned dwelling place with a fuller image of the *chora* as a maternal playing space where boundaries, identities and gender differences are annihilated.

Antonie's suicide, which is explicitly domestic, is an entirely fitting climax to his confinement. Its details seem to invoke local surroundings to lend immediacy. Directus reports that

> . . . he his bodie piers'd; and of redd bloud
> A gushing fountaine all the chamber fill'd.
> He staggered at the blowe, his face grew pale,
> And on a couche all feeble downe he fell . . . (1625–8)

When Cleopatra draws him in through a window to her tomb, she realises the masculine nightmare of being immured and annihilated in 'darke horrors dwelling place' (1588). In contrast, her wish 'to have one tombe with thee' (Antonie) (421) may be read socially as an atavistic desire to return to the state where husband and wife were incorporated within the idealised household community, or psychologically as a homecoming to the utopian *chora* of fullness where both sexes co-habit equally.

Just as the *chora,* by virtue of its infinite adaptability and openness, is beyond representation, so the utopian climax imagined by Cleopatra is beyond the limits of the text or performance. Her suicide is a struggle to reach it, to transcend the empty house and body that have become like sepulchres. She closes her first scene with the words 'Meane season let us this sadd tombe enclose, / Attending here till death conclude our woes' (694–5). These lines are eerie, defining the household as a tomb for the living. The effect of Cleopatra's expressions of claustrophobia would doubtless have been extremely sinister in a domestic reading. Spoken aloud, her hurried questions seem to invoke the patriarchal spirits of the absent Earls of Pembroke:

> . . . can I yet live,
> Yet longer in this Ghost-haunted tombe?
> Can I yet breathe!   (1835–7)

In the household context, her request to the Fates, 'O Sisters, you that spinne the thredes of death!' (1839), is a plea for release from the domestic labours needed to sustain that family line.

Cleopatra's suicidal determination may well be informed by the *ars morindi* tradition cultivated by members of Mary's family, including her mother.[42] It should also be read in spatial terms. The translation shows that, for women, death is a relief which 'doth unclose / The doore, wherby from curelesse woes / Our wearie soul out goeth' (1271–3). Cleopatra's final line looks forward to the opening of that door. Her words 'fourth my soule may flowe' seek for the same transcendence imagined by the 'house-confined maids' of Psalm 68 who anticipate flying away from the hearth to 'freer skyes' where their new selves may shine like doves. For Cleopatra, self-annihilation perversely enacts the affirmation of an autonomous self. She commits suicide to join Antonie, but by so doing, she rejects her responsibilities to children, dynasty and kingdom. Her allusion to infinite space in the final line 'fourth my soule may flowe' constitutes an unspecific but powerful form of independence. In translating and perhaps performing or reading this text, Mary Sidney enacts her own powerful position as mistress of the household, keeper of her brother's texts, facilitator for Garnier's meanings. On the other hand, the translation is a vehicle to express her fantasy of transcending the role of translator, editor, and housekeeper, to find a literary home as author of herself.

HOME AND HOMELAND: *THE TRAGEDY OF MARIAM*

The devastating effects of separating domestic and public space and identity according to gender are re-examined in Elizabeth Cary's *The Tragedy of Mariam* (1604/6), though in a much more satiric way. Cary had strong connections with the Sidney circle; the presence and function of stoical discourse in *Mariam* may show influence of Mary Sidney's ideas. Even more so than *Antonie*, though, *Mariam* is a tragedy of State. Marta Straznicky has said it reveals an author 'who is anything but domesticated, a woman author who in fact shares a politically charged cultural literacy with the intellectual aristocracy of her day'.[43] While this is undoubtedly true, the play's political dimension is, in fact, bound up with its domestic context. Cary deliberately exploits the trope of household as commonwealth to offer a double perspective on the play's scenes. Karen Raber and Danielle Clark have drawn attention to the interrelationship of private and public domains in the play, and Rosemary Kegl has argued that it puts the genre of closet drama into crisis by introducing elements of the public stage.[44] By considering the play's settings in spatial terms we can see how it reconfigures the household as a public arena to explore relationships between home and homeland.

Mariam's use of a doubled setting of State and household is an early example of what Stanley Vincent Longman has called the 'floating stage', which respects the confines of the stage space but makes them 'correspond to the boundaries of a generalized locale': Judea.[45] Cary deviated from her source by setting all the action in Jerusalem. Doris and Herod both greet the city streets as though outdoors and the Nuntio reports Mariam's procession to her public place of execution. Constabarus releases the Sons of Baba from a secret hiding place somewhere in the city, while other scenes apparently take place within the royal palace and its prison. By shifting scenes within a specified locale the floating stage can take advantage of the confines of the fixed stage, while at the same time inviting the audience's imagination to collaborate in filling out the world of the play. This can highlight the emotional journey undertaken by the protagonist, and engage the spectators' collective social conscience. *Mariam*'s floating stage encourages immediate identification with its heroine's tragedy on a local level. Simultaneously, it obliges spectators to translate scenes produced in the household into the context of the State, thereby interrogating women's place in the analogy of home and commonwealth.[46]

The Jerusalem setting carries powerful metaphorical resonance. As King David's City, it evokes images of a promised land ruled over by a patriarchal dynasty (2 Samuel 7: 10–16). *The Solace of Sion and Joy of Jerusalem*, a Catholic tract, pointed out that the New Jerusalem was 'A Spirituall house' and 'A holy nation'. William Perkins's domestic conduct book *Christian oeconomie* (1609) cites the Old Testament to set up Jerusalem as a model for the family (A3) while James I's *Trew Law of Free Monarchies* (1593) noted 'Kings are called Gods by the propheticall King *David,* because they sit upon God his Throne in the earth', ruling like fathers. Thomas Tymme's more literal description of the city, which may have informed Cary's reading of Jospehus and her setting, says that, under David's descendants, Jerusalem was 'an earthly paradise'.[47]

Cary's play blatantly rejects the idealised view of the patriarchal family as a triumphant Jerusalem. State and household are contested spaces dominated by complex power struggles. The play's numerous references to David's city and dynasty are to a lost, irrecoverable, and not altogether attractive homeland from which the characters have moved away. Constabarus outlines the traditional family values that inform the old Jerusalem. Swearing by David's temple on Mount Zion, and quoting from the *Proverbs* of Solomon, 'our wisest Prince', he tells Salome that 'a virtuous woman crowns her husband's head' and exhorts her to 'be both chaste and chastely deemed'.[48] These tenets are rejected outright by Salome and cause tragedy for Mariam.

In the play's Jerusalem, Herod doesn't have a direct blood claim to the throne (it depends on his marriage to Mariam, and the murders of her grandfather and brother). 'Must he, vile wretch, be set in David's chair?' objects Alexandra (1.2.8). She supports her grandson's right to the 'majestic seat of Solomon' (1.2.63) on the basis of his maternal descent from Mariam, true heir to 'that gold-adorned lion-guarded chair' (1.2.66). What is more, Herod's Jerusalem, unlike David's, is not a triumphant, conquering regime. The Judea of the play is subject to the colonising power of Roman empire. Read in its household context, the play's Jerusalem is the little commonwealth over which Herod rules absolutely, but Rome is the overarching power of central government that he must obey. The husband's enforced displacement from his home to the Court is shown in Herod's journey to the 'world commanding city, Europe's grace' and the temptations it offers: statues, 'Roman beauties' and 'shows' or entertainments (4.1.21–5). On a more public level, the play's focus on Roman imperialism intersects fascinatingly with the final stages of the Counter-Reformation mission in England. Whatever Cary's personal religious sympathies at the time, the characterisation of Herod and Mariam under the shadow of Rome may comment obliquely and satirically on the desperate attempts of a Protestant nation state (Herod) to establish itself by persecuting recalcitrant nonconformists who cling to an older tradition.

The colonial context for the drama's setting makes Rosemary George's work on the politics of home especially pertinent. George sees the colonial novel as inaugurating a fictional translation of domestic ideology into the expanded space of nation and empire.[49] *The Tragedy of Mariam* is an earlier literary deconstruction of the opposition that has traditionally been maintained between private and public spheres, the two genders and the coloniser and colonised. Because of the compromised legitimacy of Herod's claim, he, Mariam, Alexandra and Salome are examples of the heterogeneity of colonial subjects, sometimes colonising, sometimes colonised in their constant search for a home and homeland where their desires can be fulfilled. In spite of Herod and Salome's political power in Judea, derogatory references to their race as 'base Edomite[s]' (1.2.6) marks their failure to establish imperial dominance over David's dynasty. Relying ultimately on Roman approval to secure his throne, Herod is, in fact, a dispossessed person not truly at home in his household or kingdom. It belongs more properly to Mariam and Alexandra whose native power is more deeply rooted than the tyrannical absolutism of Herod.

Occupation of stage space indicates shifting subject positions in the play. The floating stage setting of *Mariam* shows characters engaged in political struggles to establish 'home' in microcosm or macrocosm through a process of inclusion and exclusion. Mariam opens the play by claiming the household stage and the fictional setting of Jerusalem as her space. Herod's absence allows her to speak with 'public voice' in an uninterrupted soliloquy about affairs of state and the contradictory subject positions which male expectations offer her (1.1.1). The illusion of widowhood places her in a temporary position of control over herself and her surroundings, with a power like that wielded by many aristocratic women in their husbands' prolonged absences from home. With Alexandra's entrance, the women's voices enact recovery of a mother tongue that, although repressed in the presence of the patriarch, is always ready to 'deal in this reversèd state' and to 'revolve' the 'great affairs' relating to household business and its political contribution to the State (1.2.125–7). Jerusalem is now a female-dominated commonwealth: Sohemus has yielded up 'the regal dignity, the sovereign power' of David's tower and city into Alexandra's hands (3.3.75–8).

Salome's attempted appropriation of David's city is even more extreme. Mariam and Alexandra are still tied to patriarchal tradition, but Salome, understandably, rejects the regime which classifies her as a 'mongrel issued from rejected race' (1.3.30) because of her Edomite ancestry. Superficially, Salome's desire is for a home outside Judea, with Silleus in Arabia. In fact, her desire to recreate her 'native country' in her own image is much more powerful, as revealed by her telling words 'I would not change my Palestine for Rome' (1.5.38). To make Jerusalem a home Salome rejects its patriarchal dynasty. Her determination to 'wrest' Mosaic law into her own hands to divorce Constabarus is a bold proto-feminist claim for equality. With absolute independence, dramatised in a lengthy soliloquy, she claims 'I'll be the custom-breaker and begin / To show my sex the way to freedom's door', controlling the stage space and the entrance of the lover whom she plans to move into Constabarus's 'room' as her mate (1.4.49–50, 58). Salome's conflict with her husband in Act 1 Scene 6 constitutes a radical departure from patriarchal order. Constabarus cites the authority of the Ark of the Covenant, David's City and fourteen hundred years of tradition; Salome briefly rejects all this with the words 'My will shall be to me instead of law' (1.6.80).

Salome's assertion of her desire (primarily political rather than sexual) is the most extreme form of a female autonomy that has filled the spaces created by Herod's absence. Constabarus expresses shock at the transformation of his homeland:

> Are Hebrew women now transformed to men?
> Why do you not as well our battles fight
> And wear our armour? Suffer this, and then
> Let all the world be topsy-turvèd quite. (1.6.47–50)

Inversion of gender conventions within the household, where women assume authority to proclaim their wills in lengthy soliloquies, make their own laws, and divorce themselves from their lords and masters, leads to global chaos.

The first three acts of the play feature openings: the sons of Baba are released from prison into the city, women's concerns expand beyond domestic to national scale, and Pheroras is released from the claustrophobia of a dynastic family marriage and 'made my subject self my own again' (2.1.8). Even the lowly Graphina is persuaded to open her mouth and speak, her name possibly figuring covert female writing rather than being written on. Herod's former wife Doris can return to her 'native town' (2.3.11) and claim it as her royal home, publicly asserting her identity as 'by right your Queen' (2.3.2) in Jerusalem's streets. Significantly, these extrovert movements are dependent on the confinement of Herod within the sepulchre, and on spectators' imaginative powers to read beyond the household stage and perceive a political drama of State. They impose their own extrapolated image of place upon the physical stage, expanding its material dimensions to correspond with the biblical city setting represented. *The Tragedy of Mariam* asks spectators to re-evaluate their perceptions of the household, to recognise the interdependence of family and State, and the significance of woman's position in both.

Pheroras's vision of Herod's body leaving the tomb (2.1.81–2) proves ominously prophetic and the latter part of the play is characterised by an opposite movement in which scenes close down. Herod's homecoming parallels that of Doris, in that he too publicly greets the streets only to be disappointed by a frosty human reception. Act 4 Scene 3 is liminal in spatial, emotional, political terms: Mariam and Herod confront each other, each claiming the public space of stage and city. Mariam's mourning clothes continue the illusion of widowhood and independence. Since Herod is alive they are, in effect, a declaration of divorce. They also announce Mariam's primary loyalty to her murdered grandfather and brother, and, implicitly, claim ownership of Jerusalem as well as the household. The next scene, where Herod believes Mariam is trying to poison him (4.4.), highlights the national dimensions of betrayal by physicalising the Old Testament image of 'The Cup of Wrath', whose contents curse the Kings of Judah with madness and bring the destruction of Jerusalem (Jeremiah 25: 15–18).[50] As a student who 'was most perfectly well redd' in the Bible',[51] Cary surely deployed this prop with a vivid sense of its threatening scriptural resonance. The poison of doubt that pollutes King Herod's mind does lead to the breakdown of his sanity and his regime.

Mariam's arrest begins the process of confinement that she had foreseen when she learned Herod was still alive: 'And must I to my prison once again?' (3.3.33). While the expansive scenes of the opening movement relied on the fluid qualities of the floating stage, these increasingly introverted spaces narrow down the action to the fixed limits of the physical household in which the closet drama was written and possibly produced. The inverted spatial dynamic of the play may be influenced by Cary's own physical surroundings in early marriage. 'The first yeare or more she lived att her owne fathers; her husband about that time went into Holland, leaving her still with her owne frinds,' the biography by her daughter notes (p. 108). Her family home, Burford Priory, was certainly expansive enough to entertain a royal progress in 1603, although what kind of household entertainment was offered to the royal guests has not been recorded. It was built using the classic 'E' shape design. Burford was a nurturing environment where Elizabeth (née Tanfield) was given space to read, to learn a range of foreign languages, and even to intervene in a court case. From these liberal beginnings, she moved to less happy surroundings when her mother-in-law requested her to move to Berkhamstead.

Her mother in law having her, and being one that loved to be humored, and finding her not to apply herself to it, used her very hardly, so farre, as att last, to confine her to her chamber; which seeing she little cared for, but entertained herself with reading, the mother in law tooke away all her bookes, with command to have no more brought her; then she set herself to make verses. there was only tow in the whole house (besids her owne servants) that ever came to see her, which they did by stealth, one of her husbands sisters, and a gentlewoman that waited on the mother in law. (p. 109)

Mariam was probably written in Berkhamstead Place, a long building of two storeys, in Totternhoe stone and flint, looking down on the ruins of Berkhamstead Castle, a motte and bailey fortress.[52] The play's frightening picture of Herod's return probably owes nothing to Henry Cary's own return home. Indeed, early relations between the couple seem to have been happy. Nevertheless, Cary's move into the more restricted spaces of her husband's house, where she was confined and deprived of her books, may have exacerbated fears about what her future as a *femme covert*, under her husband's rule, might bring.

How one should respond to unjust absolutism like Herod's is a key issue for Cary, relating to ownership of space in the household, nation and on stage. Calvin's *Institutes of the Christian Religion,* one of the texts we know Cary read when she was twelve, cited Nebuchadnezzar (who conquered and enslaved the Israelites as punishment for the sinful rule of Judah's kings) as an example of the sovereign's absolute rights. Calvin noted 'even worst kinges are ordeyned by the same decree by which the authoritie of kinges is stablished', citing this as a general tenet on proper subjection for wives and children.[53] Mariam's steadfast resistance to Herod in Act 4 Scene 3 certainly departs from the spirit of Calvin's words. However, her largely passive response to execution does conform to Calvin's view that subjects are given 'no other commaundment but to obey and suffer', allowing God to 'breake the bloody scepters of proude kinges, and overthr[o]w theyr intolerable government' (501v).

Men as well as women suffer under Herod's tyranny. The Sons of Baba are released only to be re-entombed and re-condemned. Constabarus's response – a misogynistic attack on all women, including female spectators – confirms how patriarchy can be psychologically as well as physically confining. He and the sons of Baba welcome death as an all-male 'blessed' retreat (4.6.73). In Act 4 Scene 6, Constabarus idealises a 'Golden Age' (2.2.18) of homosocial bonding modelled on that of 'Jesse's son [David] and Jonathan' (2.2.26). His hate for the revolutionary female autonomy beginning to emerge at the opening of the play is released at Herod's return, and his diatribe confirms that women have no significant place in the patriarchal Paradise of David's city based on Old Testament tradition.

Women's response to exclusion and confinement is dramatised vividly in a prison scene between Mariam and Doris (Act 4 Scene 8). Mariam is physically imprisoned at Herod's will, while Doris has been excluded by his rejection of her. Doris's journey from the open city streets to the palace gaol spatially enacts her emotional and cultural imprisonment by conventional definitions of female identity. Doris can envision no role beyond that of Herod's wife and helpmeet. The physical boundaries of the fixed household stage give substance to her claustrophobic self-introduction: 'I am Doris that was once beloved, / Beloved by Herod, Herod's lawful wife' (4.8.59–60). Doris's inability to see beyond the walls of the household poignantly recalls the emotional tragedy of wives left alone in their 'proper' place, while their husbands sought new pleasures abroad. Her insistence that she has fulfilled all the criteria required of a wife, by bringing noble birth, riches, 'beauteous babes', and unswerving loyalty to Herod, haunts Mariam. Doris is the ghost of the wifely ideal celebrated by Solomon, the 'virtuous woman', 'chaste and chastely deemed', whose honour 'crowns her husband's head' (1.6.20–3).

Doris pursues Mariam like 'Some spirit sent to drive me to despair' (4.8.55–6), unsettling the heroine's ethical standing. The moral and emotional force of Doris's words works with the prison setting and household stage to bring ideological pressure to bear on Mariam and her nonconformist stance. Perhaps, in performance, this moment dramatised the pressures Cary herself felt in transgressing the boundaries of modest, wifely behaviour by producing (in written, published, and possibly theatrical forms), a play. The oppressive weight of tradition is imaged in Cary's second use of the biblical poisoned cup metaphor. Doris has prayed that her rival will meet the 'cup of wrath that is for sinners found / And now thou art to drink it' (4.8.76–7). Although Herod's wrath literally destroys Mariam, the condemnatory power of the Old Testament God is also alluded to here.

Salome claims that Herod's return 'Will give my foot no room to walk at large' (3.3.85). She manages to create a home in Palestine by reconfiguring her desires within the smaller compass of a patriarchal script. By serving

Herod's power and exploiting his weaknesses she establishes herself as the effective Queen consort. Salome is a female version of the petty tyrant; her early attempt to rewrite David's laws ends in failure and Cary comments satirically on the woman whose introverted passions can look no further than power games within the family. Alexandra's surprising and cruel rejection of Mariam, reported in Act 5, points even more obviously to the unsatisfactory alliance between women and patriarchy.

By refusing to compromise and 'enchain' Herod with a smile, Mariam creates a radical separation between wife and husband, female subject and patriarchal tradition that rules household and nation. Herod's execution order makes literal the divorce of the head and the body, depriving her of the usurped sovereignty that he believes should be his alone. This is brilliantly figured in theatrical terms by the exclusion of Mariam from the performance space. After confining her to prison, Herod pushes Mariam offstage, critically fracturing the play's genre as closet drama with 'strangely lunatic' ravings that threaten to out-Herod the Herod of the popular stage (Chorus 5, 29). The absent patriarch returns from court and metropolis, invading the household stage with a dominant public style of shows and entertainments. Kegl argues that Herod's presence explodes the dynastic idiom of household theatrical tradition;[54] even more than that, the play self-consciously stages an unjust (male) invasion of a female cultural and theatrical space which has the power to provide pleasing entertainment and make significant political interventions, independent of male authority. Mariam's potentially gripping theatrical dominance on the scaffold is never fulfilled; it is sent back to the closet in the Nuntio's report of her death. The play's tragic climax thus concludes the increasingly claustrophobic process of confinement by denying spectators the spectacle they desire and expect.

'Her body is divided from her head' reports the Nuntio (5.1.90). In family terms, the execution comments bitterly on the effects of the husband's return to the household. In national terms, Herod's frantic sentences mean he has literally no body to rule over – other than his sister and mother-in-law. Cary condemns patriarchal absolutism in the household for cutting off a maternal line and producing only an introverted and essentially sterile community. Herod's kingdom has no future as his lunatic ravings acknowledge:

> 'Tis I have overthrown your royal line.
> Within her purer veins the blood did run,
> That from her grandam Sara she derived,

Whose beldam age the love of kings hath won.
Oh that her issue had as long been lived! (5.1.178–82)

Cary's feminised version of Old Testament law, with Sara and Mariam substituted for Abraham and David, acknowledges woman's proper authority in the household and the State.[55]

Sympathy for Mariam is encouraged by allusions to Christ. Cary mobilizes the New Testament associations of Jersualem to suggest that the new attitude to female subjectivity offered by her heroine cannot be tolerated in the sinful world of the present but will transcend the limits of women's current circumstances as a sacred truth. Tymme's *Briefe description of Jerusalem* informed readers that although 'King david's house' had been disgraced (A4) Jerusalem's glory was re-established when 'as in a Theater, Jesus Chirst wrought our salvation' (B2v). *The Tragedy of Mariam* dramatises its heroine as a feminised Christ, martyr to a short-sighted and insecure patriarchal tyranny. Persecuted and excluded from the stage, her fate is tragic. However, the powerful Christian associations look forward to future salvation for women readers and spectators. The Nuntio hints that a revived Mariam will 'come attired in robe of heaven' (5.1.146) after a three-day interim, suggesting her ability to transcend the physical and cultural limits of the play. Even offstage, Mariam has power to upstage her mother and to break the framing effect of the Nuntio's gaze by looking back at him. Her integrity looks forward to a new Jerusalem where women can find a home as fully realised sovereign subjects.

Mariam's redemption of Jersualem is finally a much more radical reappropriation of patriarchal space than Salome's. By moving from Old Testament to New Testament associations, Cary rewrites the paternal authority of David's city as an image of feminist heaven 'in Sara's lap' (4.8.50). The final lines of the play confidently assert the prophetic truth of its message: 'This day alone, our sagest Hebrews shall / In after times the school of wisdom call.' Cary's vision colonises and usurps Solomon's seat as the fountain of feminist wisdom. In this sense, *The Tragedy of Mariam* is a text that reaches beyond its home in the early seventeenth-century household. It uses the floating stage to show wives and widows in action as governors and mistresses. Their subsequent confinement on the return of the patriarch comments astutely on the illogical ideology that defines woman as *femme covert*. Beyond this, its feminist reconfiguration of the Jerusalem setting through the Christ-like figure of Mariam offers what Amy Benson Brown calls 'a textual half-way house between the given homes of our culture and those yet to be imagined'.[56]

Early drama by women invariably provides a space in which the interface between the literal home ('real' in a physical or cultural sense) and the imagined home (where one feels one really belongs) can be negotiated. Rachel Fane's household entertainments allow us to glimpse how a young woman tested the boundaries between her imagination and the places she was destined to occupy as the keeper of her husband's house. Fane (1613–80) was the daughter of Mary Mildmay and Sir Francis Fane and grand-daughter of Lady Grace Mildmay (1552–1620), growing up at Apethorpe Hall (figure 5), where we have evidence of a family tradition of household theatre.[57] The manuscript copies of entertainments she wrote in her teenage years and preserved among her papers are an amalgamation of imaginative fantasy and physical performance. They feature fairies, goddesses, personifications of the seasons and of abstractions like Temperance and Mirth, and yet they are simultaneously acutely sensitive as to *how* these figures are to be represented. Numerous stage directions specify entrances and exits, movement within the theatrical space, use of props, music, how actors are to be dressed, and, in one piece, names of performers.

The argument that Fane's stage directions refer to actual performances is strengthened by the contrast between their non-fictive, imperative tone and the record of an imagined performance in Fane's papers. A scene in her play fragment, for example, begins 'Enter a Dutches named ortigamus With riche atier Being atended by 2 Jentil women', while her plan for rewriting a masque, written in continuous prose, uses conditional and future tenses to propose a production:

I have considerd of this & like all very well – but for want of actores I intend to leave out ye antick & in their stead to have robin goodfellow come . . . [th]en the musicke shall playe [th]en after Daphne & Appollo, I would have 8 litle fairies bring in a litle bower wth ye 3 litle children, & dance rownd abowt [th]em.[58]

This gives a fascinating insight into Fane's ability to think and write as a director. She undertakes to revise an unworkable piece, drawing on the resources available to her, and with comic reference to their limitations. Without the professional actors necessary to present an 'antick' or 'antimasque', she will open her production with a joke about their absence: Robin Goodfellow is to come in with 'a flash of fier before him & so scare away Nobody & his company, & follow [th]em him selfe'. The interlude with fairies and children in a bower seems specifically designed for eleven young performers available to her at Apethorpe, the most likely performance venue.

Rachel's younger brothers and sisters and her cousin are named in the cast list for a pastoral Christmas entertainment (discussed in chapter 2) alongside three other children, including the five-year-old Richard Burten, who were probably family dependants or servants. A 'Dick Burton' was part of Rachel's household after her marriage, where her account book notes payments to him and for repairs to his boots and washing of his linen.[59] Although Rachel had no offspring herself, she took responsibility for the nurturing and education of numerous children after her marriage. Ned Lewin, whom she called 'my boy' was brought to her from Northamptonshire in 1642 when only three months old, for example. The inscription on her monument in Tawstock church records that 'in domestic, civil and religious affairs she had a genius exceeding that of a man, and such a motherly disposition that scarce a greater existed in the world'.[60]

Rachel Fane's genius in domestic, civil and religious affairs appears in embryonic form in the dramatic writings of her teenage, where she works out her future role as an aristocratic householder. In particular, her drama engages with her grandmother's advice on household duties and responsibilities: 'I thought good to set them down unto my daughter and her children, as familiar talk and communication with them, I being dead, as if I were alive,' Lady Grace Mildmay pointed out.[61] Rachel was seven when her grandmother died but her dramatic entertainments continue a lively dialogue with Grace's prescriptions on godly conduct for women. Grace Mildmay repeatedly states the importance of wifely subjection.[62] In contrast, the fragment of a play composed by Rachel places woman at the head of the household, exploiting the physical domestic space at Apethorpe Hall as part of its gender politics. It was probably designed for performance in either the Great Hall (close to the kitchen and store rooms) or the Long Gallery whose overmantel suggests it was used for music and entertainments.[63] In Rachel's script the male prologue entreats 'Your ro[o]m' of the patrons (either her parents or her eldest brother and sister-in-law) and the character of Duchess Ortigumus takes over. She begins by commanding the household in her husband's absence but quickly moves into the role of householder in her own right on his sudden death.[64] Widowhood was a topic on which Rachel's grandmother had offered detailed advice and the play probably had immediate resonance since Rachel's father died on 21 March 1629. In a poem 'A New Yeers Gift to my Lady' (1630), Rachel exhorts her mother to recreate herself like Thetis 'Remaide, Refin'd Re-set againe' (fol. 6r). The widow character, after ordering herself and her chamber to be dressed in black, certainly shows no hesitation in taking responsibility for the family affairs. She tells her young son that 'this besi [busy] world gives noe time to griefe' and has already used her 'witts' to contrive an 'invention' for the future. Fane engages sympathy for the widow's growing self-determination by deliberately resisting the stereotype of widowhood. Female agency is even stronger in the following scene, depicting a governor Amenores, 'in her chayre of state'. The spectacle of female command would have had an especially powerful effect in domestic performance since Apethorpe Hall's rooms had frequently been graced by royal visitors.[65] Performed in the Great Hall, where James I had sat under his canopy of state, Rachel's Amenores 'in her chayre of state' would have illuminated the dominant role of women as queens in their own households.[66]

Rachel Fane also reclaims the house as a place of one's own by critically rewriting the role of housekeeper and the women's work that threatened to reduce the home to a space of duty and self-erasure. As a noblewoman, Fane's experience of housekeeping was probably more managerial than that of her servants but it still constituted a form of housework. In the play fragment, the Duchess Ortigamus and her gentlewomen seem to be subjected to the kind of routine that Irigaray and Grosz claim distances women from their dwelling places. They are under pressure to finish feminine exercises of needlework and preserving in good time. Regera is told to contact the drapers about a petticoat and 'send for it home that you may goe in hand with it presently'. The Duchess carefully estimates the 'halfe a dosen suger lofes' which must be quickly ordered to preserve '20 or 30 pounds of apels' before oranges and lemons arrive at the house, insisting that Regera 'write up on the pots how much of everything you put up'. In performance at Apethorpe, the Great Hall venue would have reinforced the prescription of domestic labour. The characters appear to follow the principles of assiduous housekeeping in a Latin inscription on the fireplace which translates as: 'Would thine house stand? Be faithful to thy trust, / Nor thoughtless spend beyond fair bounds and just.'[67] Such scrupulous attention to household quantities was echoed in Rachel's management of the estate of Henry, Lord Bath, whom she married at the age of twenty-five on 18 December 1638. Her personal account book rivalled those of her husband's stewards for its keen interest in the financial administration of the houses, giving substance to the encomium that in domestic affairs 'she had a genius exceeding that of a man'.[68]

As well as exceeding gender expectations within her domestic role Rachel Fane exceeded the role itself by self-consciously putting it into play: re-presenting it in entertainments and thereby subverting its all-consuming effect. Her grandmother saw 'all times ill bestowed in books of idle playes and of all such fruitless and unprofitable matter' (p. 24). Fane pointedly registers a different view in the first scene of the play fragment, where the Duchess tells her second gentlewoman Pantifa-lus, 'as for your part minion, I see nothing com gentils out of your hands but play bookes & toys'. Using the authoritative figure of the Duchess to ventriloquise Grace, Fane subverts her grandmother's judgement by appropriating it as part of her script. She playfully accepts that she is not a good housekeeper. Instead of sewing or preserving she transforms housework into entertainment. Played out in the Great Hall at Apethorpe, which was close to the housekeeper's room, the still-room, and the store room, her scenes of women's work take on the power to transform the everyday. They enact what Henri Lefebvre describes as a three-point interaction 'from the quotidian to the non-quotidian through festival (whether feigned or not, simulated or "authentic"), or again from labour to non-labour through a putting into brackets and into question (in a half-imaginary, half-real way) of toil'. By staging women's work, closet drama like Fane's reverses the usual process in which female identity is erased by tasks, and puts toil itself under erasure. We see 'a movement from the space of consumption', in which women are confined to producing or reproducing in order to sustain the family and community, to 'the consumption of space via leisure' in which the household becomes the site in which women's drama is written and consumed.[69]

Fane addresses the transformative power of theatre directly in a short scripted exchange between Temperance and Mirth. Lady Temperance declares 'Wisdom's th' only spring and gide' (fol. 4v).[70] Mirth, however, offers a defence of herself (and, by implication, the author), telling Temperance that she intends 'by my endeavours, but to publish forth / your vertu' (fol. 4v). Festivity is a different form of work designed to enhance female virtue in a carnivalesque process. To illustrate, Mirth brings on the pillars of the household: 'the gentlemen usher the taylor the buttler the koocke other wilse translated in to an ase an ape a fox & a catte' (fol. 4v). The strangely costumed officers perform an 'antike dance', and household order is dramatically inverted for the interlude that is both the performance itself and the holiday period for which it was composed.

HOUSEWORK TO DOMESTIC PLAY: JANE CAVENDISH AND
ELIZABETH BRACKLEY

Claiming ownership of the household as a space for play rather than work
is addressed more fully by Lady Jane Cavendish (1621–69) and her
younger sister Lady Elizabeth Brackley (1626–63) in their co-authored,
five-act manuscript play *The Concealed Fancies* (*c.* 1644–5).[71] Like Lady
Rachel Fane, these authors and their protagonists are members of the
social elite, relieved by servants of physical domestic labour, though not
from managing it. The ability to transcend domestic labour and indulge
in play-making is one of the privileges of noble birth that the play
celebrates. In Scene 3, the cook Gravity complains of his mistresses 'those
wits will ne'er be housewives' (1.3.8–9) and the behaviour of the heroines
supports this introduction. *The Concealed Fancies* models its two household settings on the Cavendish family homes, Welbeck Abbey and
Bolsover Castle. It exploits an autobiographical dimension to display
the authors' wit in renegotiating their position as mistresses rather
than housewives. The play's two houses are owned by the exiled Lord
Calsindow (a dramatic characterisation of the authors' father, William
Cavendish). In his absence, they become a playing space for Luceny and
Tattiney, and the three cousins Sh., Cicelly and Is. (whose names are
never given in fuller form in the manuscript). The heroines' roles were
clearly designed for Jane (Luceny and Sh.), Elizabeth (Tattiney and
Cicelly) and their younger sister Frances (Is.). The identities of authors,
actors and characters are often deliberately elided in metatheatrical references to acting 'your scene[s]' (1.4.3), as if to acknowledge the creative
opportunities offered to Jane and Elizabeth by the play and playing space.

The heroines' conduct is far from what was expected of a dutiful
housewife. The ideal home-keeper, based on Proverbs 14: 1, was 'helpful
and profitable, to the state and familie of her husband, and her owne.'[72]
Her industry, elaborated in Proverbs 31, was devoted to regulating the
consumption of supplies and ensuring the maintenance of all items of
property on her husband or father's estate. As John Cleaver pointed out,
this was a full-time job:

Her eye will be to the provision of the house, that it be well dressed, and seasonably
ministered unto her people . . . The vertuous woman whom I commend, dealeth
not in her vocation remissely, and by halves, but addresseth her selfe with
removeall of every impediment to the serious performance of her duety . . .
She flieth about her worke, and setteth on it with a settled resolution . . . As
she sitteth up long in the night, so testimony is given of her [Proverbs 18–19]

and how she bestoweth her time before she goeth to bed, not in idle discourses, not in gaming or vaine sports, not in banquetting or preparing of juncates, nor in vaine fruitlesse exercises: but *she layeth her hands on the spindle, and her hands take holde of the distaffe.*[73]

Duty and pleasurable entertainment are diametrically opposed. The housewife's dedication of her energies to domestic work was especially self-denying since, whatever control she exercised over material and human resources, in most cases the household finally belonged to a man. Feminist historians have been eager to discover the existence of a subculture in which women were able to express themselves through the ownership and the use of material goods that surrounded them in their households. However, in everyday contexts, the overbearing pressure on women to see themselves as part of a family whose interests must be served before their own probably suffocates such possibilities of agency.[74]

Drama introduces a third element of festival through which the household and its contents are transformed from the quotidian to the non-quotidian, in Lefebvre's equation. In *The Concealed Fancies,* as in Fane's play fragment, the fictive space of drama enables a feminist re-appropriation of goods and space for recreational purposes. An imagined locale is superimposed on a physical household through the processes of composition, reading and possibly production. This is another example of a play for which we have no recorded performance history but there is a strong tradition of Cavendish family theatre that would have provided a supportive family context for a production of Jane and Elizabeth's play. In addition to writing collaboratively for the professional theatre, William Cavendish turned the family homes at Welbeck Abbey and Bolsover Castle into 'play' houses on more than one occasion.[75] In a masque he wrote as a 'Christmas toye' for his 'Sweet daughters', the second lady scorns 'the Liberall Siences off huswifreye as makinge Butter & Cheese, with the Education off Sum Polin & Piggs'. This is the punishment of being 'Damn'd for the Countrie', from which they hope for relief in the masque.[76] Two other lavishly mounted entertainments would have established the idea of household performance for Jane and Elizabeth. They probably saw *The King's Entertainment at Welbeck* (1633), and *Love's Welcome to Bolsover* (1634), written by Ben Jonson and produced at the Cavendish homes.[77]

A performance of *The Concealed Fancies* at either Welbeck Abbey or Bolsover Castle would explicitly commandeer the props or costumes specified in the text as part of the entertainment. In addition, the drama implicitly appropriates an excess of other objects in the venue as part of the setting. By transforming the household into a stage in a realised or imagined performance, the authors energise the particular cultural references of the household 'stuff'. Objects and garments associated with the Cavendish family would acquire a liminal status in performance. As Peter Stallybrass has cogently argued, a costume 'hovers between a fetishized identity from the past' and 'its new possibilities once it has been appropriated' as part of a performance.[78] In a private theatrical such as a Cavendish production of *The Concealed Fancies*, the fetishisation effect would be all the more pronounced since objects would be displayed in the same place, and possibly handled by the same people, as in their previous life.

This would create a range of conservative and subversive effects. Clothes and objects associated with Cavendish and Brackley's absent male kinfolk would function as material reminders of their authority. They could be put into play to express the authors' desire for the safe return of their governors, and/or appropriated to raise questions about that authority. For the Cavendish sisters, fully present in the household, a different festishisation of goods would signal subversive new possibilities. The use of Jane, Elizabeth and Frances's wardrobe to dress the characters of Luceny, Tattiney and the cousins would literally embody the possibility that these witty, self-assertive heroines are aspects of the Cavendish sisters. Objects are radically reconfigured by the script. When the lovers Courtley and Presumption sing to pictures of their beloved mistresses, for example, real pictures of the Cavendish daughters were probably imagined as props. As mistress-manipulators of the entertainment, Jane Cavendish and Elizabeth Brackley demonstrate their arch ability to step outside framed images of femininity and control representations of themselves.

The Concealed Fancies actively translates household to stage through its opening address to female spectators: 'Ladies, I beseech you, blush not to see / That I speak a prologue, being a she' (Prologues 1–2). These self-conscious words, written and spoken by a woman (probably one of the authors), announce that the house in which women are normally consumed by work becomes a place in which they are privileged leisured consumers and producers of entertainment. The heroines prioritise play over housework as they interact with a network of servants, the living fabric of the household. The servants are caricatures whose dominant features probably represent the personalities of staff in the Cavendish houses. Jane's poem 'The Caracter', in the same presentation manuscript as the play, includes cameo portraits of Cavendish's 'servants', and could be the starting point for the roles of Mr Proper, Mr Friendly, Discretion, Pert, Toy, Care and Pretty. In a coterie performance of *The Concealed Fancies* with household servants in role, private jokes about the actors' idiosyncrasies could be shared by the audience. The poem concludes with a self-referential picture of 'the Ladies' who 'sitt / All day to give their Caracters of witt', as though Jane and Elizabeth are caught in the act of writing.[79] Such intellectual and creative skill was not in line with house-wifely duty; as John Cleaver sharply observed, 'many times the most wittie wives, are the least thrifite huswives' (p. 209).

In the play, the 'wits' Luceny and Tattiney and their cousins at Ballamo pointedly ignore the promptings of their servants, whose names – 'Proper', 'Gravity', 'Discretion', 'Sage' and 'Grave' – signify the proper attitudes of their mistresses towards positions of responsibility. According to Cleaver, the good housewife 'is not slothfull, spending her time idely and looking to nothing, but setteth her own hand to worke, and looketh to all that be about her, that they shall performe their duties' (p. 554). Far from spending their time in fruitful or necessary occupations, Luceny and Tattiney are still in bed, according to Mistress Sage (1.3.7). Their complete indifference to Gravity's work as a cook seems symptomatic of a failure to take on the supervisory role of mistress. With a pointed reference to the authors, Gravity comments that poetry is far more interesting to them than what is left in the pantry for dinner (1.3.42–4). The sisters indulge in what Cleaver would define as 'idle discourses' and 'gaming or vaine sports': improvising witty ripostes to their suitors, in the form of speech or song, or even making bets with each other.

The cousins who occupy the second setting of Ballamo Castle are no better than Luceny and Tattiney. Sh. flatly refuses to look at the account books sent to her by the steward Caution, even though she has not seen them for a fortnight:

Go formality and tell his formalityship I have other business than to stupefy my brain with how many quarters of malt is bought, and in that how much I am cozened, neither care I how many scores of sheep have been plundered from me. (4.3.15)

A more blatant rejection of Cleaver's model of domestic duty can hardly be imagined. Sh.'s excuse is that Caution is testing out whether she trusts him or not, but Caution later claims he knows of no such plot (4.6.4–10), which makes her determination not to see the books for a whole month seem even more outrageous. The shock effect of these lines would have been heightened if they were spoken in the walls of Welbeck or Bolsover, as Jane and Elizabeth surely envisaged.

Sh. ignores 'the serious performance of her duety', as recommended by Cleaver, and leads her cousins off to 'rarer recreation' (3.4.79). They break into their father's cabinets, an inversion of the male invasions of space elsewhere in the play. Sh. knows that locked inside are 'our friends cordials' (3.4.29), Elizabeth Grey's recipes for restoratives, which the Cavendish sisters may have seen in manuscript since she was a relative.[80] There are also confections and preserved fruits, all part of an aristocratic feminine world of domestic creativity, knowledge and pleasure.[81] The danger they represent – in the form of temptation to stray from the path of housewifely conservation and subjection – means that they have to be locked up.

SH.	Take one of these cakes, and you cousin, they're very good ones.
CICELLY	We never saw these before, come we'll put them up.
SH.	No, take another, he'll never want them.
IS.	Truly, if he knew he would wonder how we durst offer to look of them.
SH.	I wish he saw us in a prospective. (3.4.39)

Stealing the father's fruit in the form of cakes, cordials, 'preserved nutmegs' and 'morabollans' or plums (3.4.56), recalls Eve's consumption of the fruit of knowledge which transforms her from an obedient daughter into an active consuming subject. In performance, of course, playing the scene would necessitate consuming household goods. It re-enacts the aristocratic banquets at which sweetmeats were shared amongst spectators during entertainments. Sharing food with the audience would reinforce the idea of *The Concealed Fancies* as a communal enjoyment of leisure by writers, performers and spectators.[82] Sh.'s allusion to Lord Calsindow watching them 'in a prospective' (through a telescope) grants him a God-like view-point, overseeing their transgressions. It also refers to William Cavendish as the most significant reader or audience for the piece, whose distant approval for the play is sought in a special Prologue and Epilogue. Sh.'s wish to be seen satisfying her appetite registers a need for masters of the house to accommodate women's desires and pleasures.

The Concealed Fancies challenges the legitimate model of housewifely conduct with a subversive celebration of female creativity, pleasure and consumption. The 1639 English translation of Du Bosc's *The Compleat Woman* had formally introduced the model of the leisured, educated lady, but acknowledged that not all readers would agree with its idealisation of a woman who was not 'Mother of a family, who can command her servants and who hath the care to comb and dresse her Children'.[83] Cavendish and Brackley's comic character, Lady Tranquillity, represents an excess of leisured self-indulgence, the nightmare of an invading housewife-to-be whose appetites threaten to consume all. Lady Tranquillity's name signals her fondness for relaxation rather than work. She vows to keep to her bed in order to 'plump up my face' (1.2.10) and looks forward to preparing her costume and make-up for 'Five hours without interruption!' (2.1.39). The kitchen boy reminds the cook that this lady likes 'a great dinner' (1.2.33). If, as seems likely, Lady Tranquillity is based on rumours about a prospective marriage between William Cavendish and Margaret Lucas, then Jane and Elizabeth's grotesque dramatic caricature offers their father a humorous warning about the risks of remarriage. Their portrait of Lady Tranquillity draws an important distinction between their re-working of household duties and Lady Tranquillity's passivity. In a comment rich with metatheatrical resonance, Lady Tranquillity notes that the witty daughters 'can give such characters as to make a lady appear, or not appear' (1.2.13). Behind the idea that Luceny and Tattiney will represent Lady Tranquillity to their father, is a celebration of the authors' power to rewrite themselves as leisured wits rather than domestic managers.

The English Civil War provided a crucial new element to the spatial politics of the household, accelerating the emergence of female claims for subjectivity and authority in the immediate absence of male governors and the wider climate of change. The case of Jane Cavendish and Elizabeth Brackley was fairly typical. In 1643, William Cavendish had fled into exile, along with their brothers, leaving Welbeck Abbey and Bolsover Castle under the protection of Jane, Elizabeth and their younger sister Frances. Both family seats were besieged by the Parliamentarian forces. When the Earl of Manchester captured Welbeck on 2 August 1644, he reported that 'Newcastle's daughters, and the rest of his children and family are in it, unto whom I have engaged myself for their quiet abode there.'[84] Ten days later, Bolsover Castle also surrendered to the Parliamentary troops.[85] It seems probable that the sisters remained in Welbeck, writing, and possibly producing, *The Concealed Fancies* in late 1644 or early 1645. Although they were effectively prisoners in their homes, the fictive space of *The Concealed Fancies* reveals the peculiar opportunities offered to women during the Civil War.

Like many women whose male kin were away from home, the heroines govern aspects of their own lives with remarkable autonomy. The cousins at Ballamo paradoxically have more personal freedom as prisoners in the castle, than when they are rescued by the Elder and Younger Stellow, Luceny and Tattiney's brothers. Once the Parliamentary soldiers leave, Sh., Cicelly and Is. enjoy ten lines of 'liberty' (5.1.3) from thoughts of duty or marriage before Ballamo is repossessed by the royalist heroes on behalf of patriarchy. In the main plot, Luceny and Tattiney are free to conduct their own courtships, teaching their lovers a more liberal attitude to women's place in the home, like that which seemed to operate in the Cavendish household. In this sense, the heroines' 'concealed fancies' are not romantic desires, but their wish to establish relationships in which each may 'continue [her] own' (2.3.108), rather than being subsumed in marriage by a husbandly 'rod of authority' (Epilogue, 88). *The Concealed Fancies* was a playing space for Jane and Elizabeth to negotiate their relationships to husbands and suitors. The play's jokes about the younger sister teaching the elder how to behave refer to the fact that by 1644–5 Elizabeth was already married to John Egerton, Viscount Brackley but was apparently still living with her family.[86]

The authors use the domestic playing space invoked by the script to put the heroes' ideas about husbandly authority on trial. Courtley's more progressive view is that his partner will pay lip service to the deferential wifely pose in public but will enjoy equal status with her partner at home. The heroines' opinions, and the existence of the play in manuscript, family reading or coterie performance, testify to the accuracy of Courtley's model. In contrast, Presumption's deeply conservative view of husbandly authority is a threat that is simultaneously subverted by the script in which it appears. Presumption announces his intention to use his aristocratic country house to quash Tattiney's assertive spirit, exploiting the rural isolation that invariably heightened wives' emotional insecurities. He intends to cut Tattiney off from the fashion and company of London, returning with praise of the ladies' beauty to provoke her jealousy (3.3.22–37). In addition, he will draw on the traditional power of 'my honourable old house' and his own respected position at its head. Examples of local deference will teach Tattiney the 'fashion to obey' (3.3.44). Her housework will prevent leisured play. Presumption declares, 'I would have her take the week books which is the only way to make her incapable of discourse or entertainment' (3.3.37).

Presumption's manifesto must have had a remarkable effect in performance, attempting to re-appropriate the house and stage for patriarchy. It echoes the siege outside which threatens to take over the space in which Luceny and Tattiney (their authors, and their contemporaries in the Civil War) have begun to act. Presumption articulates the immanent re-assertion of male power and, simultaneously, its suspension within the carnivalesque interludes of the play, and beyond it the chaotic world of the Civil War. The woman's work of taking the 'week books' will purportedly make Tattiney incapable of 'discourse or entertainment', but the female-authored play flatly contradicts the effectiveness of 'Presumption'. With the married Elizabeth in role as Tattiney in an imagined or realised performance, it is clear that her ability for discourse and entertainment is in no way diminished. Coterie jokes undermine Presumption's words. For example, his determination that 'she shall not stay with her own friends or family after she is married' is flatly contradicted by Elizabeth's experience since she did just that.

Luceny and Tattiney's united rejection of Presumption's household model forces a turning point and a change of setting. Tattiney sends him a letter informing him of their retreat to a convent, to which he remarks 'Alas, I never shall enjoy my dear / For she my rigid thoughts certain did hear' (3.3.13). Neither Luceny nor Tattiney is on stage in Act 3 Scene 3, but their omniscience is linked to the identities of Jane and Elizabeth as writers and offstage performers, watching like careful governors of their household. The nunnery scene warns that the sisters (characters and authors) would choose nuns' livery rather than total eclipse as a *femme covert* in Presumption's type of home. In retirement, Luceny and Tattiney grieve for their exiled father, 'an understanding man' whose discourse, unlike Presumption's, 'uses not to be dull catechising' (3.3.54). Their prayers for his return are also for the return of a more liberal attitude to women's position in the household. Jane and Elizabeth dramatise their own reluctance to leave the sanctuary of the Cavendish home in which women are given room to 'write but what [they] think'.[87]

Courtley and Presumption invade the nunnery. The stage direction 'Courtley's discovery & Presumption' suggests that they have tricked their way in by disguising themselves as suppliants alongside 'Two Poor Women' whose laments echo those of the heroines.[88] The 'Poor Men's' loves and losses follow the selfish desires of the suitors:

FIRST POOR MAN [COURTLEY]   One that I loved as my soul rejected me.

LUCENY   Take this, and be assured, you shall grow wiser or [ere] have your mistress love you. . . .

SECOND POOR MAN	And my grief is I loved a woman and she
[PRESUMPTION]	would not marry me.
LUCENY	Take this as a scourge to whip your folly
	away. (4.1.6–18)

It is not surprising that Courtley and Presumption's 'discovery', or removal of their disguises to burst into triumphant love songs, does not achieve the desired effect. Luceny and Tattiney are only likely to be converted to marriage by a miracle, so Courtley and Presumption are obliged to stage one.

They appear disguised as gods to bring Lord Calsindow home in a spectacular climax celebrating the restoration of the father in the Royalist tradition of the court masque. If costumes from the Jonson entertainments were still in the Cavendish houses, Jane and Elizabeth may have imagined Courtley and Presumption disguised as the two Cupids of *Love's Welcome at Bolsover,* who descend 'from the Cloudes'.[89] In *The Concealed Fancies* the heroes enter with a song 'sung by 2 Gods coming downe out of the skye'[90] to usher in Lord Calsindow as a symbol of paternal authority: a father who gives away his daughters in marriage, a king who commands his subjects in the little commonwealth of the household. The vertical axis from 'Gods' to father conveys an impression of awesome authority to spectators for, as Lefebvre notes, 'verticality and great height have ever been the spatial expression of potentially violent power'.[91] The central hallway of Bolsover Little Castle would have provided an ideal indoor space for such a spectacular descent and may have influenced the authors.[92] Luceny and Tattiney's roles as domineering mistresses seem to be eclipsed by the appearance of these divine commanders. They dutifully change their nuns' robes for 'garments' brought by the gods, symbolising a shift from withdrawal to betrothal, and voice no objections when their father gives them away to Courtley and Presumption.

The supreme position of the husband or father is brought into question by the highly ambiguous nature of the sequence, however. While the authors seem to be imitating the court masque with nostalgia for the conservative traditions it celebrates, they raise suspicions about the godly authority of Courtley and Presumption: 'Are you god-cheaters? / Or are we not ourselves?' (5.2.9) Luceny and Tattiney ask. The role of dominant husband as divinely-appointed head of the family is as artificial as Courtley and Presumption's disguises. Domestic setting and performance conditions deconstruct the power of the husbands-to-be. Without the resources available for a full court masque, the grandiose appearance of gods descending from the sky looks like an over-ambitious attempt to stage a divine spectacle within the household.

This is perhaps just what Jane and Elizabeth intended. In an England where royal masques no longer displayed the monarch's authority and the theatres were closed, the aristocratic household became a last bastion of patriarchal authority and traditional performance, but the ground rules had changed. Unlike earlier closet dramas such as the tragedies of *Antonie* or *Mariam,* the comedy of *The Concealed Fancies* demonstrates how, in the Civil War, households became spaces in which women took centre stage far more permanently than ever before. In the hands of noblewomen like Cavendish and Brackley, traditional assumptions about authority, autonomy and subjection within the home were questioned in ways that mirrored the wider culture of change in the commonwealth.

BELONGING AND EXILE IN MARGARET CAVENDISH'S DOMESTIC DRAMAS

The plays of Margaret Cavendish, step-mother of Jane and Elizabeth, widen the gap between traditional and innovative images of the house-hold, exploring home as a place whose meanings shift between the extremes of utopian safe haven and violent prison. Cavendish's dramas, more than any studied so far, demonstrate Wiley and Barnes's thesis that home is 'always a form of coalition' between the individual and the community, between belonging and exile.[93] Such restlessness applies in generic terms too, since contradictory (or complementary) references in the prologues, epilogues and scenes suggest that Cavendish's plays cannot find a true home in either professional or household stages, real or imagined. This does not mean that they lack a theatrical dimension. In the epistle dedicatory to the 1662 volume Cavendish tells her husband that her plays are not to be presented for *'publick Condemnation'* either now or in the future (A3) but her apology for plays *'like dull dead statues'* (A3) is not to be taken at face value since her attention to theatrical dimensions constitutes an appeal for *'the hands of applause from the Spectators'* (A3v), even if the performance is imagined rather than realised.[94] Sophie Tomlinson explores how the 1662 volume emphasises the importance of recreating an imaginary performance with 'My brain the Stage, my thoughts were acting there' (A2).[95]

Neither does Cavendish's insistence on the priority of the printed text constitute a rejection of performance *per se.* Marta Straznicky's argument for a complementary relationship between reading and theatricality in closet drama seems particularly relevant to Cavendish's plays.[96] In a Prologue addressed to Readers she sees drama from the point of view of the practitioner, arguing that household theatre is educationally superior to its professional counterpart because noble performers do not act for '*mercenary profit*'. They can learn '*grace of Behaviour*' and '*increasing of Wit*,' in the performance and then '*practise their actions when off from the Stage*.'[97] A sense of place for Cavendish's plays is complicated by the overlap between imaginary, domestic and professional stages alluded to in the scripts. She sometimes imagines a utopian professional theatre as the proper home for her plays, but her representations of home are also influenced by more immediate contexts: the Lucas household, the Rubenshuis, and later Bolsover Castle and Welbeck Abbey. To find a generic home, Cavendish's plays employ a shifting coalition between the three-dimensional, material surroundings of the buildings where she lived, memories of English public theatres and private theatricals, and imaginative visions for future performances.

Undoubtedly the most important reason for instances of coalition in Cavendish's drama is the fact that it spans the transitional period from the Civil Wars to the early years of the Restoration, the earliest plays written while Cavendish was in exile on the Continent, before 1655, and the later ones finally published in 1668, after the restoration of public theatres. Between 1642 and 1660 the great house was a refuge for royalist drama by both men and women with three times as many closet dramas written than in the previous four decades.[98] Simultaneously, however, the aristocratic household was in a process of fragmentation and change, literally so in the case of properties taken over by the Parliamentary armies, the fate of Cavendish's family home and those of her husband. The country house was also disappearing in cultural terms: from a physical and social entity to what McBride calls 'a fungible commodity in an emerging capitalist economy that can be displayed and exchanged' more easily than land itself.[99] In the later seventeenth century, the country estate was transformed discursively from a source of wealth into a simulacrum, a symbol of wealth and legitimacy in the newly commercialised economy.

Cavendish's first volume of plays offers numerous discursive reconfigurations of the aristocratic household in this changing cultural landscape. On one hand, a preface to the 1662 *Plays* confidently rejects the principle of unity underpinning traditional structures of drama and the household, claiming that her characters do not need to '*have a relation to each other, or* [be] *linked in alliance as one Family*' (A4). On the other hand, her plays frequently look back to the security represented by that traditional home. Cavendish's own experiences, dispossessed of her childhood home in Colchester, displaced in exile as part of the English court in Oxford and Paris, then as mistress of William Cavendish's exiled household in Antwerp, lends a particular charge to her nostalgia for the country house. Even when William returned with Margaret to Welbeck Abbey and Bolsover Castle, they were effectively rural exiles from the court of Charles II.[100]

'This unnatural war came like a whirlwind, which felled down their houses', Cavendish comments in her autobiography. The plundering of her family home by Parliamentary sympathisers, and the subsequent deaths of her brothers Charles and Thomas Lucas, must have been deeply distressing.[101] A Royalist newsbook reported that on 22 August 1642, St John's Abbey in Colchester was invaded by twenty men who 'rusht into the Ladies Chamber' and laid hands on Margaret's mother, sister and sister-in-law, threatening 'to pull down the house, unless they thrust her out'.[102] The mob ransacked the buildings and gardens, and then broke into the family tomb in the church. In her autobiography, Cavendish condemns their barbarity, remarking 'they would have pulled God out of heaven, had they had power, as they did royalty out of his throne'.[103] Cavendish's alignment of the household, the monarchy, and heaven indicates her conservative bias. Attacking the home is sacrilege.

Her tragicomedy *The Religious* (1662) demonstrates the seductive power of home as a cradle of security. We can begin to glimpse the full emotional resonance of *The Religious* by considering it as a literary reworking of Margaret's memories of her childhood home, which functions as a trope for the wider loss of home felt by royalist families. Gaston Bachelard has argued that the house in which we were born is physically and emotionally inscribed within us since it has 'engraved within us the hierarchy of the various functions of inhabiting'. As well as being the repository of memories, it travels with us, moving across time, existing at levels of daydream and reality, as St John's Abbey appears to do in Margaret's play. Bachelard asserts, 'the houses that were lost continue to live on in us', exerting pressure on us 'as though they expected us to give them a supplement of living'.[104] For Margaret Cavendish, this experience must have been particularly acute. In addition to the effects of loss through exile, the material destruction of her childhood home magnified its quasi-religious topophilic power. That home was, of course, founded on loss in the Dissolution of the monasteries: Camden's *Britannia* pointed out that St John's Abbey was 'now ruinated, and converted into a private dwelling house'.[105] During the 1648 siege of Colchester, the house was largely destroyed and Margaret's brother Charles was taken to Colchester Castle and shot by the Parliamentarian captain. In spite of this context, *The Religious* avoids sentimentality by dramatising the claustrophobic pressures of arranged marriage in the main plot, and by pushing its representations of the household as sacred haven into parody in the sub-plot. Both rely extensively on the material presence of the household.

In the main plot, the tragic separation of the young lovers is physically dramatised by means of a grate and curtain. Lady Perfection determines to 'take a Religious habit and enter into a Religious Order' to avoid the attentions of the Arch-Prince and maintain her chaste commitment to Lord Melancholy (p. 544). The feminine cloister and its interface with the masculine world are presented very differently from the sororal playing spaces I examine in chapter 4. *The Religious* constructs '*the Grate of the Cloyster*' (p. 550) as a site of heterosexual erotic exchange between Lady Perfection and Lord Melancholy; it is a threshold between sex and death-drives. Their suicide tryst, to intermix blood on a double-ended sword passing through the grate, aims to transcend the body's mortal 'Cage' to find a 'resting place' together (p. 551). As Lord Melancholy pushes the sword point through the grate, Lady Perfection grasps it and unties the cord to her gown, while he holds the other end and strives to unfasten his doublet, commenting impatiently that the buttons are 'like troublesome guests at Marriage Nuptials' (p. 553). The tragedy resolves when they reject a future of parenthood and are admitted to the cloister as a chaste married couple. The Arch-Duke pessimistically notes that 'happiness lives more in Cloysters than in Courts, or Cities, or private families' (p. 555).

In dramatising this scene, Cavendish's contemporary surroundings in the Rubenshuis in Antwerp seem to have exerted as powerful an influence as memories of her home. We know that the building contained two large studios: one for Rubens, measuring fourteen by sixteen and a half metres, with a height of between nine or ten metres, and one (apparently lit from above rather than with windows) for his students. With three exits, the former room would have been an ideal playing space. However, it is the portico of the Rubenshuis that Cavendish probably thought of as a setting for the cloister scenes of *The Religious*. The eighteenth-century Mols note records that, in the previous century, the three archways of the portico were covered with grilles or railings separating the courtyard from the garden.[106] Above the archways were stoic captions from Juvenal's tenth satire, which speak precisely to the situation of Cavendish's star-crossed lovers. Their suicidal resolutions are aptly glossed in the inscription 'ORANDVM EST VT SIT MENS SANA IN CORPORE SANO // FORTE[M] POSCE ANIMVM ET MORTIS TERRORE CARENTVM // NESCIAT IRASCE CVPIAT NIHIL' ('We should pray for a healthy mind in a healthy body, for a courageous soul which is not afraid of death, which is free of wrath and without desire').[107] Although there is no record of a performance of *The Religious*, Cavendish evidently associated the Rubenshuis with her dramatic output since the title-page of the 1662 *Plays* depicts her in the archway occupied by a statue of Hercules.[108] Perhaps dramatising a cloistered scene in the Rubenshuis portico was Cavendish's way of giving a 'supplement of living' to the childhood abbey home she had lost forever in England.

The sub-plot of *The Religious* explores retreat to the family home through Mistress Odd-Humour who fetishises her small wicker chair as a symbol of her childhood. The piece of furniture is the focus of the entire plot and Cavendish relies on its physical properties to create meaning and humour. On a textual level, the chair has an ontological dignity, functioning like Bachelard's examples of drawers, chests and cabinets as a topos of the nest and its uterine comforts. Like the nest, it is marked with 'the sign of *return*'. The chair exemplifies Bachelard's poetics of intimate space as one of those special objects which are animated because they are so heavily invested with the power of memory associated with home.[109] Mistress Odd-Humour tells her maid Nan

I, using to sit in this Chair from my Childhood, I have a Natural Love to it, as to an old acquaintance; and being accustomed to sit in it, it feels easier than any other seat, for use and custome makes all things easy, when that we are unaccustomed to, is difficult and troublesome; but I take so much delight to sit and work, or Sing old Ballads in this Chair, as I would not part from it for any thing. (p. 530)

Mistress Odd-Humour clings to the chair and the traditional maidenly virtues it represents as a retreat from the uncertainty of marriage. When a suitor approaches, she quickly recognises her place in 'a Merchants Trafficking' (p. 535), vowing that she would rather lose a husband than the chair. She can rely on her mother's secrecy to indulge 'my Childish humours' (p. 545), but when her maid is bribed 'to betray the life of my Chair', her father burns it and she is forced to 'see the Martyrdome' (p. 549). She is subsequently obliged to marry (p. 554), losing, with the chair, her quasi-religious devotion to single life.

In performance, the tragic import of these scenes is undercut by their broad physical comedy. Unlike the shell, the chair-home does not grow with its owner. Mistress Odd Humour's self-determination is inevitably compromised as spectators watch her struggling to get her 'Britch' in and out of the tiny seat (p. 531). The material limitations of the prop telegraph a clear message to the audience about the cultural limitations of the traditional household and the spinster's life of sewing and singing. Cavendish's personal hesitancy about marrying is comically re-cast in the play as an immature confinement of the self.

Nevertheless, the seductive and dangerous appeal of the feudal household recurs in other Cavendish plays: *The Several Wits, The Unnatural Tragedy* and *The Matrimonial Trouble I and II*. The rise of a commercialised culture that outmoded the ancient image of the country house had perverse effects on Cavendish's dramatic representations of it. Cavendish's great households are haunted by an immanent sense of loss, and an often-disturbing nostalgia for the traditional values they represent. In *The Several Wits* (1662), for example, the intelligent, virtuous Madamoisel Solid laments the decline of an old order in which the female soul 'keeps at home' (p. 83). To her distress, the country household is deserted nowadays. Community values and personal integrity have vanished as the soul moves away to the selective economy of the city. The soul

is never at home, but goeth wandering about, from place to place, from person to person, and so from one thing to another, and not only the soul wanders thus, but all the Family of the soul, as the thoughts and passions; for should any thing knock at the gates of the soul, which are the senses, or enter the chambers of the soul, which his the heart and the head, they would find them empty, for the thoughts and passions, which passions are of the Bed-chamber, which is, the heart and Presence-chamber, which is the head wherein they ought to wait, are for the most part, all gone abroad . . . (p. 82)

This distressing picture of moral and intellectual vacancy is the effect of increased social mobility in the Civil War years. To leave the protective walls of the country house is to move into a marketplace driven by fashion where religious, legal, civic, moral and personal certitudes lose their foundations. Gossip surrounds the changing fortunes of every family and individual. The fashionable characters, including Madamoiselles Caprisa and Volante are, to some extent, victims of the *beau monde*.

Homes break up in the frantic maelstrom of acquisitive desire: 'with such a house, or houses, or Lands, or with such Jewels, or Plate, or Hangings, or Pictures, or the like' (p. 83). They no longer have any emotional or cultural integrity in a society where they are displayed and exchanged as material objects rather than sources of security, wealth and legitimacy. Madamoiselle Solid's conservative values seem close to Margaret Cavendish's view that, in a home, 'order in less fortunes shall live more plentifully and deliciously than princes that lives in a hurlyburly . . . for disorder obstructs; besides it doth disgust life, distract the appetites, and yield no true relish to the senses'.[110] Solid deliberately inverts commodity culture to argue that 'the Pallacesses of fame may be furnished and adorned by the wit of a poor Cottager' whose native merit could spin, weave and thread 'fine and curious Tapestries', and whose imagination, wit and poetry would create pictures, sculpture, and elaborate fountains for home and garden (pp. 111–12). Home has become a utopian vision rather than a physical place. There are glimmers of hope for the future in the matches of Madamoiselle Doltche and Monsieur Noblissimo (probably a semi-autobiographical portrait of Margaret and William's courtship), and Madamoiselle Solid and Monsieur Perfection. However, as Perfection points out, 'we cannot make any choice upon certainties but uncertainties' (p. 90). Home remains provisional, out of reach.

The uncertainties of the metropolis as compared to the rooted order of the country house appear even more starkly in *The Unnatural Tragedy* (1662). Monsieur Malateste's first and second wives have contrasting but equally unsatisfying experiences of his country house. The aptly named Madam Bonit and Lady Malateste behave as the good and bad housewives in Proverbs 14: 1, explained by John Cleaver: 'A good woman coming to a house scarce wall-high will set up the roofe and furnish the rooms: but a lewd huswife, finding a house already built and stored will raise the foundation of it and quickly empty it of all the furniture' (p. 78). The two women exemplify a transformation between old and new orders escalated by the Civil War. Cavendish's play does not reiterate a patriarchal moral distinction between the women. Instead, it demonstrates that each is a victim of the masculine modes of thought that have obliterated the debt all human beings owe to the maternal *chora*, and thereby rendered women homeless within their own homes.

Lady Bonit, who conforms to society's expectations of the good woman as a living representative of domesticity, is left with only the outward shell of a home. Her house is the site of endless work with no value or recognition. She sews bands for her husband, dresses simply, eats abstemiously and even surrenders her jointure (pp. 326–9). She is praised as 'virtuous and wise', beautiful, wealthy, well born and 'of a sweet disposition' (p. 349), but her conformity to the conventional patterns of housewifely virtue is self-destructive. When Malateste has an affair with her maid Nan, Lady Bonit remains Griselda-like, preferring to 'be bury'd in silent misery' rather than attract public scandal (p. 339) and dies shortly afterwards. Like the earlier example of Cary's Doris, Lady Bonit is Irigaray's image of woman robbed of her existence, dispossessed of any place of her own by a male construction of her identity:

I was your house. And when you leave, abandoning this dwelling place, I do not know what to do with these walls of mine. Have I ever had a body other than the one you constructed according to your ideas of it?'[111]

The unnatural tragedy that can result from looking perpetually inwards to home, as Bonit does, is dramatised more extravagantly in a sub-plot centred on incest.[112]

Lady Bonit's successor is expected to take over her subservient role. The servants carefully prepare the country house with all the best furnishings, including, significantly, a set of bed hangings depicting the Old Testament story of Abraham, Sarah and her maid Hagar (p. 348). However, Lady Malateste immediately registers her dislike: 'Fie upon it, I hate such an old-fashioned House; wherefore pray pull it down and build another more fashionable' (p. 351). The house and her assigned role as house-keeper within it spell the certain erasure of her autonomy and are rejected outright. In line with her self-definition as an independent, consuming subject, she redefines the house as a dazzling luxury commodity that no longer has any organic connection to the surrounding community or even to the landscape. It is to have 'a Bell-view and Pergalus' (pergola), checkered floors inlaid with silver, a large winding staircase, and, illogically, vaulted lower rooms and flat-roofed upper ones. Outside, she insists that her husband 'take in two or three Fields about your House' to make elaborate, geometrically arranged gardens with 'Fountains and Water-Works' (p. 381). This capital investment in display, typical of the late seventeenth century, is a female-authored symbolic redefinition of the household.[113]

Madam Malateste's extravagance extends beyond the country house to the metropolis (p. 357), and likens her to the foolish housewife who 'spares not to lavish out and misspend'.[114] Indeed, she finally loses the family estate in gaming and revels. Monsieur Malateste dies recognising his first wife's virtues (363) so, at a superficial level, the play dramatises the loss of the traditional household as an 'unnatural' tragedy. Simultaneously, it questions that judgement by granting Madam Malateste dramatic space to voice an alternative. She complains that her husband's estate is 'a dull place, where I see no body but my Husband, who spends his time sneaking in after his Maids tails' (p. 357). Her refusal to tolerate his affair with Nan is far more dramatically satisfying than Lady Bonit's passivity. In an ensuing argument, she defines the country house as a conservative site of patriarchal tyranny:

MONSIEUR   It is my delight and profit to live in the Country; besides, I hate the City.
MADAM   And I hate the Country.
MONSIEUR   But every good Wife ought to conform her self to her Husbands humours and will.
MADAM   But Husband, I profess my self no good Wife: wherefore I will follow my own humour. (p. 358)

Paradoxically, Madam and Monsieur Malateste are well matched: her abuse of the family estate in the city exposes an equally exploitative gender bias at the heart of the traditional household. It may be a perfect home for her husband, but the 'delight' and 'profit' he finds in the country is bought at the expense of his wife and servants. Cavendish gives further dramatic space to the rehearsal of this critical message in the *The Publick Wooing*, and *The Matrimonial Trouble I and II*. In the latter play, Lady Jealousy exposes the sexual double standard: 'These are Laws that neither the Gods nor Nature have prescribed', she complains; men, it seems 'make what Laws they please' (p. 453).

Cavendish's reservations about the household as home dominate *The Matrimonial Trouble* (1662). This two-part play, in which servants make up nearly half the characters, is Cavendish's most minutely detailed consideration of the little commonwealth. Her invocations of domestic spaces and rituals are even more prominent than those noted by Lisa Hopkins in William Cavendish's plays *The Humorous Lovers* and *The Triumphant Widow* which encode 'memories of an older way of life in which parts of a house and geometric shapes both had symbolic as well as literal meaning'.[115] The stark contrasts of comfort and violence, affirmation and alienation in Margaret's scenes suggest that, for her, exile did not provoke a simple longing to return home to an older way of life.

The Matrimoniall Trouble opens with a discussion about ordering beef suet for a venison pastry, immediately foregrounding the material comforts offered by home. The play is overburdened with a wealth of realistic domestic details. Cavendish approaches the never-ending duties for the housewife very differently from her step-daughters (in *The Concealed Fancies*), by overloading the scenes with reminders of this oppressive climate. Characters' needs for a posset, caudle, or mulled wine are ministered to on stage, with Cavendish as overarching maternal provider.

The provision or withdrawal of material necessities is a finely graded marker of social differences in the play. When Briget Greasy becomes Sir John Dotard's mistress, laundry maid and housekeeper, for example, her fellow servants note that, where previously her shoes were cobbled two or three times over, now she has two new pairs in three weeks. Women's desires are bought at the expense of the household and implicitly condemned in the play. Lady Wanton's profligacy is marked by her gift of five hundred pounds' worth of her household linen to Monsieur Amorous in the form of shirts, caps and handkerchiefs (p. 481).

Cavendish makes it obvious that the household's comforts are purchased at a high cost for the female provider. Lady Sprightly, who is expected to govern in her mother's place by caring for siblings and managing servants, points out the 'trouble, care, labour, vexations and disquiets belonging thereunto' (p. 436). The unavoidable presence of the household in the play gives material force to the responsibilities of domestic government and self-discipline, an effect emphasised in any domestic performance or reading. A theatrical prop, such as a cordial or candlestick, would not have existed in symbolic isolation, as on a theatre stage, but would have called into play the range of other household objects in the immediate vicinity.

Lord Widower's affair with his servant Doll Subtilty makes Sprightly's role particularly difficult, setting up a competitive relationship between the young women over the position of house-keeper. Doll says Lady Sprightly is 'fitter to dress Babies, and order a Closet, than govern a great Family, which is a little Common-wealth' (p. 432). Although the household is inescapable, Sprightly's reading teaches her how to negotiate a place of her own by actively managing it and her father. By proclaiming her intention to marry the butler, she undoes the double standard and forces Lord Widower to promise that he will not marry or enslave himself to Doll. In a feminist inversion typical of Cavendish's drama, the daughter teaches her parent about his responsibilities, reminding him that fathers who are ruled by Mistresses can 'incaptivate their Children, or ruine their Estate' (p. 456).

The quotidian world evoked by the gossip of the servants, the costumes and props, heightens the emotional traumas experienced by the characters. Making starvation, arguments and physical violence seem disturbingly everyday domestic occurrences. Food and mealtimes are especially important symbolic markers. The cameo plot of Lady Poverty, whose husband has spent his estate on whores and drink, dramatises the housewife's struggle to keep her family from starvation, and her rescue by a community of friends (pp. 481–2). Voluntary starvation marks another deviation from the household norm for Lady Hypochondria and Sir William Lovewell. Although they are a loving couple, the dictates on conventionally gendered behaviour alienate them emotionally and spatially. Lady Hypochondria listens hesitantly at her husband's closet door, fearful of his health, and of disturbing him. She is 'a stranger' there. Having internalised the idea of woman as the weaker vessel to ridiculous extremes, she uses it to claim her husband's attention. Self-starvation is a part of this technique, and Cavendish may be indulging in a nervously jokey piece of self-mockery. Her autobiography notes that she keeps a frugal diet, drinks water, and that, because she does not take much exercise when meditating and writing, 'I do often fast.'[116] Her letters to William anxiously anticipate her role as wife and comment frequently about her illness, but she assures him 'my health will be according to your affection'.[117] In the play, Lady Hypochondria's excessively emotional behaviour is a result of the pressure to behave discreetly as an invisible figure in her husband's house. She claims that her miraculous fasting is not for public record, 'only troublesome to my self, and to those I naturally love, as Husband, children, Father, Mother, Brothers and Sisters' (p. 465). It is, however, a self-conscious disruption of the domestic community and can be read as a symptom of the emotional and cultural pressures inadequately contained within the early modern household.[118] Lady Hypochondria's decision to fast in her chamber signals a potentially tragic suppression of emotional needs. Only by 'coming out' physically to shoot an invader who threatens her husband's life and the security of the house, can she release her need to love and be loved. She tellingly requests that the chains of discretion and temperance that have imprisoned the expression of love in the household can now be lifted.

When even mutually loving relationships produce scenes of troublesome domestic life, the audience are encouraged to wonder, like Mistress Single, 'who would Marry?' (p. 473). Incidents of physical violence in *The Matrimonial Trouble* heighten these doubts. The servant Roger Trusty kicks Lady Hypochondria's maid, and Sir Henry Courtley threatens to strangle Lady Jealousy (pp. 459–60). In the plot line tracing Sir Humphrey and Lady Disagree's marriage, verbal and physical violence are routine. There is every appearance of order in their noble household: the chaplain observes that Lady Disagree is 'a good Huswife, and very orderly in her House, as concerning what she is to take care of, or to direct' (p. 472). This makes the couple's invariable disagreements over trivial matters all the more disturbing. Their incompatibility causes a deep fracture of the basic principles of household government, seen when the chaplain points out that Lady Disagree's duty is to obey:

PERSWADER   the Husband is the Master of his Family, the
                 Governor of his Estate, the Ruler and
                 Disposer of his Children, the Guide and
                 Protector of His Wife.
LADY DISAGREE   Yes, he protects me well indeed when he breaks
                 my head. (p. 467)

Lord and Lady Disagree desecrate the hearth, sacred heart of the home, by throwing fire irons at each other. Their marriage is held together by the surrounding community but such social glue is inadequate without co-operation between husband and wife, depending ultimately on wifely subjection. The couple's incompatibility points to a deeper fault in the structure that underpins domestic order.

The play's traditional festive ending illustrates the brutal shortcomings of the patriarchal household as a home. There is an outward semblance of order: the table is '*furnish'd with meat*' and wine, the lord, lady and guests take their proper places, but the feast is without substance or depth. It parodies the idealised picture of feudal harmony celebrated in traditional country house discourse (pp. 486–7). Sir Humphrey Disagree claims his traditional place: 'Surely I will be Master', but his wife challenges him: 'Surely I will be Mistris of this Feast' (p. 486). Lady Disagree is no longer at home in the country house. She vocalises the discontent experienced by generations of women. Family breakdown is played out at the table, as napkins and plates are hurled and '*in the strife and bussle, down goeth all the Pots and Dishes*'. The supposedly festive climax descends into a 'hurlyburly'. A maidservant poignantly observes 'in truth it is a sad Feast', but spectators are free to consider what exactly makes it sad (p. 487).

Nostalgia for the old order, and the role of Mistress of the Feast, is superseded by recognition that woman's conventional position in the male household is itself sad, empty, inadequate. Lady Disagree's demand to be mistress of the feast on her own terms reiterates the views of many female characters, writers and domestic performers from the late sixteenth and early seventeeth centuries. The noblewomen who lived in households whose walls offered protection to nurture writing and theatre were, indeed, a privileged elite. Although they were not numerous, their position was a powerful one. From here, they were able to open up playing spaces in which women's identities in the home and wider homeland could be re-evaluated. Emotionally charged scripts such as Sidney's *Antonie*, Cary's *Mariam* and Cavendish's *Unnatural Tragedy* critique the tragedy of a lost *chora* or maternal home which holds fulfilment for both sexes. The lack experienced by men, who must alienate themselves from it by moving outside, and by women who occupy it as a discarded, devalued territory, is a major preoccupation of women's domestic drama. Deserted wives are extreme examples of the household's oppressive effects. The protective arena of a demarcated playing space provided opportunities to interrogate or undo those effects. The settings invoked by women's closet plays and the material surroundings of the great houses where they were composed could be utilised to deconstruct the inadequate living spaces allotted to them. The self-effacement caused by women's domestic work could be subverted or evaded through dramatic re-presentations. Even within the walls of the male-authored household, women's drama opened doorways through which they could create temporary but viable places to inhabit as women: homes of their own.

CHAPTER 2

Gardens

In *Partheneia Sacra* (1633), Henry Hawkins introduces the Virgin Mary as a circular garden 'compassed-in with a wal', which he illustrates at the opening of the book (Figure 2).[1] Image and text present the garden in theatrical terms as 'a goodlie Ampitheater of flowers, upon whose leaves, delicious beauties stand as on a stage to be gazed on; and to play their parts, not to see so much as to be seen' (p. 5). Knowing how to read the staged features of the garden is vital. Hawkins warns visitors that care is needed before he will 'leade thy Reader into the Maze or Labyrinth of the beauties therin contained' (p. 2). The metaphorical garden is both the Virgin and his own book, featuring images, poetry and moral essays. He points out that reading a garden (or his book), takes as much effort as reading a tapestry or an emblem. The scene should be enjoyed in an initial survey, then each element scrutinised and returned to its context:

as the manner is of such as enter into a Garden, to glance at first theron with a light regard, then to reflect upon it with a better heed, to find some gentle mysterie of conceipt upon it . . . Then liking it better, to review the same again and so to make a Survey thereupon to the same use. (p. 3)

Each 'Symbol' in the garden or text deserves careful attention. At first, the reader will enjoy its aesthetic appeal and 'dallie with it as it were with some natural and apt *Character* upon it'. After analysing its moral meaning, the reader returns 'with a fresh review on the Symbol itself', and is able to compare this to the wider context of the whole. Time and concentration are needed; Hawkins recommends that the reader 'sit downe awhile' in contemplation in order to help his 'discoverie of the hidden mysterie' (pp. 3–4).

Hawkins's words clearly demonstrate the complexity of the garden for early modern readers. It is an idealised feminine terrain (the sensual bride of the Song of Songs and the purity of the Virgin Mary), identified with theatre and with a journey into the unknown. Beneath its aesthetic appeal

Figure 2. The *Hortus Conclusus* or Virgin Garden from Henry Hawkins, *Partheneia Sacra*
[*By permission of the Trustees of the National Library of Scotland*].

lie hidden mysteries to be discovered by the careful reader. Hawkins draws
attention to some key associations of the garden. His comparison of verbal
and horticultural texts makes him a highly appropriate guide to reading
the garden as venue and setting for women's drama. Firstly, *Partheneia
Sacra* exemplifies the gendered association of woman and nature that is
typical of Western culture and early modern literature. Texts from male-
authored gardening books to women's own letters and fiction, assume a
close relationship between women and the land. In a very frosty letter to
her mother-in-law over the ownership of Longleat House, for example,
Lady Maria Thynne replied to Joan's accusation that she wasn't managing
the estate properly by telling her 'whereas you write your ground put to
basest uses, it is better manured than my garden. . . I should answer that
comparison with telling you I believe so corpulent a Lady cannot but do
much yourself towards the soiling of the land, and I think that hath been,
and will be all the good you intend to leave behind you at Corsley.'[2] Here,
'land' is set in relation to corpulence and manuring. The estate's fecundity
is inseparable from female corporeality and, in Maria's insult, the intellectual or strategic skills of her mother-in-law's management are eclipsed
by her physicality.

On a more idealistic note, Aemilia Lanyer's description of the garden at
Cookeham presents Margaret Clifford, 'great mistress of that place', in
perfect harmony with her environment:

> The walks put on their summer liveries
> And all things else did hold like similes:
> The trees with leaves, with fruits, with flowers clad
> Embraced each other, seeming to be glad,
> Turning themselves to beauteous canopies,
> To shade the bright sun from your brighter eyes:
> The crystal streams with silver spangles graced,
> While by the glorious sun they were embraced:
> The little birds in chirping notes did sing,
> To entertain both you and that sweet Spring.
> And Philomela with her sundry lays,
> Both you and that delightful place did praise.[3]

Lanyer describes Cookeham from the outside rather than the inside, using
an organic setting to construct an empathy between woman and place and
an idyllic relationship between women (Margaret Clifford, her daughter
Anne, and Lanyer herself). The plants, hills, trees, streams, birds and
animals create a venue where female community and learning can flourish
equally 'naturally'.[4]

What kinds of freedom did the garden, as opposed to the household, offer women? A character in *The French Garden: for English ladyes and gentlewomen to walke in* (1605) may have given voice to many readers' views when he declares 'God grant me always the key of the fields, I would like it better than to be in bondage in the fairest wainscotted or tapestried Chamber and with the best cheere that one could make me in it, for as there was never foule love, so there is no faire prison' (NIV–N2v). Architectural forms in these man-made sites invariably create problems for the construction of female subjectivities. Rooms, structures and buildings that are generally designed and owned by men, automatically privilege the legitimisation of male identities (although we must remember important exceptions to this rule such as the buildings of Bess of Hardwick, for example).

For most early modern women the garden outside offered a more open environment in which to nurture a unified sense of self. An example from the first book of Lady Mary Wroth's *Urania* (1621) demonstrates the point. The love-struck Pamphilia is drawn from her chamber to the gardens as a sympathetic arena in which to explore her feelings. Passing from one garden to another, she goes through a door into a wooded area 'delicately contriv'd into strange, and delightfull walkes; for although they were fram'd by Art, neverthelesse they were curiously counterfeited, as they appeared naturall'. She reaches an ash grove, with a 'purling, murmuring, sad brooke', flowers of sweet scents and colours, and recognises it as an external correlative of her own interiority: 'Seeing this place delicate without, as shee was faire, and darke within, as her sorrowes, shee went into the thickest part of it.' Pamphilia's self-consciousness is spatially realised: she 'goes in' to herself and the wood simultaneously. The grove enables her to fashion selfhood out of her experience of suffering and to give it form through writing. Pamphilia, exemplifying the problems of authorship faced by Wroth, uses her affinity with the wooded grove to literally express her pain. She realises her feelings by projecting them into the skin of an ash tree, where she carves a sonnet. '*Keep in thy skin this testament of me*,' she asks, to '*testifie my woes*'.[5] The tree is a living text; Wroth's narrative constructs the organic environment as actively sensitive to human emotions, able to give them a voice. The natural arena is a uniquely enabling space for Pamphilia: speaking through and with nature, she can establish an identity that is partly independent and partly relational. By moving away from architectural forms, as Pamphilia does, women dramatists can access 'natural' environments different from those of the home, court, convent or city. External settings or venues seem to encourage more open expression for characters and their authors. Outside arenas can, arguably, create space for the development of more independent, female-centred subjectivities.

We should not, however, be deceived into thinking that outside settings offer a return to a pure or spontaneous nature. Invariably, early modern texts advertise the need for a masculine civilising force to cultivate the savage feminine 'wild'. As image and text in Hawkins's *Partheneia Sacra* show so clearly, the garden is a piece of nature firmly enclosed by man-made boundaries. It exemplifies a productive patriarchal marriage between nature and man, an ideal nursery from which inspiration and wonder can grow. Sir Hugh Plat's gardening book *Floraes Paradise* (1608) praises the 'true and philosophicall Husbandman' as 'he that knoweth how to lay his fallows truly, wherby they may become pregnant from the heavens, and draw abundantly that celestiall and generative vertue into the *Matrix* of the Earth'.[6] Mother Nature must be inspired by divine virtue through the civilising work of man. The garden is therefore as much artifice as nature, for female writers too. In Wroth's text the walks are 'fram'd by Art' and 'curiously counterfeited, as they appeared natur-all'. In Aemelia Lanyer's Cookeham, they are dressed in 'liveries' like the servants of the Dorset household, while the trees spread canopies like the decorated hangings within the hall. All supposedly natural phenomena 'hold like similes' and are metaphorically paralleled with the court: even the streams 'spangled' with the touch of the sun recall the jewelled costumes of the nobility displayed before the monarch. Lanyer's anthropomorphic tropes remind us that early modern women who set or designed their plays to create in-garden performances, were engaging with a highly complex social space, delicately suspended between culture and nature. The garden recalls Paradise, the *hortus conclusus* of innocence and security, enclosed and pure. The walled gardens of large country houses were frequently secularised versions of the monastic cloister, even more obviously so when the household had been set up on the site of a dissolved religious house, such as Welbeck Abbey, home of the Cavendish family, or Wilton, on the Pembroke estate. The garden is also a site of contemplation and self-discovery, both stasis and journey, like the monastic cloister. Here, one has the space to travel metaphorically, intellectually, spiritually. Further, the abundant feminised landscape celebrated in the Song of Songs makes the garden a place of sensual love or *locus amoenus*. With so many different meanings, it is a natural 'heterotopia', Foucault's term for a contradictory site which has the 'curious property of being in relation with all the other sites, but in such a way as to suspect, neutralize, or invert the set of relations which they happen to designate, mirror, or reflect'.[7]

In the Elizabethan and Jacobean garden the physical ordering of space and of living objects within it is highlighted in the knot. Ornamental knots are a material tying together of nature and culture in the processes of pruning, shaping, training of plants. The knot garden is therefore also a 'not' garden in social terms: a place where paternal law constrains natural instincts especially for female subjects. The nurturing and fashioning of natural growth is a botanical equivalent of the social tutelage that restrains human desire. For early modern woman, the garden teaches proper spatial practice. It functioned like a conduct book imprinted on nature. Since the emergence of print culture and the idea of landscape were simultaneous developments, reading the carefully patterned garden was, in effect, a physical equivalent of studying the lessons on female modesty and virtue printed in popular books like Vives's *Instruction of a Christian Woman*. Walking within the walled alleys and pathways of the garden, or viewing its ornamental knots from above, was a means to control the early modern woman's experience of nature, while simultaneously suggesting that the typical cultural constraints on her behaviour grew out of nature. The formal garden was a site of surveillance of nature and of self-policing through surveillance. Given such boundaries, can the garden offer any more freedom than the house to women dramatists?

As an extension of the house, the garden may simply reproduce the structures and strictures of that man-made environment. One school of thought argues that the Renaissance garden developed as did the great house. It became more ostentatious, a vehicle for display, and, simultaneously, divided between public and private spaces. According to Roy Strong, 'privy' gardens, and formal rituals of exclusion or admission to them, mirrored the proliferation of 'privy' chambers in the great houses.[8]

However, as Scott Wilson has argued, the size of the garden, the presence of irregularly placed supplementary buildings in its grounds, and the porous quality of its boundaries with the uncultivated natural environment beyond made it very different from the fixed architecture of the house.[9] Sir Henry Wotton's *Elements of Architecture* (1624) noted 'a certaine contrarietie betweene *building* and *gardening*: For as Fabriques should bee *regular*, so Gardens should bee *irregular*, or at least cast into a very wilde *Regularitie*.' Looking from above, the viewer should be confronted 'rather in a delightfull confusion, then with any plaine distinction of the pieces'.[10]

If ordered patterns and (k)nots told a narrative of restraint, the blurred boundaries here suggest that an irregularly ornamented garden could also be a place of liberty, a site of contrived disorder and pleasure. Walks, mazes, arbours offered the artful contrivance of a journey into the unexpected. Smaller buildings within the garden, such as the lodge or the banqueting house (the sites of possible outdoor performances), were dangerous supplements to the main edifice. It is no accident that they became known as 'follies' towards the end of seventeenth century. They were material manifestations of excessive or transgressive desires that could not be held within the household: blood sports; the non-nutritious, luxurious consumption of wine, sweetmeats and pastries at banquets; the pursuit of love. Although women's desires probably did not always find a place here, women's drama could perhaps find playing spaces within the 'very wilde Regularitie' of the garden, whose heterotopic nature as a counter-site to the rest of society, offered unique opportunities to represent, contest, and invert the conventional tropes for female conduct. It is important to remember that early modern women's identification with nature did not necessarily carry associations of inferiority. Closeness to nature could also signify power: the power to challenge or contest the masculine project of cultural mastery. The need for greater vocal projection in open-air performances already transgresses the idea of 'low' speech, which Lear finds such 'an excellent thing in woman' (5.3.274). Outside settings and venues offered early modern women strategic playing spaces to unsettle what is 'natural' about gendered behaviour.

The garden's living spatial identity allies it more closely to theatre than to print culture, as is hinted in Henry Hawkins's phrase the 'goodly Ampitheater of flowers'. In theory at least, the garden provides a more 'natural' venue for dramatic performance than the house. It is a kind of theatre: patterned or organised like a play's scripted moments of speech, movement, plot, and yet at the same time it has an organic life of its own, just as does any individual performance of a script. No reader of the garden notices exactly the same elements and, of course, these change according to season, time of day and weather conditions. Robin Lane Fox, Garden Master at New College, Oxford, points out that gardening (like theatre) is a transient art, but all the more powerful for that: 'If gardening loses its connection with artificiality, transience, and extravagant experiment, it will have lost most of its dimensions.'[11] Wotton captures the range of perspectives which characterise the garden and theatre, arguing that by means of 'severall *mountings* and *valings*' (elevations and descents) the '*Beholder*'of the garden is taken to 'various entertainements of his *sent,* and sight' and 'every one of these diversities, was as if hee had beene *Magically* transported into a new Garden'.[12]

Like a play, a garden purports to be a place of entertainment and ease, yet its carefully landscaped terrain, complete with sculpted topiary and stone, maps out a clear narrative or message to the visitor. As Pugh notes, the garden is inextricably linked to the realities of power, violence, wealth and political intrigue; although it pretends to be a retirement: 'these themes are "suspended in disbelief", hanging conveniently and uncertainly between theatre and real estate'.[13] Even though Pugh is discussing the later eighteenth-century garden his point holds for sixteenth and seventeenth-century examples. The garden's ostentatious display of allusions to the family or to prominent visitors in its statues, fountains and inscriptions, is held in play to be 'discovered', just as a dramatic performance fictionalises the serious messages it telegraphs to its audience. A close parallel can be drawn between pastoral drama and gardens, where the artificial world that is self-consciously created imitates that of the garden. In pastoral, nobles masquerading as shepherds enjoy a country holiday in which the real work of caring for a flock is subordinated to the demands of the (usually romantic) narrative. Similarly, in the garden, the realities of nature are shaped and trained to further an ordered, spatial narrative. Women's pastoral dramas can usefully be analysed under the heading of 'gardens', because even though their highly artificial rural settings move beyond terraced knots into the fields of the family estates, the generic characteristics which govern pastoral demand the same balance of natural expansion and careful restraint found in gardens. Scenes in the *Pastorall of Florimène*, performed at court, for example, move between rural settings and 'a spacious Garden, with walkes, perterraes, close Arbours and Cypresse trees'.[14]

In addition to being a living art form like theatre, the garden is also a public statement in the sense that it is more like an oral performance, accessible to many ears, than a text offered for private reading. Brian Stock draws a useful parallel between reading a landscape and reciting the memorised lines of an oral text, in which a good deal is pre-read or already understood, and the narrative proceeds *in media res*, with the repetition of selected motifs. Such reading encourages a greater sense of community so that, unlike a printed text, a garden landscape 'permitted the viewer to live in two worlds at once: that of the private reader and that of the public beholder'.[15] As with the spectator at a performance, each visitor's experience of the garden at any given moment is unique, as perspective, view and position change. Nevertheless, all these different, partial readings are produced and sustained within the garden-as-theatre.

COMING OUT IN LADY JANE LUMLEY'S *IPHIGENIA*

The garden's public, communal dimensions are essential elements of Lady Jane Lumley's (1537–77) scripted translation of Euripides' *Iphigenia at Aulis* (*c.* 1557).[16] The outdoor setting of this play, close to Diana's altar where Iphigenia is to be sacrificed to the goddess, has close affinities with the 'Wilderness' or outer garden at Lady Lumley's home, Nonsuch (Surrey), as Gweno Williams has shown.[17] The Grove, Fountain and Temple of Diana and banqueting house, which Thomas Watson thought 'worthy of Diana herself', are described in most detail in Platter's *Travels in England* (1599):

At the entrance to the garden is a grove called after Diana, the goddess; from here we came to a rock out of which natural water springs into a basin, and on this was portrayed with great art and life-like execution the story of how the three goddesses took their bath naked and sprayed Actaeon with water, causing antlers to grow upon his head, and of how his own hounds afterwards tore him to pieces. Further on we came to a small vaulted temple, where there was a fine marble table, and the following mottoes (in Latin) were inscribed here thus – on the nearest wall: 'The goddess of chastity gives no unchaste counsels; she does not counsel disgrace, but avenges it; they are the fruits of an evil mind and an evil spirit' . . . Then I beheld a pointed tower spurting out water, and a rock from which issued water. We next entered an arbour or pavilion where the Queen sits during the chase in the park. Here she can see the game run past.[18]

Although these symbolic ornaments to Diana were probably built after 1579, the first record of the banqueting 'pavilion' occurs in 1550 when Sir Thomas Cawarden, Master of the Revels at Court, had it added to his duties as Keeper of Nonsuch and 'the Bankettynge House within the Park there'.[19] In 1556, the Earl of Arundel, Lady Jane Lumley's father, acquired the Palace of Nonsuch. Marion Wynne-Davies has convincingly dated *Iphigenia* after 1557, when Jane Lumley and her husband John were in occupation. Her manuscript is on paper with a glove and flower watermark, which belonged to the crown, and was frequently used by Sir Thomas Cawarden who only relinquished control of Nonsuch after a pitched battle with Arundel and Lumley's men. Jane's use of his notepaper to compose a script designed for performance in the Banqueting House was a doubly pointed way of establishing the family's ownership of Nonsuch. Wynne-Davies argues persuasively that *Iphigenia* was written with the banqueting house as its intended venue, pointing out that Lady Jane Lumley showed special interest in a parallel banqueting house at Gorhambury, owned by Sir Nicholas Bacon. She requested copies of the sententiae painted on its walls, possibly part of the extensive decorations for a visit by Queen Elizabeth in 1572. In Jane's commonplace book, two sententiae follow the manuscript of *Iphigenia*, one of which, '*nemo poluto quest animo mederi*', closely resembles one of the inscriptions noted by Platter.[20]

Queen Elizabeth's three-day visit to Nonsuch in 1559 offers a possible link between Lady Lumley's interest in Latin sententiae, banqueting house decoration, and her free translation of *Iphigenia*, the first English version of Euripides' tragedy. When the Queen visited Arundel, Jane, his only living daughter, would have been the hostess, since her brothers and sister had died in 1556–7. It is not difficult to trace the influence of these events in Jane's choice of dramatic translation, although other influences, such as the execution of Jane's cousin, Lady Jane Grey, were probably equally significant factors.[21]

The diary of Henry Machyn records that Elizabeth was entertained on Sunday 6 August with a magnificent 'soper, bankett, and maske, with drums and flutes, and all the mysycke that cold be'. He also points out that the Earl of Arundel 'mad her a grett bankett at ys cost, the wyche kyng Henry the viij builded', which suggests that Arundel had refurbished the banqueting house for her visit. The following day Elizabeth stood to watch hunting, and at night saw

a play of the chyderyn of Powlles and ther master Se[bastian], master Phelypes, and master Haywod, and after a grett bankett as [ever was s]ene, with drumes and flutes, and goodly banketts [of dishes] costely as ever was sene and gyldyd, tyll iij in mornyng; and ther was skallyng of yonge lordes and knyghtes.[22]

Although Paul's Boys performed regularly at court only two plays are definitely known as theirs up to 1576, the first of which is *Iphigenia* 'a tragedy', performed at court on 28 December 1571 or 1 January 1572. This play is lost. Wynne-Davies's suggestion that it may be Lady Jane Lumley's translation, first performed by Paul's Boys in 1559 at Nonsuch, is an intriguing possibility. Under the leadership of Sebastian Westcott, the company seems to have specialised in presenting works in the pathetic-heroine tradition so the translation of *Iphigenia* would have appealed.[23] Machyn's account of the day, with hunting, play, banqueting and 'skallyng' (climbing) suggests that the dramatic performance could also have taken place outside near the banqueting house on that summer evening.

Iphigenia would have been an appropriate piece to present to the young Queen who had recently answered Parliament's request that she choose a husband by declaring her determination to live and die a virgin.[24] In William Birch's 'Song Between the Queen's Majesty and England' (1559) she pledges herself to the nation: 'Here is my hand / My dear lover England, I am thine both with mind and heart.'[25] Euripides' play shows Iphigenia grow from a child in the private world of the family to 'an adult, a member of the citizen body of Athens'.[26] In Jane Lumley's version, as in Queen Elizabeth's speech, the potential for marriage matures into a public role as the servitor to one's country. Iphigenia is brought to Aulis under the pretext of being married to Achilles in order to be sacrificed to the goddess Diana. The virgin sacrifice for Diana's favour is needed so that the Grecian army can sail to conquer Troy. Iphigenia tells her grieving mother that she will lose her life for 'the welthe of grece, whiche is the most frutefull countrie of the worlde'. She sacrifices herself so that the soldiers' wives and children can live in peace from the angry Trojans, and 'I shall not onlie remedie all thes thinges with my deathe: but also get a glorious renowne to the Grecians for ever.' She reproves her mother: 'remember how I was not borne for your sake onlie, but rather for the commoditie of my countrie' (802–10). Elizabeth had dedicated herself to England in remarkably similar terms just a few months earlier, instructing Parliament that she would never marry at the risk of the kingdom 'for the weal, good and safety whereof I will never shun to spend my life'.[27]

Lumley's *Iphigenia* is not just a story for or about a queenly spectator, but a play that explicitly transgresses the confinement of women to the private, domestic sphere. It expands the field of legitimate female action beyond the doors of the household. Euripides' text (337 BC) sets up an opposition between the onstage, public arena and a private domestic space behind the *skene* or backdrop, an innovation in Greek theatre which demarcated the masculine outdoors and feminine indoors.[28] Lumley's translation highlights the gendered opposition and Iphigenia's extraordinary movement into the public domain. The stage is always an outdoor, masculine place. Agamemnon tells Clytemnestra 'it doth not become you to be amongste suche a companye of men' (465–6) and Achilles is equally surprised to see Clytemnestra, asking who she is, that 'beinge a woman dare come amongste suche a companie of men?' (489–90). Achilles agrees to champion Iphigenia but restricts her indoors and offstage, deeming it 'not mete, that she shulde come abrode'. He advises Clytemnestra 'it is beste therefore you kepe hir at home' (590–3).

Lumley's *Iphigenia* blatantly defies such advice, literally turning the *skene* inside out in its celebration of a heroine who appropriates the open stage for herself. The outside setting of *Iphigenia* is not an automatically feminised place like the *hortus conclusus* of Henry Hawkins's *Partheneia*. It is an open space, perhaps essentially androgynous, but traditionally occupied by men. The play re-places woman in that public arena, and in doing so, broadens opportunities for the sex in immediately material and wider symbolic terms. A performance in the gardens at Nonsuch would have exemplified the heterotopia's function to invert gender relations in the pre-Elizabethan public world, which the garden as stage happens to mirror in its re-presentation of a female protagonist in the public arena. Significantly, Clytemnestra and Iphigenia arrive in a chariot to be greeted by a Chorus of noblewomen (374–5). In an outdoor performance, the chariot would have made a very effective entry down the central sandy pathway through the heart of the Wilderness to the grove of Diana and the banqueting house above on its mound. Perhaps Jane Lumley anticipated and witnessed a scene like that depicted in Hoefnagel's 1568 picture of the Queen Elizabeth arriving at Nonsuch in her chariot.[29]

Lumley's translation of the Greek play offers a compliment to the self-declared virgin queen who offered herself on the stage of the world for the good of her country. Its setting near the temple of Diana at Aulis could thus have been one of the earliest examples of the cult of Diana so central to Elizabeth's iconography. John Lumley's lavish decoration of the sites surrounding the banqueting house with allusions to Diana and Elizabeth would have commemorated the event, giving concrete form to the myth created there by the performance of *Iphigenia*. Watson, writing in 1581, sensed that it was a woman-centred place since 'Diana herself, guardian of the groves, lurks in the shadows.' In Diana's grove stood a pinnacle topped with a pelican, a symbol of maternal sacrifice adopted by Elizabeth.[30] Perhaps this was the spot where, in performance, Iphigenia 'whos bewtifull face and faire bodi anone shalbe defiled withe hir owne blode' (909–10), presented herself as a sacrifice to Diana.

Once Agamemnon has summoned Iphigenia to the stage, she defies the shame of public exposure and preserves her sovereign identity by determining to direct her own fate. She refuses to play dutiful daughter to Agamemnon's tyrannical father, or to be a defenceless maiden to the lone champion Achilles. *Iphigenia* proposes that it is altogether unfitting for a father to demand the ultimate sacrifice of his daughter. Lumley's translation emphasises its unnaturalness and Agamemnon's shame. The Chorus of noblewomen give their voices to Clytemnestra's objections 'for it is not lawfull that a father shulde destroy his childe' (695). The translation's critique of women's subjection to an apparently unnatural paternal authority would undoubtedly have pleased the young Queen who had cautioned Parliament never to impose its will on her. 'I must needs have misliked it very much and thought it in you a very great presumption, being unfitting and altogether unmeet for you to require them that may command', she observed, 'for a guerdon constrained, and a gift freely given can never agree together.'[31]

Lumley's heroine, like Queen Elizabeth, must give herself away as she chooses, not as her father commands. Achilles declares he would 'counte my selfe happi if I mighte obteine the O Iphigeneya to be my wife'. His self-centred desires, as one who ranks 'myne owne pleasure above the commodite of my countrie' (762–3) contrasts starkly with Iphigenia's stance. Like Elizabeth's suitors, he is rejected in favour of patriotic self-sacrifice. His admiring words 'I wonder gretelie at the bouldenes of your minde' (840) point to the new status Iphigenia has realised as a sovereign subject.

Beyond Elizabeth I, a wider, interested audience of women is hinted at in Clytemnestra's request that Iphigenia send a message to her offstage 'sisters' and to the 'other virgins' (857–61). The Chorus who comment on events bring a community of Greek noblewomen on stage and into the public arena alongside Iphigenia, forming a link between offstage female spectators and the bold heroine. Although Lumley reduces their lines from the Greek original, their sparse comments on female agency and parental responsibilities strike home, like moral sententiae. They sympathise with Agamemnon 'so much as it becommethe women to lament the miserie of princes' (311–12), but, more significantly, they define themselves as occupying a happy medium. They are 'mooste happie, which being neither in to[o] hye estate, nor yet oppressed with to[o] moche povertie, may quietly enjoye the companie of their frindes' (366). Like the translator Lady Lumley, they openly acknowledge that they will not achieve 'perpetuall renowne for ever' which belongs only to exceptional figures on the public stage, of the order of Iphigenia or Elizabeth I. Nevertheless, they have a place on the margins of the action, and their presence in the public domain suggests that they share the heroine's 'bouldenes of mind' and independent spirit.

If *Iphigenia* was performed around the banqueting house at Nonsuch that venue obviously worked very differently from the model of Jacobean banqueting outlined by Patricia Fumerton. She argues that banqueting houses and the entertainments enacted there offered a 'special place for subjectivity arising' since they are deliberately displaced from the central places and normal conditions of living within the house.[32] *Iphigenia* certainly relies on a more open arena in its setting, which could have been emphasised by the garden venue to develop new female subjectivities. Fumerton's argument that the banqueting house was essentially a 'hollow place set apart from the communal whole' does not hold for Lumley's Elizabethan text, however. Iphigenia's public self-sacrifice offers a new vision of the golden age in which women play a leading role in civic life. If Elizabeth was the prime spectator, she was also represented as the prime public actor.

The extra-mural banquet offered Elizabethan women something very different from the retreat into privacy that it offered Jacobean men: space and licence to celebrate a newly-won sense of identity in the realm of public experience. The insubstantiality of void stuffs and masques may have reproduced a fragile Jacobean private self, but *Iphigenia* works in the opposite way to conventional banqueting tradition. It does not dramatise 'a quest in which an endlessly frustrated search for private subjectivity was displaced into repetitive, ritualistic acts of preserving the flesh'.[33] Instead, the flesh disappears completely: Iphigenia's sacrificial body vanishes from Diana's altar and is replaced by a sacred hart. Perhaps Lady Jane Lumley's idea of banqueting is a very maternal one, in line with Elizabeth's: the deliberate self-consumption of the private individual in favour of full communal identity. On a spiritual level, it could also symbolise the disappearance of the Catholic host in favour of the Protestant 'hooste' or national community, which the Catholic Earl of Arundel and Lord John Lumley were obliged to recognise. The latter's involvement in the Ridolfi plot may have prompted his fellow recusant, Master Sebastian Westcotte, to revive the play at court in 1571–2, as a reminder to Elizabeth of the history of the Arundel family's loyalty. If so, the shift from private garden to royal court mirrors the way in which Elizabeth legitimised women's entry onto the public arena and appropriation of the more rigid architectural structures of the house and palace.

REWRITING QUEENS' GARDENS

Two more female-authored entertainments for Elizabeth make use of outdoor environments to rewrite the typical equation of woman and nature. Each is a deliberate female appropriation of space to repoliticise the closed, sterilised territory in which male authors inscribe Elizabeth and women more generally as part of the landscape. Lady Elizabeth Russell and Lady Mary Sidney Herbert wrote pieces to greet Elizabeth I to their estates in 1592 and 1599. *Speeches Delivered to Her Majestie this Last Progress, at the Right Honourable the Lady Russels at Bisham* (1592) self-consciously casts the landscape as woman's terrain: to be controlled by Lady Russell (author of the entertainment), by her two daughters (who performed the parts of shepherdesses), and by the Queen. A complex interweaving of nature and artifice characterises the scenes but, unlike the masculine cultivation of landscape and plants in most georgic and pastoral literature, artistic control is always in the hands of female figures.[34]

The entertainment enacts a politics of visual pleasure amenable to feminist analysis. It does not represent oppressive images of feminised landscapes or of women's bodies as terrain. Instead, it actively engages with the familiar tropes, opening them up in ways that challenge the authority of the originals. The female gaze is, as Catherine Nash has observed, central to such feminist re-appropriation of the landscape. By authorising 'the validity of a feminine heroic approach to landscape through a distanced and elevated viewing position, the power and natur-alness of the masculine heroic is subverted'.[35] In the Bisham entertain-ment, the most powerful gaze is that of a woman: Elizabeth I, and after her, the gazes of Elizabeth Russell and her daughters.

In the first scene, the Queen's influence permeates the woods forcing Sylvanus to his cave. A wild man admits that her presence has transformed him: 'my untamed thoughts waxe gentle, & I feel in my selfe civility' (A2–A2v). The Queen's ability to tame nature reverses the usual model of husbandry in which the untamed feminine is trained to conform to patriarchal laws: here, the savage man is brought under the benign control of the artful Queen. As she draws nearer to the house, the second scene, featuring Elizabeth and Anne Russell as shepherdesses, extends the trope of female artistry. Sybilla and Isabella firmly resist Pan's coarse wooing and reduce him to their servant 'fitter to drawe in a Harvest wayne, then talke of love to chaste Virgins' (A2v–A3).

A central feature of the scene's composition is the shepherdesses embroi-dering samplers in the open air 'at the middle of the hill' (A2v). Thomasina Beck has demonstrated a close relationship between the arts of needlework and gardening in early modern culture; indeed, the same patterns were used for the designs of embroidery and knot gardens.[36] The sisters' needlework on the hill thus materialises their power to civilise nature through art. Their samplers depict the beastly transformations of Jupiter to satisfy his lust, and the elevation of chaste virgins to goddesses. Needlework is purportedly an activity associated with feminine modesty and subjection, and part of the scene's purpose would have been to recommend Elizabeth and Anne

Russell as ladies-in-waiting to the Queen.[37] Embroidery is also a metaphor for constructing the world according to one's own agenda. Under the auspices of the Virgin Queen, the power relations of classical myth are reversed, the naturalness of the masculine heroic is undermined, and women dominate nature. In celebration, the sisters embroider roses, eglantine and heart's ease (all flowers associated with Elizabeth I), thus erasing any distinction between culture and nature. Significantly, the flowers are 'wrought with Queenes stitch' (A3). At the top of the hierarchy, Elizabeth controls her own self-representation through a powerful iconography. Inspired by this example, Lady Russell artfully creates a series of rural speaking-tableaux to compliment the Queen on her powerful model of chastity and self-possession. The Russell daughters show themselves dutiful disciples of this ideology in their actions (rejecting Pan) and their own artistic endeavours.

The Virgin Queen creates a different model of husbandry, as the entertainment triumphantly concludes. Elizabeth's chastity does not isolate her from the living world: in her, 'nature hath imprinted beauty, not art paynted it' and wit has bred learning 'but not without labour' (A3v). Elizabeth's promotion of female labour, learning and independent virginity leads to a wonderful harvest across the country, where 'our Cartes' are 'laden with Corne' and 'our Rivers flow with fish' (A3v). At the doorway to the house she is greeted by Ceres, who graciously surrenders her crown of wheat, 'the honour of your peace' (A4v), to the Queen. It is the chaste mistress, not the paternal master, who controls fertility within the kingdom. Elizabeth Russell, widowed for the second time in 1584, was, like her queen, mistress of her household. Her entertainment promotes parallel examples of female self-possession for Queen, Countess, and virginal Ladies-in-Waiting.

A more radical rewriting of pastoral encomium is seen in the Countess of Pembroke's 'Dialogue Between Two Shepherds Thenot and Piers in Praise of Astraea'.[38] The dialogue was probably never performed since the Queen's visit to Wilton in August 1599 was cancelled,[39] but the Countess surely designed it for outdoor performance to greet Elizabeth because much of its meaning and subversive power can only be fully realized in an outdoor setting. Wilton House was on an estate dominated by sheep farming. Before the elaborate reconstruction of the gardens by de Caus in 1632–6, its formal knots would have been relatively close to the Wiltshire Downs outside the walled gateway on the eastern front. John Aubrey commented 'the downes are intermixt with boscages that nothing can be more pleasant, and in the summer time doe excell Arcadia in verdant and rich turfe and moderate aire . . . The innocent lives here of the shepherds does give us a resemblance of the golden age.'[40] Mary Sidney Herbert probably anticipated her shepherd characters greeting Elizabeth somewhere just outside the gateway. This location, beyond the pale, enabled the Countess to move outside the conventional rhetoric of courtly praise. The natural surroundings of this living theatre immediately cast the brittle limits of pastoral encomium into relief.

'Thenot and Piers in praise of Astraea' sets the pastoral lyric style of the former shepherd against the critical scepticism of the latter. The balance between their viewpoints of artifice and reductive realism would have been materialised at the gateway to Wilton House, with the formal gardens on one side and the fields on the other. The shepherds' competitive dialogue to praise the Queen directly addresses the problem of Elizabeth's identity as both a goddess (Astraea) and a natural woman. Thenot's extravagant praise of her as 'a field in flowry Roabe arrayd', matches her representation as Astraea in the Rainbow Portrait (1600), but seems all the more artificial if spoken outside, amid the realities of nature. Here, Mary Sidney's dialogue deftly enacts Philip Sidney's opinion that 'Nature never set forth the earth in so rich tapestry as divers poets have done.'[41] She refuses to limit her praise of the Queen to the conventional tail rhymes that her neighbour, Sir John Davies, uses in his *Hymnes to Astraea* presented in November 1599 in London.

Instead, Mary Sidney Herbert strikes out much more boldly to reclaim a nature truer to the rural surroundings at Wilton. Piers's objections to comparisons that make Astraea 'the like, the same' as the natural environment carry more weight and humour in an outdoor setting. He wryly points out that Astraea's beauty cannot be exactly like the sun, since (in an English summer at least), 'darknes oft that light enclowdes'. The countryside at Wilton undercuts the pastoral idyll and the dazzling image of royalty. Hannay's feeling that the piece 'may subvert its own genre of pastoral panegyric' is borne out when Piers silences Thenot with the words 'nought can praise her'.[42] The failure of language is supplemented by the silent script of the landscape in which the dialogue is spoken.

Piers seems to promote Astraea as divinely transcendent, beyond the reach of language or praise. Nevertheless, his rootedness in the rural world also leads him to appreciate Elizabeth's materiality. Divine virtue and wisdom are powerless unless embodied by Astraea: 'Nay take from them, her hand, her minde, / The one is lame, the other blinde.' An appreciation of Elizabeth as a woman who grows, ages and will die like every other living thing on earth is hidden under Piers's protestations. Claiming that 'nought like to her the earth enfoldes', his references to nature and its imperfections do just that, enfolding her in earthly shackles. The net effect is, ironically, to emphasise the praise and love due to a Queen who is not a goddess but a woman who has transcended the normal limitations of her sex. Elizabeth outdoes the crooked, 'manly Palme' or the lowly 'Maiden Bay', because she stands upright 'and still high doth growe'. The organic image, echoed outside Wilton House, would have offered a powerful example of natural female growth. It is not surprising that Mary Sidney Herbert, the presiding spirit and Mistress of Pembroke, preferred this to the more conventional floral tributes as a way to greet her monarch.

DIGGING DEEPER: LADY MARY WROTH'S *LOVE'S VICTORY*

The women's scripts explored so far have used the garden's heterotopic qualities to invert or neutralise the given cultural relations between woman and the outside world, either natural or public. However, Hawkins's reading of the garden in *Partheneia Sacra* reminds us that garden space functions on physical, social, psychological and spiritual levels simultaneously. As Foucault points out, 'the heterotopia is capable of juxtaposing in a single real place, several spaces, several sites that are in themselves incompatible'.[43] Heterotopias are thus like theatre, he goes on to argue, and Anne Ubersfeld's work on the poetics of stage space has explored the juxtaposition of different sites within a theatrical performance. As well as representing a physical fictive world (the garden or pastoral setting), stage space can simultaneously figure a sociocultural or sociopolitical network (gender relations within that setting), or a topography of the mind. The enclosed performance arena, like the walls of the garden, brings together these layers functioning 'as a mediation between different ways of reading the text'.[44]

Lady Mary Wroth's play *Love's Victory* (1615–18) makes full use of the multi-faceted quality of dramatic pastoral to explore the sensual, sociopolitical and psychological aspects of romance.[45] Wroth constructs a deliberately fantastic pastoral; her shepherds and shepherdesses follow a psychological journey within a rural setting that is simultaneously a topography of the mind and heart. Climeana's song captures the new emotional territory into which they venture:

> O mine eyes, why doe you lead
> My poore hart thus forth to rang
> From the wounted course, to strange
> Unknowne ways and pathes to tread? (2.311–14)

Wroth takes the audience, as well as the characters, into new paths and unknown ways of thinking. The play makes brilliant use of the metaphor of garden as journey to lead spectators to accept that women's direction of romance (through the guidance of female characters under the overarching control of the female author) is something natural by the end of Act 5. The reader of an early modern garden must follow a planned route or narrative, passing from the formal knots or parterres, into the surprises hidden in bowers in the garden labyrinth or its wilderness. Here, the visitor appears to lose him or herself in order to discover a self. Likewise, in *Love's Victory*, characters and spectators pass through the groves, deepening their self-knowledge and emotional maturity in various scenes that are held securely within the fixed outer boundaries of fictional tragicomedy, presided over by Venus and Wroth herself.

Like all pastoral, *Love's Victory* draws on the recurrent horticultural motif of the garden of love or *locus amoenus*, a place of opportunity in which the subject journeys into a realm where 'the imagination concede[s] the helplessness of its rapture and the strangeness of its discovery'.[46] Supporting characters like Rustic and Dalina are genuinely rustic in their closeness to the material realities of country life, but the play's primary focus is on the noble protagonists' imaginative journeys through the garden of love. The physical landscape of the play is therefore to be read in emotional and psychological terms. Sylvia Bowerbank has persuasively argued that the topography of Wroth's prose romance *Urania* foregrounds nature as an animate force coexisting with human desires. She coins the term 'pathetic stylistics' to describe the strategic construction of the natural order's complicity with the noble human subject in a subtle interplay between self and setting. The investment of women's emotions in distinct locations is particularly important in the creation of a sense of place.[47]

A similar process is at work in *Love's Victory*, whose landscape is brightly decorated with flowers, but also subject to the cold of winter's blast. It is experienced differently by each character according to his or her fortunes in love. John Money's model of mapping the developing psyche provides a useful tool for analysing the emotional geography of the play. He proposes that the 'gendermap' and 'lovemap' are the two organising schemas within the mind. The former is an evolving representation or template depicting the details of one's gender identity / role, which includes a wide range of non-sexuerotic ideation, imagery and practice. The 'lovemap' is a template depicting the idealised lover, love affair, and programme of sexuerotic activity projected in imagery, or actually engaged in with the lover.[48] The natural settings of *Love's Victory* can be read as a garden of love, a maze through which characters move, guided by their gender and love maps. Open ground, with meadows, walks, grass and flowers, is the temperate zone in which feelings are expressed and love can prosper. Wroth's harmonious setting uses the typical features of the *locus amoenus,* as outlined by Henry Hawkins: 'It is the Paradice of pleasures, whose open walks are Terrases, the Close, the Galleries, the Arbours, the Pavillions, the flowerie Banckes, the easie and soft Couches. It is, in a word, a world of sweets, that live in a faire Communities together, where is no envie of another's happiness, or contempt of others povertie' (p. 6).

Traversing this terrain is dangerous, however, since the garden of pleasure contains hidden surprises. The shepherd Lacon sings of how he came upon Venus and Mars in a bower, and was led by Cupid to fall painfully in love with 'a heaven'ly mayd' (372), an experience shared by the other shepherds, most notably Lissius. For women too, Cupid's dart transforms the lovely place into a place of love where the subject cannot rest. Falling in love (or 'limerence'), the central experience of Wroth's play, is a critical stage in the development of the subject's mental maps. It destabilises the individual because it is an experience where he or she tries to project his/her idealised gendermap and lovemap onto the desired other. Like entering the labyrinth, the would-be lover risks losing him or herself in order to win an extended identity with the beloved. The garden here becomes an expression of desire as a split, a rift, between needs and wants, since its fantasy escape world offers an illusion of plenty but cannot provide for physical needs.[49] The settings of *Love's Victory* physicalise the lovers' highly charged emotional chemistry during limerence. The sun, frequently a metaphor for the lovers' passions, threatens to grow too hot, and several characters withdraw to the woods, which are governed by Diana's bow instead of Cupid's. Chastity and restraint are the dominant forces here. The shady fringes of the wood, where the shepherds and shepherdesses retire to play games in each act, are a liminal space of flirtation between desire and restraint. They are like the arbours or shaded walks skirting the garden.

The protagonists' journeys through physical and psychological land-scapes offer male and female spectators routes through the confusing experiences of romantic love. What is clear, however, is that the open pleasure garden, associated with the pursuit of desire, and the shady woods of chaste restraint offer different opportunities to men and women, both in *Love's Victory* and beyond. For women, the pleasure garden is a

dangerous place of temptation. On the title illustration of Richard
Brathwait's *The English Gentlewoman* (1631) (Figure 1), for example, the
virtuous gentlewoman is accosted in a garden by 'Complement', a fantastic gallant, and is obliged to 'make knowne her neglect of him by
sleighting or putting him aside by her hand'. The feminine virtue 'Estimation' defensively guards 'an Arbour'. Honour is also a withdrawn
figure. In contrast to Fame, who stands exposed on a grassy mount, the
virtuous woman is shown 'Retiring from the Theatre of Honour, and
reposing in a securer harbour: Where she is *inclosed* with a *flowry grove of
Osyers*, implying *privacy*.'[50] Brathwait's advice on behaviour reinforces the
message. He warns women 'Chastity is an *inclosed Garden*, it should not
be so much as assaulted' (p. 42).

Love's Victory appears to duplicate the cautionary messages of Brathwait's
text. Dalina and Climeana's gendermaps are shown as unsuitable guides
to the romantic territory of the play. Dalina has to rework her former
independence as a proud and fickle mistress into more conventional
receptive humility. Climeana's belief that 'love's passages' afford 'large
scope' (3.228) for the open expression of female desire is deeply mistaken.
When she declares her feelings like Fame on the mount in Brathwait's
picture, Philisses reprimands her as 'shameful' and spectators are left in
no doubt that the garden of love does not offer equal 'scope' to everybody.
The mismatch between her gendermap, which includes assertive female
behaviour, and Philisses' lovemap, in which his beloved is a much quieter,
submissive partner, makes for a deeply uncomfortable, embarrassing
exchange.

Far more successful is Musella, who conceals her love for Philisses,
apparently even refusing to listen to his compliments in public (1331–2).
Only in the 'secrett guard' of the 'blessed woods' (4.5) can she hide to
overhear his declaration of love before revealing her own. Wroth creates
an ironic, empathetic identification between her chaste heroine and the
setting, which functions as the medium through which the couple bond.
Philisses projects his lovemap and his ideal image of womanhood onto the
surroundings he addresses in soliloquy. The trees are sympathetic, their
hearts and minds are constant and they are, above all, silent: 'No Echo
shrill shall your deere secrets utter, / Or wrong your silence with a
blabbing tongue' (4.13–14). Musella, hidden on stage, matches his ideal
picture of a chaste, silent woman. The heroine is '*inclosed*' in an Arbour to
preserve her honour and estimation, like Brathwait's feminine virtues.
Her lover's words here do not offer much hope for liberation in the
future.

The male characters in *Love's Victory* learn to adapt their gendermaps to accommodate traditionally feminine types of behaviour, but only in the Forester does this change carry permanent weight. Philisses' self-doubt in love leads him to new territory. The clear pathways of self-expression, imaged in the open flowered meadows, grass, and walks, are drained of the sweet pleasures they once held: 'Waulks, once so sought for, now / I shun you for the dark' (1.47–8). Introspection, self-neglect, and passivity takes him into the woods, the feminine zone of retreat. Here he learns to express his feelings for Musella and to trust Lissius, but even at the end of the play his gendermap and appreciation of Musella are not much modified. His heroic offer to die for her initially fails to recognise the strength of her love, which will make happiness without him impossible.

Lissius's transformation through love is even more superficial. Rather than retreating to the woods when Simeana rejects him, he makes a very public, ostentatious display of his grief:

> Tell fierce Simeana she hath murder'd mee,
> And gaine but this that she my end will bless
> With some though smallest griefe for my distress;
> And that she will but grace my hapless tombe
> As to beehold me dead by her hard doombe. (4.172–6)

This is a mimic performance of feminine passivity and subjection, a drag act, delibertately adopted to impress, rather than a genuine reorientation of his gendermap or lovemap. Although Simeana and Lissius are reconciled, she must accept the double standard which allows him to 'sitt too privately' (4.275) and flirt with another woman. What the men learn about trust and expressing their feelings is, in fact, part of male-authored pastoral tradition, especially the bonding of Lissius and Philisses through trust and marriage (via Simeana).

The Forester, associated closely with the woods, is something of an exception. For love of Silvesta he embraces a more feminine world of chastity and restraint, 'nott seeking gaine' (1.262). This 'new image of love' surprises Lissius because of its non-possessive quality, 'strangest' in that it neglects 'the fruitfull ends of love' (1.265–74). Wroth presents the Forester as a man who has learned to respect and even enjoy Silvesta's independence at a distance, although he still finds this difficult. At the end of the play, he offers his life to preserve that 'unma[t]ched' self (5.413), not as a gamble to win her love.

Lady Mary Wroth radically re-landscapes heterosexual romance by positioning female protagonists, relationships between women and female-centred spaces as the creative forces behind harmonious pastoral community. In Act 3, when the shepherdesses gather under the trees to discuss their experiences of love, competitive relations between women are shown as painful. Climeana and Simeana both want Lissius while Phillis and Musella are both in love with Philisses. These tensions cannot be resolved but they can be aired safely, without loss of honour in an all-female space. Musella and Silvesta's relationship is more idealistic because competition between rivals (for Philisses) has been transcended by love for each other based on respect for differences. Miller rightly observes that the play promotes discourse between women as a motivating and sustaining force in which they can negotiate identities.[51]

In addition, *Love's Victory* presents powerful female figures whose elevated viewing position allows them to direct the plot, offering female spectators on and offstage a controlling perspective over the garden of love. Silvesta's chastity gives her an elevated viewpoint. Far from being a constraining force (as it is for Musella and the other shepherdesses), it allows Silvesta to transcend the boundaries of romantic love that previously tied her to Philisses:

> I have wun chastitie, in place of Love.
> Now love's as farr from mee as never knowne,
> Then bacely tyde, now freely ame mine owne.
> Slavery, and bondage with mourning care
> Were then my living, sighs and tears my fare,
> But all thes gone, now I live joyfully,
> Free, and untouch'd of thought butt chastity. (1. 156–62)

Silvesta moves quickly and easily between the settings of the play; she watches the lovers with understanding, attaining something close to omnipotence in directing them towards the love's victory of the title. Above her, the presiding spirit and most important spectator of the romantic journeys is Venus. As a mother, she is shadowed onstage by Musella's mother who can enforce Musella's marriage to Rustic (albeit through the demands of her dead father's will). The goddess is much more powerful than her human counterpart, who fears that Musella has been flirting wantonly with Philisses. Venus can rise above patriarchal boundaries on female behaviour in her dual persona as goddess of passionate, outlawed desire, and goddess of regenerative, fruitful harmony.

Venus unites the romantic landscape under her purview to create pathways for the fulfilment of female desire. She inspires both the sun-drenched walks of passionate desire and the fierce independence of the shady woods. It is therefore no surprise that the wilful yet loving Silvesta is her 'instrument' (5.71). As Irene Burgess has remarked, Venus is also the figure of the playwright, 'a woman who exceeds others in passion and power and is able to construct a world for herself, based on her ability to go beyond normal womanhood'.[52] The capricious goddess who subjects humans to the power of love but grants them a fantastic happy ending is Wroth, the creator of a pastoral idyll in which her own fantasies of romantic fulfilment within the Sidney family community could be enacted. In this sense, the garden of love's victory is a manifestation of Wroth's feminine self, just as the wooded grove discussed earlier becomes a sympathetic externalisation of Pamphilia's mental and emotional identity in *Urania*.

Love's Victory reworks the Sidney family romance; its love story of Musella and Philisses, for example, presents a happy resolution to the relationship between Lady Mary Worth and her cousin, William Herbert, Earl of Pembroke, and, a generation earlier, the frustrated passions of Philip Sidney and Penelope Rich.[53] Alexandra Bennett argues that the play has a wider courtly dimension, satirising the royal entourage from which Wroth had been expelled.[54] However, at the time of composition and possible performance, the courtly site is eclipsed by the presence of the Sidney family. *Love's Victory* is a drama of retirement, firmly sited in the culture and material surroundings of the Sidney family. The play is not a drama of private family relationships but Wroth's active refashioning of herself through the authoritative literary models of her uncle, aunt and father.[55] In addition to contributing to the popular vogue for pastoral tragicomedy (*c.* 1590–1616), *Love's Victory* follows a Sidney tradition of using pastoral romance as family recreation, functioning as a sequel to *The Countesse of Pembrokes Yvychurch* (1591), dedicated to Wroth's aunt.[56]

The Countesse of Pembrokes Yvychurch suggests an audience and performance style for *Love's Victory*. We have no firm evidence as to where (if at all) it was produced, but it is safe to assume that the play was designed for a Sidney family performance.[57] The script encodes Wroth's adulterous love for her cousin in such romantic terms that Durrance, the married home of Sir Robert and Lady Mary Wroth, is an unlikely venue. Rustic, probably based on Sir Robert, is utterly lacking in pastoral imagination, as his lyric proves:

> Thy Eyes, doe play
> Like Goats with hay,
> And skip like kids flying

From the sly fox;
So eyelid's box
Shutts up thy sights prying.
Thy cheecks are red
Like Okar spread
On a fatted sheep's back;
Thy paps ar found
Like aples round
Noe praises shall lack. (1.341–52)

Rustic's attitude to the landscape, the livestock and Musella as a potential mate, is essentially georgic, a style for which Sir Robert Wroth was also well known.[58] In the happy union of Philisses and Musella, *Love's Victory* celebrates the transcendence of pastoral idyll over georgic husbandry, romantic passion over economic, paternally sanctioned matches. Naomi Miller has commented on how Wroth's sonnet sequence *Pamphilia to Amphilanthus* develops the garden metaphor of seasonal change in feminine terms to explore the possibility of rebirth.[59] *Love's Victory* extends that possibility: its tragicomic plot plays out a family celebration of new-found freedom after Robert Wroth's death.

The most obvious venue for Wroth's fantasy of retreat to an innocent dreamworld of family romance would have been the Sidney home of Penshurst, where she was born and grew up (though with visits to the Continent and to other Sidney estates). She seems to have returned here after her husband's death.[60] The first extant survey of Penshurst by William Burgess (Figure 3), suggests an ideal setting for the romantic journeys in *Love's Victory*. Although created in the eighteenth century, it appears to map the estate retrospectively as the seat of Wroth's mother and father. It defines Penshurst as belonging to the heirs of Robert Sidney, and the first item in the key is 'Lady Gamage's Bower,' a feature singled out for special attention in a large escutcheon at the bottom right of the Survey (the top just visible in Figure 3), announcing 'the bower Erected by Lady Barbara Countess of Leicester Viscount Lisle Baronness Sydney of Penshurst Lady of Coytey Wife to Sr Robert Sydney, Knight of the Gareter and Early of Leicester only Daughter of John Gamage. . .'[61] The bower itself is small (the second circular group of trees down from the house, with a single tree to the top right); but the Survey defines the grounds as a female area of influence. The two main gardens nearest to the house are set out formally, each divided into four squares, one featuring a fountain and the other an orchard. Beyond the garden walls, the park features tree-lined walks (each tree with an individually painted

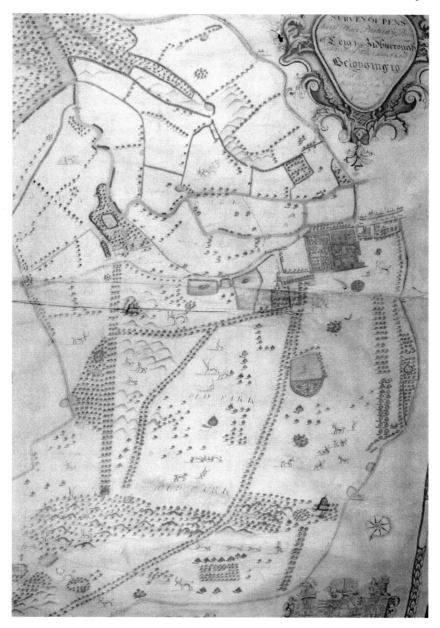

Figure 3. William Burgess, *A Survey of Penshurst*, showing surrounding parkland with domed garden house, wooded walks and bowers [*By kind permission of Viscount De L'Isle from his private collection*].

shadow), lodges, specially planted bowers and fenced areas, woodlands, a pond and a well in the old park. The broadest walk ends in a large 'kissing beech' marked on the key. In addition, there are two large, domed pavilions, one amongst hills and one in trees. Whether these woodlands, shady walks and parkland palaces could have formed the basis of the fictional landscapes of Wroth's *Urania* or her *Love's Victory* cannot be known, but the details of the Survey are certainly suggestive.

It is possible that Wroth envisaged or perhaps realised a private production in the Penshurst surroundings in the tradition recorded in *The Countess of Pembrokes Ivychurch*. Fraunce's example of communal, oral performance in the woods is a pattern repeated by Wroth's shepherds and shepherdesses. It is an intriguing possibility for the play's own production, which could readily have been staged under the trees at Penshurst. Margaret Hannay suggests that the Countess 'may well have taken part in a reading of *Love's Victorie*', where her own romance with Sir Mathew Lister was refigured in the love plot between Simeana and Lissius.[62] In the *Pembrokiana* circle, spectators, listeners or readers of *Love's Victory* could trace a private family message within the familiar landscape of the narrative or the open 'public' place where it was performed.

An alternative venue was the Great Hall of Penshurst, which Swift suggests Wroth may have used.[63] The Great Hall occupies a central position in the physical layout of the Penshurst estate, and would have been a highly appropriate venue for the play in practical and ideological terms. As a performance space, its roomy, high-vaulted wooden ceiling artfully recreates the boughs under which the shepherds and shepherdesses gather, while its balcony creates an ideal elevated perspective for Venus, suggesting her influence over players and spectators. A 1627 inventory lists 'tapistrie hangings of boskage worke otherwise called ymagery worke and forrest worke' and a picture of Cupid in the 'Great Chamber', decorations which recalled the *locus amoenus* in the gardens beyond.[64]

The Hall has even greater metaphorical significance. Don E. Wayne has pointed out an 'implicit or underlying "map"' in the arrangement of buildings and archways at Penshurst 'which charts the transformation of Nature from the wild state of the surrounding forest, through the Arcadian fields and park, into the paradise of the garden'.[65] The Hall at the centre of the Penshurst buildings, representing the Sidney family, is the agent of transformation. Figure 4, a detail of Penshurst Place from the Survey, shows how one looks from the Hall through the gardens and into the park. A letter from the estate Steward at Penshurst reminded Robert Sidney that the Northern Tower 'was raised askewe, and as Kerwyn saythe your father would have it

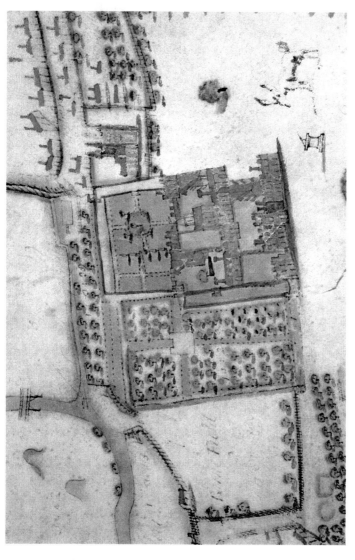

Figure 4. Penshurst Place and immediate gardens, showing view from Great Hall to west (left) through gardens to park. Detail from Burgess, *A Survey of Penshurst* [*By kind permission of Viscount De L'Isle from his private collection*].

soe, because that he might see clene thorowe the howse into the garden'.[66]
On the Survey, clear sightlines exist from the Hall to the left (west) of the hall
through the gardens, and out to the park due to the realignment of the tower.
In the allegocial progress traced by Wayne in Jonson's 'To Penshurst', the
natural garden is then returned to the Hall, where the Sidney family's virtue
transforms and restores it as an image of paradise regained. A family performance of *Love's Victory* in the Great Hall would have enacted just this
pattern. Its highly artificial setting brings the garden and estate back into
the Hall to be represented by the Sidneys. The play's multi-layered pastoral
scene thus brings together three key semantic fields: the material presence of
the flourishing Sidney estate visible from the large windows; the cultural
prestige of their noble connections with that natural environment; and a
psychological journey of development through romance. With Wroth and
her cousin William Herbert as Musella and Philisses, the comic resolution
enacts a family drama of restoration: of rebirth into a paradise of love and
hope for the future.

REGENERATING AND RESOWING: RACHEL FANE'S DRAMATIC ENTERTAINMENTS

Indoor performance obliges us to consider what different dynamics are at
work when 'nature', in terms of an outdoor setting, is imported back into
the house. The popularity of natural motifs in interior design, especially
tapestries and embroideries, suggests a desire on the part of early modern
people to make the regenerative qualities of the garden literally part of the
fabric of the house. An even more literal example of importing the garden
was proposed by Sir Hugh Plat, in his popular gardening book *Floraes
Paradise* (London, 1608), directed to improving 'the lives & healths of the
Nobility and Gentry of this Land' (A5v). Plat enthusiastically recommended the installation of 'A Garden within doores' in 'a faire gallery,
great chamber or other lodging' which could catch the sun. The room was
to be decorated with living 'hearbs and flowers, yea & fruit if it were
possible' (p. 31). From numerous window boxes, herbs, flowers, climbing
vines, plums and apricots could be trained to grow 'about the sides of
your windowes, and all over the seeling of your roomes' (pp. 36–7). Most
extravagantly, Plat suggested the following living canopy, and hearth
decorations for the indoor garden:

You may also hang in the roofe, and about the sides of this roome,
small pompions or cowcumbers, pricked full of Barlie, first making holes for

the Barlie (*quaere* what other seedes or flowers will grow in them) and these will bee over-growen with greene spires. . . And these are Italian fancies, hung up in their roomes to keepe the flies from their pictures: in Sommer time, your chimney may be trimmed with a fine banke of moss, which may be wrought in workes being placed in earth, or with Orpin, or the white flower called *Everlasting*. At either end, and in the middest, place one of your flower or Rosemarie pottes. . . (pp. 34–5)

Plat gives detailed instructions on how to pot outdoor plants, indicating a practical side to his directions for the indoor garden. It represents a belief that the garden's cornucopia, its examples of natural growth, are restorative features. Bringing them into the house will enhance the 'life and healths' of the gentry by integrating them into a wider cosmological order.

Bringing natural settings into the walls of a house in live entertainments constitutes a dramatic equivalent to Plat's garden, but how are women positioned in the restorative pattern? Does their reintroduction of natural motifs enact what Lefebvre sees as an appropriation of the closed, sterile, dominant space of the master's project, by establishing a more democratic 'natural space modified in order to serve the needs and possibilities of a group'?[67] Or do the walls impose limits on the use of nature as a feminine or maternal power? While women's embroidery using flowers, leaves, and animals seems to celebrate them as mistresses of nature, as on the frontispiece to *The Needlewoman's Excellencie,* all these patterns were designed by men. Like the garden, and more particularly the knots within it, embroidery is training of female hearts and minds according to male patterns. Lady Alice Egerton's performance as the Lady in Milton's *Comus,* performed in the Hall at Ludlow Castle, is a dramatic example of such a pattern. However radical the masque's politics, it prioritises passive chastity as the primary female virtue. Even though Alice is rescued by Sabrina (a role probably performed by her sister Lady Mary Egerton Herbert), female power is strictly subservient to that of male commanders in the family, the State and the heavens.[68]

The highly wrought domestication of nature indoors still offers unique opportunities for women, however. Lady Anne Drury's closet, decorated with green-bordered panels depicting outdoor scenes, creates a series of portals to outside. Its decoration suggests that withdrawal to the contemplative, private space paradoxically opens doors to wider horizons.[69] Similarly, drama set outside and presented within the house creates a mixed or joint experience that functions as Foucault's model of the mirror: 'it makes this place that I occupy at the moment when I look at myself in the glass at once absolutely real, connected with all the space which surrounds it, and absolutely unreal, since in order to be perceived it has to pass through this virtual point which is over there'.[70] Dramatic representations of the natural world are very effective 'virtual points' through which perception of the cultural space presented by the house has to pass. Superimposed directly on it, they activate the questions raised earlier about whether the garden is an extension of the house or different from it, and the similarities are as disturbing as the differences. Outside settings offer an image that is simultaneously natural and artificial. As such, they are uniquely suited to unveiling the filter of 'naturalness' that masks ideologies governing behaviour in the house. In Wroth's *Love's Victory,* the uniqueness of male suffering in Petrarchan courtship and male authority *per se* are rendered deeply questionable by the play's 'natural' female-directed romantic narrative.

The ideology governing the country estate is explored by Lady Rachel Fane (1613–80), whose pastoral entertainments can be read as a 'virtual point' through which she learns to grow within and beyond the cultural borders set on women's behaviour. At one level, Fane represents the country estate of her family along the lines of Ben Jonson's 'To Penshurst', as an organic part of the natural environment. At the same time, she adapts the performance of pastoral masque to suit her own purposes. Rachel Fane wrote these short pieces between the ages of thirteen and sixteen, but it is mistaken to dismiss them as juvenile trivia. Barbara Ravelhofer shows that children featured prominently in court masques of the period, expressing through their movement and appearance a purified version of the culture in which they had been raised. In particular, child performers created a vital link between the mythicised or historicised past of their culture (in terms of family, and nation), and its future.[71] Rachel Fane's entertainments perpetuate the conservative feudal ideology by making deliberate use of the juvenile cast to celebrate the regenerative power of her family but she re-presents it with a pointed, woman-centred agenda. Her drama brings the rural landscape into the aristocratic household under the beneficent view of the aristocratic spectators. She recreates her family in the style of the court masque, as semi-divine overseers of the natural cycle of the seasons.

In an entertainment that has become known as 'The Wishing Chair', Puck's ability to call up the four seasons, who are brought on in chairs, grants the audience an atemporal omnipotence suggesting the permanence of the Fane family's demesne in their Apethorpe estate. It is possible that Rachel wrote 'The Wishing Chair' with reference to the courtship and betrothal of her brother, Mildmay, and Grace Thornhurst in early summer 1626 since it expands Mildmay's courtship sonnet 'Comparing Fid[elia] to the 4: Seasons – and the 4: times of the Day'.[72] The seasons change according to the wishes of a 'fantastycal man'. His dissatisfaction with the extremes of each season functions as a mini-antemasque and is succeeded by the harmonious uniting of the seasons and rural community by the noble spectators, who join the performers in a country dance. Fane's stage direction reads:

Yn ye springe & ye sumer wth 2 of ye sheaperdisses, & ye gide [th]at brought ym in take out ye companie for cuntrey dances, wch shall be 8 dances yn ye spring ye sumer wth ye 2 others dance their masking dance yn ye other seasons ioyn to ym & dance, yn they sit & ye sheaperdesses dance their dance.[73]

The graceful integration of differences through dance makes the fantastical man praise 'thise beautious train', implicitly the noble spectators, and the 'harmonie yt wth ym cam'. The entertainment follows the pattern of courtly compliment in celebrating the Fane family as the bringers of perfect peace. Following their intervention 'every creatur' can retire to sleep safely.

The ideological power of Fane's pastoral is increased when we consider her entertainments in spatial terms in the context of the Long Gallery at Apethorpe where they were probably performed. This room, 110 feet long, 15 feet high and just over 20 feet wide runs the whole length of the eastern façade of the courtyard, and is perfectly symmetrical with nine bays letting in extensive light. Long galleries like this gave what Timothy Mowl calls 'an almost external dimension to the house.'[74] At Apethorpe, spectators could easily descend to the loggia and gravel garden immediately below the Gallery, or go up to the roof walk before, during, or after the performance. From these positions, the garden constituted a threshold between the aristocratic household and the surrounding rural landscape and community. An early eighteenth-century sketch of Apethorpe's East Front (Figure 5) gives an impression of what the family, in their elevated position, would have seen. In front, across the walled gravel garden with its two summer houses, they looked over the wider expanse of the well-ordered estate, while to the left, they oversaw the village community whose livelihood must have depended largely on the great house. The long gallery's shaped and stepped gables are in a local style, increasing this sense of integration between the noble family and their surroundings.

What kind of a stage the Long Gallery provided at the time of Rachel's manuscripts is not clear, although the plays written by her brother Mildmay and performed at Apethorpe in the 1640s detail three separate doors, three flat revolving wings on each side of the stage, and a curtained

Figure 5. View of Apethorpe Hall, East Range [*By permission of The British Library*].

area at the rear. Rachel's entertainments and Mildmay's poetry and drama share similar pastoral settings. Mildmay's *Don Phoebo's Triumph*, for example, features the hero sitting in 'a Chaire Hemisphericall' and addressing the seasons, so perhaps the symbolic use of chairs, as in Rachel's 'Wishing Chair Entertainment' was a common staging feature of the Fane family drama, with specific pieces of stage furniture.[75] Music and dancing are characteristic components of the Fane family drama; when the shepherds or nymphs of Rachel's entertainments call for music, the meaning behind their patterned dance or song was spelled out clearly for spectators in the Long Gallery. The magnificent fireplace displays a statue of King David playing the harp and bears the inscription

> Rare and ever to be wished sound here
> Instruments which faint spirits and muses cheer
> Composing for the body, soul and ear
> Which sickness, sadness, and foul spirits fear.[76]

Rachel Fane's pastoral entertainments take a cue from the verse to use music as a charm against the ills that could harm the household and estate.

The noble family are celebrated as the centrepoint of harmonious productivity in Fane's Christmas entertainment, written *c.* 1626–8. As in the 'Wishing Chair', music, song and dance bring seasonal and social opposites together in an organic whole. Fane's cast list includes members of the extended household as well as her brothers Antony, George, William and Robert, her four-year-old sister Frances and her cousin Margaret Wortley (11). Juvenile performance symbolically perpetuates a feudal ideal of harmonious community based on social difference. 'Won cester michell', aged nine years, was probably a family retainer or tenant, while Mary Falconer (aged eleven) and Richard Burton (aged five), may have been maintained and educated under the charitable provision of Rachel's mother.[77]

The entertainment begins with a rural antemasque representing the household traditionally, with an apparently conservative message. A garlanded jester (probably played by Jesper Michell), who resembles a green spirit of renewal, apologetically announces 'The worst does first for 'tis ye fashion', and introduces a May Day celebration. With pipe and tabor, and a maypole, 'from woods wher may doe fluresh to day' (fol. 2r), the rural company dance 'amores' (love dances), before paying tribute to their noble patrons (fol. 2r). The maypole dance inside must have involved a pot or fixing device for the pole, but the very act of bringing the rural festivity into the aristocratic gallery dramatises the inclusive nature of the noble family's paternal care. The Fane household list for January

1627 includes 'William Wade' and 'John Rowell shepheards' but it is more likely that the shepherds' roles were played by Rachel's brothers since there are no male speaking parts except young Cupid in the main masque. If so, the younger Fane sons continue the feudal tradition, allying themselves with the rural members of the country estate as grateful dependants on their parents' and elder brother's careful management.

Appropriately, Fane uses the symbolic gift-giving typical of pastoral and private entertainments to reiterate the message of harmonious community at Apethorpe. The jester's book of 'birds beasts flowers' contains emblems suited to each audience member. The gifts bring together the seasons of Christmas and summer, the cyclical notions of perpetuity and rebirth that the noble family protect, promote and symbolise. A female-centred dimension is subtly introduced here. Sir Francis Fane receives a marigold 'for mary's joy', while Mary (Rachel's mother), is given a fan to symbolise her taking of the Fane family name. The curious intertwining of names is the dramatic equivalent of the quartered or impaled coats of arms, displayed in the drawing rooms, and acknowledges women's importance in the living fabric of the family. Marigold is traditionally associated with charity, a virtue for which Mary Fane was much celebrated. It also wryly symbolises the rich gift (like the Christ Child), which she brings to Fane, as heiress to the Apethorpe estate.

The pattern is repeated at the next generational level. Rachel's eldest brother, Mildmay, is given a grape to celebrate his recent appointment as Lord Dispencer, 'Yo love to eat as I doe understand / Therefore a grape is good to put wt in yr hand.' Mildmay's role as the fruitful dispenser was appropriate since he had a liking for good wine, so the grape is probably also a family joke.[78] The address continues with puns on his wife's name Grace: 'at this time you have / Both grace in nature and in name.'[79] Mildmay and Grace's love forms an appropriate centrepiece to the entertainment. Possibly the May time antemasque festivities were performed earlier in the year during their betrothal and are repeated here in celebration of that relationship coming to fruition at Christmas, where Grace is visibly pregnant. The stage direction says she is given 'a mous' but the spoken lines refer to a 'tru love hart' and 'a box' to 'cloth in fast yr hart', so perhaps she was given an ornament symbolising their love, with the 'mous' for the unborn baby who is given an unnamed gift.

The rest of the presentations develop the gendered opposition between masculine culture, associated with the house and heredity, and feminine nature associated with growth. Rachel's brother Francis, a scholar, receives a book but is counselled not to work too hard, while her sister Elizabeth is given a pot of flowers to symbolise her virginal 'garden yeet unfurnischt'. The gentlewomen attending Grace receive presents too. Elizabeth Flower is told 'you love ye primrose & eake other flowers'; Lady Voisin, a Frenchwoman, is given a bird 'that you might pattern take / To fly from France to England / For ye makers sake'. The emblem's appeal evidently worked since Lady Voison makes frequent appearances in Rachel's household books after her marriage. The old shepherd winds up the antemasque with a joke about how he will be beaten by his wife for being late home, an image of female dominance that prepares for the new focus of the main masque.

The transition from earthly to higher realms is pointedly gendered: men dominate the antemasque, women raise the tone in the masque. Venus' nymph opens the masque perfuming the air with 'frankumsence'. Incense was used in rites of purification in *Pan's Anniversary* and *Love's Triumph Through Callipolis*, but Fane's script seems to recall the Christmas season, alongside the summer 'garland of flowers' worn by the nymph. Perhaps the eleven-year-old Mary Falconer played this servant role, if she was a dependant of the family. The shift from earth to heaven and male to female is pointedly marked in spatial terms. Venus (possibly played by Rachel) appears 'standing half within & half without' on the threshold of a doorway into the gallery. Cupid, who has already entered, tells her that the air is purged 'This place is bleste, 'Tis fit yr Person / Here should rest' and leads her towards the spectators. Fane's choice of presiding deities recalls Lady Mary Wroth's use of Cupid and Venus in *Love's Victory*, suggesting that Rachel could have been familiar with the Penshurst manuscript, or have heard about a performance of Wroth's play in Kent, close to the Fane seat at Mereworth.[80] In Fane's text Cupid appears 'wt bose arose & outher things fiting his atier' (fol. 2v, col. 2), and, as in *Love's Victory*, Venus promises that she will free the noble spectators and protagonists 'From my sons iniury'.

Like Wroth's play, the masque explores a tension between the forces of chastity and love, a topic that must have been highly pertinent to the teenage author and to her cousin Mary Wortley. Perhaps the pastoral entertainment gave Fane a safe space in which to play with questions about female sexuality that preoccupied her. Like the garden, the masque displays a careful interweaving of culture and nature. A precarious balance between the (k)nots of restraint and the energies of adolescent fertility is echoed in the relationship between Venus and Urania, a shepherdess who honours Diana but is not one of her followers. A 'dance of my making' led by Venus and Urania, presents a harmonious cooperation between love and chastity. The female protagonists and their nymphs gracefully 'mingel yr selfs together'. By 'coopeling ym selfes' an idealised partnership is created, its artifice heightened by the carefully orchestrated movement of female bodies in the dance. It is a spatial manifestation of the restraint that must govern female growth like the formal arrangement of flowers within knots. As a resolution of the conflicting influences on Fane herself, the feminine ideal is a hard model to live up to.

The family's power to recreate Apethorpe as arcadia is celebrated by female deities. Their blessings on the household develop the symbolism of female fertility in the flower gifts of the antemasque.

> The Godes Juno unto you gives wealth
> Pales [Pallas] like wiss wisdom & strength
> Sares [Ceres] corne & wine most plentifully can give you.

These lines progress the masque from May to summer, the success of this year's harvest now enjoyed in the Christmas feasting, and look forward to prosperity in the next. The celebration of female fertility reiterates typical equations of women with the land, but forms a strong counterpoint to the maypole and green spirit of the antemasque. Fane's lines highlight female wisdom and strength as equally vital factors for the prosperity of the household. The female deities Juno, Pallas and Ceres may allude back to Queen Anna of Denmark, who is supposedly figured in the female bust adorning the balustrade that led out of the Long Gallery over the porch.[81]

Venus, to whose beneficent power Cupid recommends the household, embodies the virtues celebrated by Anna: 'Her wisedome is soe / That she cane more good / Then I unto yo shew.' At a local level, the words pay tribute to Rachel's own mother, especially if spoken by one of her own sons or by the dependant Richard Burten. The maternal role was one for which Rachel had been taught to prepare herself too, of course, so playing the part of Venus would have been a rehearsal for her later role as Countess of Bath, in which she showed 'such a motherly disposition that scarce a greater existed in the world'.[82]

A celebration of maternity as a force of renewal, prosperity and sustaining love expands in the masque's concluding speeches. Urania summons nymphs to the house since its utopian climate offers the warmth of sunshine and plenty even in the middle of winter.

> Leave yr streames for to come hether
> Make haste I say, have noo delay
> Here that's above the weather
> A flower of May is prung today
> That like the flower of sun

> Tis clought today in lively array
> And in at night is done.
> For she descends to ascend back again
> From highest place whence she came. (2v)

The picture of Venus as a may flower or sun flower which descends to bless the earth, 'to ascend back again' to the 'highest place', carries strong religious associations in a Christmas performance. For Fane, classical pastoral is an alternative space where a feminised narrative of renewal can be foregrounded to complement the Christmas story (elaborate praise of the Virgin Mary would not have been appropriate in a protestant household). Venus has the maternal power needed to bless the family, to ensure its health and the endurance of the household.

At the same time, Fane acknowledges the fragility of her own fantastic vision, and in doing so, critically reframes the earlier celebrations of feudal perpetuity. As if looking to the immediate future in which her father, her younger sister Frances, and later her sister-in-law, Grace, would all be dead, Urania's song acknowledges 'Time stays for none, we'll take our leaves' and registers the mortality of the spectators. She goes to prepare for them 'a place most rare / Where never human that did come / Would e're desire to return'. By bringing rural and heavenly places together in the presence of death, Fane points to a space that has been lost and rediscovered. Apethorpe Hall is not the perfect world of illusion beyond the confines of the performance. At its close, the ruling maternal goddess must be eclipsed in the household governed by hierarchies of gender and class. Nevertheless, Urania looks forward to the Paradise of her own making, a world elsewhere.

GREEN SPACES OF REVOLUTION: CAVENDISH AND BRACKLEY'S *PASTORALL*

By the mid seventeenth century, the aristocratic garden was changed. The influence of Salomon and Isaac de Caus and the European mannerist style transformed the Tudor estates of Hatfield, Woburn Abbey and, most famously, Wilton, by introducing classical landscaping with innovative water features, grottos and statues.[83] The English Civil Wars changed the meanings of the garden equally dramatically: its existence and significance were increasingly unstable amid such revolutionary change, yet it became, more than ever, a site that looked back to a time of innocence and peace. In particular, it became a royalist retreat, the nostalgic evocation of a perfect kingdom ruled by the king as shepherd and deputy of the divine creator. Women dramatists such as the royalists Lady Jane Cavendish and Lady Elizabeth Brackley participated in the current of change by rewriting some of the garden's associations: its relationship with the masculine culture of the house, its complex existence as nature, artifice and theatre, and, most importantly, its symbolic meaning as a manifestation of the female self. The feminised version of the garden as paradise was the *hortus conclusus* of virgin purity, exemplified in different ways by Hawkins's *Partheneia Sacra*, and Cavendish and Brackley's *Pastorall*, a masque composed collaboratively in 1645.[84] These are interconnected by a third material text: the fountain garden at Bolsover Castle, home of the Cavendish family (see Figure 6). This circular garden attached to the Little Castle at Bolsover was reconstructed *c.* 1612–33 from the medieval curtain wall by William Cavendish, father to Lady Jane and Lady Elizabeth.[85] It bears a striking resemblance to the garden in *Partheneia Sacra* 'compassed-in with a wal' (A7), and with 'a goodlie HOUSE of pleasure, standing therin' (Figure 2). The seventeenth-century sketch (Figure 6) reproduces the image from Hawkins from the south (right) hand side, figuring the Little Castle as the pleasure house. The gaze of Hawkins's text is male, positioning the reader in disturbingly voyeuristic terms. The Virgin 'presents her self for your delights in Garden-attire' in a 'coorse and rural array of hearbes and flowers' (A1v), while the reader can 'secretly view' the garden and the 'hidden and sublime perfections therin' (4). At Bolsover, the balcony of the Little Castle and the walk on the enclosing high walls afforded similar views down into the garden. In Cavendish and Brackley's *Pastorall* their father occupies a voyeuristic position as the most powerful reader and virtual spectator of the masque. Even though William Cavendish is in exile in France (and thus absent from the scene of writing or production), he is imagined as a remote presence – reading the manuscript or overseeing his daughters' performances with a god-like omnipotence. William's eye is like a telescope to which the actors perform as though addressing him in their imagination, yet always under surveillance. Elizabeth Brackley tells him in an epilogue that she 'cannot owne / My selfe to thinke I am alone' while feeding on his 'stock of wit' (84). Beneath their effusive affection her lines betray some anxiety about never 'owning' herself, as author or person, in her father's garden.

Hawkins's instructions for reading the metaphorical virgin garden form an appropriate guide to the stylised spectacle of Cavendish and Brackley's *Pastorall* masque. His idea of scrutinising each detail and returning this to the whole, and his advice to the reader to 'sit downe awhile' in contemplation to aid his (sic) 'discoverie of the hidden mysterie' (pp. 3–4), are

Figure 6. The Little Castle and Fountain Garden, Bolsover Castle [*By permission of Sir Reresby Sitwell*].

helpful to feminists wishing to unpack layers of meaning in the *Pastorall*. In a live performance, of course, the pace of reading is obviously dictated; perhaps Cavendish and Brackley prepared the folio manuscript to allow readers to review its significance at more leisure. Even in performance, however, the *Pastorall* holds opportunities for reflection on the diverse elements presented. The significance of costume or setting is often explicitly spelled out for the spectator, who is then free to reflect on the 'hidden mysterie' of the piece. Reading Cavendish and Brackley's pastoral setting in the context of *Partheneia Sacra* and the fountain garden at Bolsover allows us to uncover an early feminist 'mysterie', hidden beneath layers of patriarchal literary tradition and property ownership.

At a superficial level, the *Pastorall* exploits the royalist trope of the English garden as a lost, or in this case besieged, paradise. Two antemasques set outside the castle walls show how civil war has ruined relationships between kinfolk and deprived the population of the fruits of their careful husbandry: 'And soe my Corne I cannot keepe / Neither can I my pretty sheepe / And I have lost fowre dozen of Eggs' (p. 61). One of the country wives is Naunt Henn, a domestic figure like the hen depicted outside the garden walls in *Partheneia Sacra* (Figure 2 bottom left). The main masque presents rarefied aristocratic territory inside the walls of the besieged castle. Here, pastoral settings are a royalist green space threatened by parliamentary forces as were the Cavendish homes in 1644. The sister-shepherdesses, roles obviously designed for Jane, Elizabeth and their younger sister Frances, show loyalty to their 'friends' in exile. In addition to its political allegory, the masque's landscape symbolises the bodies of the shepherdesses, the Cavendish sisters, and their emotions. Borrowing heavily from the trope of virgin as *hortus conclusus* in *Partheneia Sacra*, the masque performs a skilful re-appropriation of the father's estate.

William Cavendish designed the garden at Bolsover as a complement to his pleasure house, whose interior decoration created an allegorical journey through love. On the first floor of the Little Castle, William's apartments included the 'Elysium chamber', depicting the classical gods and goddesses in love, and it was from this room that the balcony looked out over the walled garden. The fountain at its centre is dedicated to Venus; small lodges set into the enclosing wall offer outdoor retreats for the pursuit of love.[86] The seventeenth-century sketch (Figure 6), with the pleasure palace and viewing balcony at the centre, depicts William's appropriation of the *hortus conclusus*. Jane and Elizabeth's *Pastorall* re-appropriates the garden as a virginal space, in contrast to conventional pastoral romance like William's prologue promising 'Amorous speeches, & sweet Roundelayes' between shepherds and shepherdesses.[87] His daughters' protagonists, Innocence, Chastity and Ver, reject suitors and romance. Innocence tells Persuasion 'I dedicate my selfe to each sweete feild / For to your Sex I'm very loth to yeild' (p. 68). It is difficult to imagine a more striking contrast with William's version of pastoral. His shepherdess Flora freely offers 'blushing Aprecott, & wolley Peache' like the trees at Penshurst, and then tells her shepherd 'what a home-borne, housewiferye can yelde, / Ile contrebute to the plentye off your feilde'.[88]

Possession of the land and self-possession are clearly equated. The struggle for control of the fields in Jane and Elizabeth's masque is not just with lovers who might wish to 'husband' the authors, but with their father who landscaped the garden of love. During his exile, they struggled to maintain the estates, under siege or capture from the parliamentary forces. In their roles as Innocence (Jane), Chastity (Elizabeth) and Ver (Frances), their determination to remain mistresses of themselves is rooted in the landscape. Jane Cavendish's stage direction notes that shepherdesses appear alone in the first scene allowing Chastity, the Prologue, to claim the feminised terrain:

> We're now become a fine coule [cool] shady walke
> Soe fit to answeare Lovers in their talke
> And if sad Soules would mallencholly tell
> Let them then come, to visitt, where wee dwell
> For wee're become a fine thick Grove of thought
> Soe fresco even our selves with teares full fraught. . .
> And this our Groto; soe who lookes may have
> A welcome to a sad Shee Hermetts Cave.   (p. 65)

As one might expect, Chastity's lines reject the garden of love offered by Venus on the fountain in favour of a politics of withdrawal and self-reflection. Although we have no evidence of performance for the masque, the garden makes an ideal venue for a coterie production. The stone alcoves in the walls could easily stage the 'groto' or 'She Hermetts Cave', and the fountain of Venus would have been a powerful material symbol of what the shepherdesses are resisting by becoming 'a fine thick Grove of thought'.

The shepherds and shepherdesses compete to define the landscape according to their desires, though in a more self-conscious way than the protagonists in Wroth's *Love's Victory,* as this exchange between Ver and her suitor shows:

CON   Come let us walke that wee may heare
      The joy of Love & then his feare
VER   Noe my remorse shalbe the gentle Spring
      Where sweetly I may heare the Birds to singe
      Which makes my fancy thoughts bravly to thinke
      I shall noe more with mallancholly winke. (p. 71)

Ver's emotions, fancies and thoughts define the spring landscape in the opposite way to Constancy. Her version of the *locus amoenus* is a different kind of lovely place from the place of love that Constancy sees in William's garden. Faithful to the trope of the *hortus conclusus,* the masque prioritises chaste sorority over heterosexual flirtation.

The shepherdesses make a nun-like retreat from courtship (just as the heroines do in *The Concealed Fancies*), deliberately excluding the shepherds from the green sanctuary they create. They rewrite pastoral in overtly Christian terms,[89] a move which seems conservative at first glance, especially since it is used to express devotion to William, the earthly father. Innocence presents herself to spectators as a shepherd and sacrifice, following a family tradition as well as the royalist one that depicted

Charles I as a religious martyr. William Cavendish is praised as a shepherd caring for his flock in Jonson's *The King's Entertainment at Welbeck* (1633) and references to lambs in the *Pastorall* carry an additional allusion since William's troops, costumed in white coats, were known as 'Newcastle's lambs'. The troops promised to dye their uniforms in their enemies' blood.[90] Innocence alludes to this, saying 'My Garments are pure white because that I / Will have no colour to hide spots of dye' (p. 66). Newcastle himself is recalled as the 'pretty lamb' whom Innocence fears to lose.

Something subversive seems to be going on beneath the proclamations of filial devotion. Innocence's 'pure white' shepherd's garments which 'do become mee soe' (p. 66) feminise the Christian trope of shepherd, implicitly reminding spectators that Jane has taken over her father's role as protector of the estate. The feminine *hortus conclusus* becomes an exclusive sisterhood of grief in the musical equivalent of a voice-over, when Chastity sings the feelings of Innocence. Here the identification between woman and garden is extended: Chastity, the woman-as-garden, externalises her sister's interiority through song, revealing that 'greifes Arrows' rather than Cupid's rule in her heart (p. 67).[91] Unlike the audience, Persuasion, the amorous shepherd following her every move, is totally excluded from this confidence, indicating both his lack of understanding and the sisters' re-appropriation of the garden of love.

Religious iconography provides a 'safe' way of expressing feminist ideas about self-ownership. Chastity, a 'shee Priest' (73), remains icily chaste even though she is married. Her suitor Careless bars her way to the grotto to complain 'You owne your selfe to bee a wife / And yet you practice not that life' (p. 73). Elizabeth Brackley probably wrote this part for herself since, as noted in chapter 1, she was married to John Egerton before the Civil War but was 'too young to be bedded', according to Margaret Cavendish.[92] The exchange between Chastity and Careless is a witty response to the earlier masque *Comus*, in which John Egerton played the part of the elder brother. There he had declared that chastity was a sacred armour through which 'No savage bandit' would 'dare to soil her virgin purity'; now his words are turned back upon him as Chastity resolves to 'live a country life' as her own mistress.[93]

Cavendish and Brackley's *Pastorall* follows a royalist remodelling of the garden during the Civil War period, where the usual pattern of moving outside to find more opportunity for self-definition is reversed. The sister-shepherdesses withdraw inwards to 'a little Table' in the 'Temple of Love', purportedly dedicated to their father (p. 76). Their devotion to William as paternal deity is spatially counterpointed by the way they rewrite the

Venus garden as a chaste temple. When the shepherd Freedom asks them to join in a country dance, the customary terpsichorean conclusion to the masque is unfulfilled. They maintain their icy iconic position as 'three Devinities of sad[ness]' (p. 80), their affections and fertility frozen. Their actions purportedly proclaim daughterly love, but preserved virginity also represents a haven of self-possession and sisterly solidarity. In what is probably the most radical rewriting of garden space, the Cavendish sisters create a virgin sanctuary that allows them to remain poised as authors of themselves in the privileged space of their father's garden, a paradise they do not intend to lose.

The *Pastorall* thus reworks many of the garden's meanings by extending the identification of woman and nature beyond those imagined in previous dramatic entertainments by women. Lady Jane Lumley's translation of *Iphigenia* and the royal entertainments by Mary Sidney Herbert and Elizabeth Russell moved to an outside arena to write woman into the public domain as a corporeal being connected powerfully with the land, rather than an idealised goddess. Lady Mary Wroth's *Love's Victory* and Lady Rachel Fane's scripts superimpose a topography of the mind and a rewriting of feudal estate onto pastoral settings, reorienting relationships between the country and the family house. Cavendish and Brackley apparently return to the conservative image of the monastic, enclosed garden but in doing so they recreate it as an all-female preserve where women set the boundaries. The relationship between the male-constructed house of pleasure and the garden is broken, the latter now functioning independently and in opposition to the master's original plan. All these scripts show how the garden's heterotopic qualities made it an open site for revisionary spatial practice. Many ancient layers of meaning were embedded in it, but because it functioned like a theatre, an organic, shifting art-form, these deeply rooted tropes could be pruned and refreshed by the planting of new ideas. Women embraced the possibilities of the garden as a place in which the seeds of their own creativity could be fruitfully planted, an expansive field where their familial, psychological, or culture-changing narratives could grow through dramatic practice.

CHAPTER 3

Courts

The early modern court was a mercurial space characterised by movement. Changing locations of royal residence were matched on a human level by the rise and fall of individual courtiers and factions bound by complex networks of ideological, religious and family alliances. Nevertheless, the buildings in which its members were set forth, 'on stages, in the sight and view of al the worlde' as Elizabeth claimed, were invariably sites of tradition and continuity.[1] Palaces like Hampton Court, Somerset House or Whitehall were invested with the symbolic power held by generations of Tudor and Stuart princes, and even new performance venues like James I's Banqueting Hall were built to perpetuate that patriarchal legacy. James told the Venetian Ambassador that *The Masque of Beauty* (1608) was designed to consecrate the birth of the great hall which his predecessors had left him built in wood but which he had converted into stone.[2] Court drama produced by women is therefore invariably an exercise in negotiation with the conservative legacy of palace buildings and the power invested there. While all courtiers had to negotiate a place, gender difference automatically alienated women, even those at the top: Queen Elizabeth and Mary Queen of Scots had to accommodate themselves as ruling princes; the Queens consort Anna of Denmark and Henrietta Maria were set at one remove from royal authority. A study of the relationship between venues and settings reveals how queens and noblewomen devised tactics of appropriation and withdrawal to establish competitive alternatives to the production of space in this national theatre.

Du Bosc's *The Compleat Woman*, translated in 1639, described the court as a place of sexual equality and performance opportunity: 'God, shewing in the same race, the wonder of women, as well as men, would have the one and other in Court, to make them appeare in the same time and Theater, as the greatest ornaments of our age.'[3] Du Bosc succinctly reminds us that the venues of court performance were already theatricalised. The court was an exemplary arena where social interaction, including that relating to gender, set standards for the population. Queens and noblewomen who actively reproduced themselves through fictional settings did so knowing that the courtly venues gave their actions heightened political, social and spiritual significance. Domestic, rural or heavenly settings automatically invoked national and supernatural kingdoms beyond the court. Female courtiers performed in sites where authority was an imitation of divine power. As Walter Montague's *Miscellanea Spiritualia, or Devout Exercises* (1648) argued, the function of courts was not merely aesthetic. Spectators should, properly, use them as a telescope to perceive divine beauty:

Instead of looking on them as flattering glasses, and mirrours which reflect only the material beauty of the earth, they make opticke glasses of them through which they do easilier take the height of the celestiall glories. . . [T]he lusters and spendours of Courts (being understood as figures of the sublimer and purer state of the kingdome of heaven) are convenient ascents for our weak apprehensions to rise up to the love and estimation of those spirituall objects.[4]

Here, courtiers carry a heavy responsibility as a refraction of the divine, mediators of a heavenly ideal. The entertainments in which aristocratic or royal performers represented themselves as 'figures' of divine power were obvious kinds of 'opticke glasses,' two-way mediating spaces in which the court configured its relationship to the kingdom and to the heavens from which it drew its authority.

The narcissistic effect of bringing together the aesthetic of the court and that of theatre produced what Baudrillard would call 'a simulacrum, never again exchanging for what is real but exchanging in itself in an uninterrupted circuit'.[5] For the Stuarts, an increasingly hysterical overproduction of absolute authority through masques failed: the real remained beyond vanishing point of the spectacular scenes that sought to represent it. For women, the court, whether as a 'flattering glass' or an 'opticke glass', threatened to become an equally destructive uninterrupted circuit, objectifying female beauty. Brathwait's *English Gentlewoman* (1631) recognised they were '*Objects* to many *Eyes*' and warned that 'the Courts glosse may be compared to glasse, bright, but brittle', where one's currency could slide from 'a thousand pound' to 'a single penny'.[6] Elite women's heightened sense of their own fragile commodity value perhaps equipped them to exploit the opportunities offered within such a culture. In Margaret Cavendish's play *The Presence* (1668), for example, Quick-Wit is told 'Lady, you are the life of the Court', to which she replies 'And the Court is the life of me, Sir', implying their interdependence as mutually sustaining fictions.[7] Lady Quick-Wit personifies an active female engagement with the court's opportunities for display that expanded over the Jacobean and Caroline period. The Stuart queens became increasingly adept at manipulating performance spaces in order to reproduce themselves within a tradition of female sovereignty strategically constructed by Elizabeth I and Mary Queen of Scots.

STAGING QUEENLY AUTHORITY: MARY AND ELIZABETH'S COURT ENTERTAINMENTS

The reigning queens, Mary and Elizabeth, manipulated settings and venues to position themselves in relation to princely authority, to their kingdoms, and to each other. Their contrasting dramatic styles drew on Continental and English influences. Broadly speaking, Mary Queen of Scots' spatial politics involved imaginatively expanding her royal household to encompass the kingdom and represent it in an international context. In 1562, for example, Mary used the marriage of Lord Fleming, brother to one of her ladies-in-waiting, to present a lavish visual spectacle to the Swedish Ambassador at Holyrood Palace.[8] The entertainment apparently had little to do with marriage; it imitated the 1560 siege of Leith using the outdoor venue of Dunsaple Loch, a fleet of model galleys, and a castle setting made of wood. Venue and setting positioned Mary politically. Recreating the English Protestants' unsuccessful attack on her mother, Mary of Guise, within the palace grounds, it declared the Queen's firm, if beleaguered, commitment to her faith in the face of Protestant opposition at home and abroad. For the Swedish Ambassador, whose visit may have been to explore a match between Mary and the King of Sweden, it telegraphed a diplomatic message about the nature of any personal and political alliances.

Mary's most elaborate attempt to represent herself as the centre point of her country and the international community was the baptismal ceremonies for James VI at Stirling Castle on 17–19 December 1566.[9] Although the masques show continental influence, their national character is very prominent in the imaginative settings invoked by the costumes of the masquers. Satyrs representing the lowlands, naiads the streams and rivers, and Orcades the highland mountains, all brought homage to the future king of Scotland. Symbolically bringing the kingdom into the palace was a pattern developed in James's British court, especially in the masques of his queen. Mary used a different, Arthurian setting to broadcast her imperial aspirations in relation to England, somewhat prophetically in the light of James's eventual succession. The lords, including the Earl of Bedford (who represented Elizabeth at the baptism), were invited to sit at a round table over which Mary presided as an Arthurian host while musicians 'lyk maidins, playing upon all sortis of instruments' entertained them. Mary's symbolic usurpation of Elizabeth's role was highlighted by Buchanan's text celebrating her as Arthur and Astraea.[10] Doubtless Elizabeth would have seen the technical problems of the masque, where a revolving stage collapsed, as rightful punishments for Mary's presumption.

Elizabeth's own courtly style was very different. Plans for masques to celebrate a meeting of the two queens in summer 1561, for example, represent the court allegorically as a self-sufficient governing female body rather than incorporating the surrounding regions and population through visual spectacle. Although we do not know how much Elizabeth was involved in their preparation, the entertainments' clever use of the occasion certainly meets her personal as well as diplomatic agenda. The proposed Nottingham venue was at a distance from the palaces that symbolically reinforced Elizabeth's princely power. This created opportunities to establish a more feminised model of monarchy, alongside the need to re-assert her national authority. While welcoming the Queen of Scots, the fictional scenes produce space in ways that radically regender princely identity: prioritising female bodies and intellects as the sites of national prosperity. An allegorised national *mise-en-scène* offers utopian images of sisterly solidarity as a source of strong government. The hall is set with a 'prison' of 'Extreme Oblyvion', but, far from being eclipsed by it, a triumphal procession of 'Ladyes maskers' bring in 'captive Discorde, and false Reporte, with ropes of gold about there necks', and immure them. Female figures dominate or embody the national settings, reflecting the Queens' common need to sustain female sovereignty. Pallas, carrying a standard with clasped female hands and the motto 'ffides', is followed by ladies as Prudentia and Temperantia riding the lions of England and Scotland.[11] The setting changes on the second night's entertainment to a castle 'called the Courte of plentye' which flows with wine during the Revels (p. 146). The castle is a concrete manifestation of the Queens' successful government through peace. For the climax on the final night, an 'Orcharde havinge golden Apples' suggests the pre-lapsarian harmony which the Queens have restored (p. 146). The Stuart Queens' masques, especially those by Henrietta Maria, were to develop the feminised pastoral image of peace as crucial to good government.

Elizabeth's own attitude to the court and its performance possibilities can be glimpsed from the translation from Seneca's *Hercules Oetaeus* that has been attributed to her. 'The court's lustre a stale guest made for me,' declares a lone, royal voice in Elizabeth's rendering of the Chorus of Aetolian women.[12] The Chorus speaks with immediate experience of the insecurity of her position, using the personal pronoun to render the Latin 'pauci reges, non regna colunt; / plures fulgor concitat aulae' [Few worship kings and not their thrones; for 'tis the glitter of the royal hall that stirs the most] (pp. 236–7):

> The love of kingdom's rule observed with care,
> But for himself a king but few regard.
> The court's lustre a stale guest made for me,
> Delighted with the shine noe woe forethought. (27–31)

The translator has a worldly, embittered perspective on how the court has changed for her. Although dazzling when viewed from outside, from her precarious position at its centre, it loses its glamour.

The spatial dimensions of the dramatic text are revealing. The monarch, as representative of the institution, is always a king but architectural metaphors and material details locate the speaker on the threshold, as though she has not, or cannot fully occupy the throne. One of Elizabeth's prayers acknowledged 'without Thee, my throne is unstable, my seat unsure, my kingdom tottering, my life uncertain',[13] and the play fragment offers a palimpsest of a woman negotiating her position as ruling monarch. The court functions as a gap or space through which insecurity crowds. Faith in oneself as ruling by divine right, and from the loyalty of others, can function as 'unpicked locks of certain trust' (4) but this may be small comfort in a bustling environment where 'the vulgar crew fill full thy gates' (8) and the broad 'golden ledge' or royal threshold, offers an 'easy way to guiles' or spiteful treachery (14–16).[14]

Elizabeth may have chosen this speech because the material details of the monarch's surroundings were so familiar to her own. The classical comparison of the monarch's unease in the palace and the peasant's peace in a humble abode take on a personal resonance from the perspective of the Queen whose bedchambers at the palaces of Whitehall, Hampton Court, Oatlands, Richmond and Windsor were frequently decorated with golden ceilings and royal purple hangings. Like Shakespeare's Henry V, Elizabeth knew feelingly that

> All Tyre, where purple woven is and made,
> Not so sound slumber doth his owner yield.
> The gilded roofs the quiet rest bereave,
> And waking nights the purple draws from ease. (66–70)

Elizabeth had greeted her people in purple velvet robes when she entered London as their queen in 1558, and wore the same colour for her coronation banquet. In spite of her love of luxurious clothes and accessories, her longing for the simple life of the milkmaid with a pail on her arm would have made the speech's description of the peasant's wife 'her ears far from the pluck of gemmy weight' (85) appealing.[15] The ideal of a middle way recommended by the Chorus was not a route open to Elizabeth. Her insecurities in assuming the throne would have found an echo in the speech's lengthy allusions to Phaeton and Icarus. Alongside her conviction that God had made her Queen, Elizabeth's sense of her own audacity in occupying the throne after Henry VIII may have informed her description of Phaeton, who stepped out of his natural place and 'of father got / To rule the reins' (103–5), with tragic consequences.

Elizabeth's progresses across the kingdom were strategic moves beyond the palace. They were extrovert, unlike Mary's orchestration of the baptismal celebrations to bring recognition of her dynasty *into* the Scottish court. A progress signalled the monarch's trust and generosity as she travelled (a word deriving from the French to work), to connect herself to her kingdom. Of course, the expense of dramatic entertainments celebrating that connection was borne by the nobility in the great houses she visited.[16] Peripatetic country house entertainments staged around the estate were a microcosm of the progress itself, using place to localise the connection between monarch and kingdom. The manipulation of space in progress entertainments, made by the authors, producers and the Queen's reactions, were thus the means by which delicate relationships between monarch, host and the country were negotiated. The entertainments written by Mary Sidney and Elizabeth Russell and discussed in chapter 2 show how female authors intervened in this political project.

The Queen, although central to an entertainment's overall effect, had less opportunity to produce the space around her and thus advance her own interests. She could ill afford to withdraw from symbolic enactments of her connection to the country, but her participation involved considerable risks. By moving away from the powerfully symbolic material surroundings that helped to construct royal 'presence' in the palaces, the Queen literally laid open her royal persona when on progress. As Michael Leslie points out, the walls and chambers that were the physical home of the court allowed the monarch to manipulate inclusion and exclusion, intimacy and distance. Although great country houses still offered a version of such architectural power, by moving outside on the estates Elizabeth was entering unknown territory: a geographical and theatrical landscape in which she had to improvise.[17] In Sidney's *The Lady of May* (1579), she made an adroit appropriation of the spectacle presented by Leicester and Sidney to sidestep their attempt to position her politically.[18] Two further examples show how Elizabeth learned to work within the boundaries set by the host's script to nurture bonds with her kingdom.

The *Entertainment at Elvetham* (1591) offered by the Earl and Countess of Hertford took great pains to stabilise the relationship between monarch and territory, offering the Queen a series of contained geographical environments in which her own place, as supreme ruler of England and the empire, was predictable and easy to recognise. Its most formal scenario featured a specially constructed 'canapie of estate', the equivalent of an outdoor throne room at the side of the lake, where she was hailed as 'A sea-borne Quene, worthy to governe Kings'. Each stage of Elizabeth's progress through the estate reassured her of the natural loyalty of her kingdom: 'plants and beasts salute with one accord', and a female chorus of Graces and Hours welcomed her to the house as 'Queene of second Troy'.[19] Elizabeth's role was to consolidate the messages of royal authority with indications of her 'great liking' and 'gracious approbation' (p. 113), and to direct the gaze of her court. She was quick to capitalise on the desirable propaganda that particular effects offered. When a Fairy Queen and her ladies danced in a garden, singing 'Elisaes eyes are blessed starres, / Inducing peace, subduing warres', Elizabeth commanded it to be repeated 'three times over, and called for divers Lords and Ladies to behold it' (p. 116).

In contrast to Elvetham, the 1591 Cowdray entertainment exemplifies the very difficult improvisatory role that the Queen sometimes had to undertake on progress. This outdoor, promenade performance used the politicised association between the monarch and the landscape to challenge the Protestant Queen to accept the loyalty of the Catholic Montague family as an inalienable part of her kingdom. At Cowdray, Elizabeth's physical move beyond the clearly defined structures of her court took her into undefined political territory regarding the status of her Catholic subjects. The entertainment's unexpected scenarios obliged her to map out her relationship to a significant proportion of her population. The Porter's speech at the threshold of the Montague house uses gender-based flattery to subtly reconstruct Elizabeth's iconic role as virgin mother of the country into that of protector of her loyal Catholic subjects. Women are active mediators of peace, while men, like the statues of porters and Lord Montague himself, must wait passively at the gates. 'Many Ladies have entred passing amiable', the Porter tells Elizabeth, but only she can secure the household and 'make the foundation staid'.[20] The liminal encounter is a form of spatial blackmail. In order to gain entry to the house, Elizabeth must accept the gift of a golden key along with the truth that Montague is a loyal subject, whose 'tongue is the keie of his heart' (p. 3).

While she is staying at 'the *Priory*', Elizabeth faces surprise encounters with the symbolic figures of 'a Pilgrime', a wild man, and a fisherman (p. 4). Emerging from the rural venue of the estate, these traditional representatives of the Old Faith incorporate her in a landscape of Catholic solidarity. Indeed, a song that followed deer hunting in the park even forced her to confront the bloody question of Catholic martyrdom in its image of helpless deer who loyally 'gaze you in the face although they die' (p. 4). The Wild Man defines the ancient Catholic population whom he represents as 'All heartes of Oke', loyal to the national cause and 'all woven in one roote' (p. 6). Doubtless the park venue substantially reinforced the symbolic power of his words, grounding his message in the earth. This is not merely a process of affirming county as well as family loyalty. It is a much more radical form of religious politics, suggesting that to be truly English *is* to be Catholic. A final dance by Lord and Lady Montague and 'the countrie people' implicitly placed the Protestant Queen at the head of a rural Catholic community. In order to unite herself with her kingdom, Elizabeth had to accept Catholic difference graciously and protectively. As the fisherman reminded her: 'There is no fishing to the sea, nor service to the King: but it holdes when the sea is calme and the king vertuous' (p. 10). Although Elizabeth appeared to move freely across the estates that made up her kingdom, this outside entertainment paradoxically cornered her into a position assigned to her by its producers. The landscape could prove a very difficult metaphor for the monarch to control. For women in the Stuart court this provided both opportunities and difficulties.

RE-SITING QUEENSHIP: THE MASQUES OF ANNA OF DENMARK

Arbella Stuart's introduction to Queen Anna of Denmark's household was to a playing space. She claims that she was thrust into an arena of childish role-play, 'so I was by the mistresse of the Revells not only compelled to play at I knew not what' but to act 'perswaded by the princely example I saw'.[21] In Stuart's description Anna, as Mistress of the Revels, has usurped Sir Edward Coke's position as manager of mirth in the court. Festivity is now in female hands. The death of Queen

Elizabeth and the arrival of Queen Anna as consort fundamentally changed the position of women at court. This, in turn, meant a significant shift in opportunities for performance. Anna brought to England, via Scotland, a distinctive continental tradition of female masquing. However, her position as sponsor or masquer in the palace venues at Whitehall or Hampton Court was very different from that of her predecessor. These were now the King's playing spaces. Under Anna's promotion, the court masque became the site of a dialogue between male and female theatrical voices. Since the masquers remained silent, the dialogue was conducted primarily through the theatrical production of space.

From the beginning Anna's household was recognised, albeit somewhat sarcastically, as an architectural and social space distinct from that of her husband. On 2 February 1604, the Earl of Worcester reported news of Anna's household to the Earl of Shrewsbury with the words: 'Now, having dealt with matters of state, I must a littel towche the feminine comon welthe.' Evidence suggests that Anna's court was indeed a place of opportunity for assertive women. Lucy, Countess of Bedford, Catherine Howard, Countess of Suffolk, and Jane Drummond were all able to forge powerful social positions for themselves here. William Fowler complained that even Anna's Scottish maid, Margaret Harteside 'with too much authority, commands and directs in her Majesty's name with insolence'.[22] Viscount Cranborne's 1605 letter 'from ye Q[ueen']s court' at Greenwich draws attention to its distinctive physical location, something that also operated at Whitehall as we can see from Anne Clifford's diary. She reports 'from the King we went to the Queens side', the physical 'sides' of the court becoming sides in the argument when Anna agrees to support Clifford's struggle over the inheritance of her northern estates. Clifford refused to surrender her claim, even when she was locked into the King's drawing chamber on 20 January 1617. Later that year, the Queen apparently made use of her own quarters to create a more sympathetic hearing for Clifford: 'the Queen sent for me into her own Bedchamber & here I spoke to the King. He used my very graciously & bid me go to his Attorney, who shou'd inform him more of my desires.'[23] Anna of Denmark's intervention effectively re-placed the King in an intimate, female-centred space to create a more just court (in both senses of the word) for Clifford.

In her own conflicts with James, Anna of Denmark adroitly established separate playing spaces as a mark of her independence and authority. Her deliberately politicised sponsorship of *Hymen's Triumph* (1614) to celebrate the marriage of her Scottish Lady of the Bedchamber, Jane

Drummond, to Lord Roxborough is a case in point. Scripted by Samuel Daniel (a Groom of Anna's Chamber), *Hymen's Triumph* was a counterpoint to Campion's *The Somerset Masque* (1613), produced by the King for the controversial marriage between Robert Carr and Frances Howard.[24] In the Banqueting Hall at Whitehall, Anna had been obliged to publicly bless the match that she opposed. She retaliated by symbolically withdrawing from Whitehall and constructing an alternative playing space for a rival marriage masque, over which she presided. The pastoral setting of *Hymen's Triumph* in Arcadia is a '*feminine*' alternative to the ruder sports of James's court.[25] Anna directed the building of a temporary theatre in the courtyard of Denmark House for the production. The palace had formerly belonged to the Dukes of Somerset of course, but under Anna's auspices, it was rebuilt and eventually renamed. The performance was partly in honour of Anna's new palace: 'in hallowing of those roofes (you rear'd of late) / With fires and cheerfull hospitality' (p. 329). The courtyard was a venue 'which the queen had wonderfully transformed with wooden boards and covered with cloth with many lights and degrees', as the Savoyard ambassador observed. This was 'the Quenes court', Chamberlain noted, and Anna was quick to use the performance of *Hymen's Triumph* to emphasise her centrality to the State, placing the French Ambassador at her side.[26] The play's rural setting made symbolic connections between the Queen and the land, emphasised in Daniel's dedication to Anna as set in 'the heart of *England*' and 'the meanes our State stands fast established'. Daniel was well placed to articulate her household's political and artistic agenda. Choosing him (rather than Jonson) to write this pastoral, her first masque, *The Vision of the Twelve Goddesses* (1604) and *Tethys Festival* (1610) was probably, in each case, an assertion of her own court's autonomy.[27] Daniel's praise of Anna as the generous heart of the nation harks back to the style of royal munificence in marriage celebrations hosted by Mary, Queen of Scots and the royal authority of Elizabeth I.

Queen Anna of Denmark was, as Leeds Barroll notes, 'temperamentally unsuited to a purely symbolic role'.[28] Her vigorous political interventions and development of a distinctive artistic culture continued the style of the queens regnant who had preceded her. James Knowles has shown how Anna used Elizabethan iconography to fashion a distinctive gendered arena where she could perform the role of Queen independently from her husband. The *Entertainment Given to the High and Mighty Princesse, Queene Anne* (1613), for example, greeted her with the words 'in Elizaes roome, / As from the Phoenix ashes did another Phoenix come'.[29]

According to Arbella Stuart, the French Ambassador noted Anna's intimacy with the people and would not 'leave that attractive vertu of our Late Queene Elizabeth unremembered or uncommended when he saw it imitated in our most gratious Queene' (p. 184).

Queen Anna's drama was, like her court, a space in which the queen regnant's power could be revived in startling new ways. Palace venues such as the Great Hall at Hampton Court and Whitehall were invested with associations of patriarchal ownership tracing back to Cardinal Wolsey and Henry VIII. Nevertheless, Queen Elizabeth had also reigned in those palaces; fictional representations within the playing space created by a masque frequently put gender and power into play. Masque was an ideal dramatic vehicle to redefine the relationship between masculine government and queenly consorts because, as an even more multi-dimensional form than a play, it defies the model of single authorship and offers multiple points of entry for female creativity. Even though women did not speak any lines, female voices could emerge through fissures in the official court discourse. The masque's yoking together of material and fantastic, fictive worlds made it inherently unstable, as Marion Wynne-Davies has argued.[30] Its special tensions could be employed by royal dramaturgs, designers, writers and aristocratic performers to resonate powerfully, and often subversively, in the court and beyond. The Venetian Ambassador's description of Anna as 'authoress of the whole' of *The Masque of Beauty* succinctly recognises her controlling power as a producer of space.[31] Anna's strategic use of performance to recite and re-site queenly authority within her husband's palaces opened with her first masque *The Vision of the Twelve Goddesses*, performed as part of the winter court entertainments for 1603–4.

The venue, Hampton Court, provided the Stuart King and Queen with a tangible opportunity to appropriate the traditions of English Tudor government.[32] The Duke of Lennox's entertainment on 1 January looked back to the all-male masquings of Henry VIII,[33] but *The Vision of the Twelve Goddesses*, performed by Anna and her ladies, drew on the legacy of Elizabeth I to introduce a new style of masque to the court of Britannia.[34] Its title was telling: it occupied a threshold position between the concrete reality of the Tudor past and dreams of a future Queen's court. Clare McManus has argued that Anna set up a dialogue with her predecessor to align herself with a tradition of female courtly authority.[35] The use of Elizabeth's clothes for the masque supports this idea. Unlike Elizabeth's Parliamentary robes, those made for Anna as Queen consort did not invest her with ruling power. However, in the Great Hall at

Hampton Court, Elizabeth's garments could be deployed to invoke queenly authority. Arbella Stuart remarked, 'the Queene intendeth to make a mask this Christmas to which end my Lady of Suffolk and my Lady Walsingham have warrants to take of the late Queenes best apparel out of the Tower at theyr discretion' (p. 197).

The Vision of the Twelve Goddesses presented a fragmented performance of Elizabeth's queenly presence by a consort of female figures. The opening setting, where Night wakens her son Sleep from a cave, transforms the Hall into a fantasy playing space, or memory theatre, co-opting Jacobean spectators to constitute the 'strange visions' of powerful goddesses from ancient times. Iris ('the daughter of Wonder') and a Sybil introduce each one with implicit reminders of Elizabeth's more recent example of female rule (43, 66). The Countess of Suffolk figured Juno 'in her Chayre / With Scepter of command' (90-1) while Astraea and Diana, so central to Elizabeth's iconography, were danced by Lady Walsingham (who had been Elizabeth's Keeper of the Queen's Robes), and the Countess of Bedford. Anna appeared as 'War-like *Pallas*', as though to highlight her 'Wit and Courage' (94-5) in artistically reciting and re-siting Elizabeth's authority. Although the goddesses ultimately paid homage to James, their physical dominance of the venue subverted the masque's explicit political function. They appeared on 'a Mountaine raised at the lower end of the hall' in rows of three, 'a number dedicated unto Sanctity and an incorporeall nature' (*Dedication*, 189). In the first row, Pallas (Anna), Juno (Lady Suffolk) and Venus (Penelope Rich) constituted a trinity of power centred on the Queen. The rows of goddesses were a spectacular, united female body, 'being all seen on the stairs at once', as Dudley Carleton noted with admiration.[36] The mountain structure displayed the masquers above the eye level of most spectators but with their feet firmly on English ground. It was an appropriate way of signalling the continuity of female rule since Elizabeth's court entertainments had used similar set pieces, including a scenic rock with a rising trap, designed by John Rose for a performance of *The Knight of the Burning Rock* in 1579, and an elaborate castle for Lady Peace, designed by Hans Eworth for a masque in 1572, possibly a rewrite of the entertainment for Elizabeth and Mary Queen of Scots.[37]

The *Vision*'s revival of female authority in a fictional setting was intrinsically empowered by the place and occasion of performance. The ancient Tudor Hall silently sanctioned the presence of ruling goddesses in Elizabeth's clothes, even as they stood opposite the Stuart King. Following the introductory tableau, their movements through the Great Hall were a cleverly orchestrated display of Anna's Court as a site of female influence. The *Vision* increased the usual number of masquers from eight to twelve as though recognising the power of women's bodies to produce queenly presence through space. Their dances on the floor of the Great Hall brought together divine authority and worldly diplomacy in the figures 'fram'd unto motions circular, square, triangular' by Anna and her ladies with 'great maiesty and Arte' (*Dedication*, 229–31). The masquers promoted the idea that was to dominate Stuart masque culture: that artistic control and the ideological power it offered was the most effective form of government.

The dancing masquers were not just attractive female bodies; they were Anna's body politic. The goddesses' movement across the Hall to the Temple of Peace set the masquers' bodies 'against the backdrop of their peers', as McManus notes, because the courtly spectators were seated in traverse, in tiered rows.[38] Choreography integrated the women-as-goddesses into the Court's social and political fabric, particularly in the concluding Revels where boundaries between the feminine commonwealth of the setting and the Jacobean court of spectators were blurred. When the twelve goddesses took out the Duke of Lennox, the Earls of Pembroke, Suffolk, Southampton, Devonshire, Nottingham, Northumberland, and the Lords Henry Howard, Knollys, and Monteagle, and Sir Robert Sidney (Anna's Lord Chamberlain), this clearly signalled the Queen's ability to control the royal Court through the selection of men she favoured.[39] A lyric beginning 'Whiles worth with honour make their choice' (193) heightened the masquers' political interventions. Those who joined in the dance implicitly accepted queenly patronage and leadership. The masquers extended Anna's influence over foreign policy in the second 'taking out' of courtly spectators. The Countess of Bedford and Lady Susan De Vere (niece of Robert Cecil), invited the Polish and Spanish Ambassadors to join the revels 'and they bestirred themselves very lively', as Carleton reported.[40] Physical movement figured the ways Anna and her ladies shaped the changing social dynamic of the Court. The rich continental heritage she brought to Britain was figured in Tethys, goddess of the sea's fecundity, who embraced Albion in 'faithfull Armes' (145–6).

Anna's next entertainment, *The Masque of Blackness* (1605), employed a different strategy to re-stage her arrival from across the seas. Its script, by Jonson, offered no explicit assertion of female command. A more subtle negotiation between the Queen's masquers' spectacular appearances and the Banqueting House venue at Whitehall is at work here. Banqueting houses, as purpose-built performance spaces, have a very high

'information rate' for those inside them; that is, they confront spectators
with a much greater density of visual stimuli than other theatre spaces and
non-performance venues, even in palaces. The wealth of visual decorations, full of colour, is intended to psychologically arouse inhabitants.
They are designed to provide pleasure, stimulus, and excitement, and to
work in concert with the masque presented there to inspire awe. For *The
Masque of Blackness* the roof of the Elizabethan banqueting house had
been redesigned 'with Clowdes and other devyses' and 'framing and
setting upp of a great stage' eleven feet square and four feet high on
wheels.[41] A competition between two-dimensional visual decorations and
three-dimensional, moving, female bodies operates in this masque and in
the subsequent *Masque of Beauty* staged by Anna. The careful deployment
of scenery was charged with national significance since the settings represented both the court and the country beyond the walls of the Banqueting
House.

In *Blackness,* James's kingdom, Albion, is a flat canvas depicting 'a
Landtschap' consisting of '*small woods and here and there a void place filled
with huntings*', the latter detail increasing its associations with the King.[42]
James would doubtless have been aware from his visit to Denmark in 1590
that the term 'landtschap' meant more than a place. It signified a polity,
and was at the centre of conflicts between a monarch or lord, and
common laws laid down by custom and established as the law of the
land.[43] From the seat of State, James commanded a perfect view of the
kingdom in the perspective scenery. In contrast to this carefully fixed
panorama, Anna appeared amid a three-dimensional, feminised, ocean
setting, symbolising her status as an incomer, a foreign princess. The
central focus of spectators' attention was a '*great concave shell, like mother
of pearl curiously made to move on those waters*' (47–8), in which the female
masquers were seated. Anna and her 'corte of ladyes', as Edmonds called
them, brought into Court an exotic otherness that upstaged both the
scenic decorations and the visual splendour of the banqueting house itself.
Carleton famously criticised their costumes as 'too light and curtisan-like'
and their blackened faces and hands 'which were painted and bare up to
the elbowes' as 'a very lothsome sight'.[44]

The spectacle of the Daughters of Niger was intended to shock, to show
how the public role of woman, previously embodied by Queen Elizabeth,
was denigrated in the Stuart Court. The blackening of the public woman
is the work of 'brain-sick men', in particular poets, like Jonson, who
compose the courtly script (132). Such prejudice has infected the purity of

the daughters' reputations; their fall is compared, as in Queen Elizabeth's dramatic translation, to the tragic presumption of Phaeton:

> As of one Phaeton, that fired the world,
> And that before his heedless flames were hurled
> About the globe, the Ethiopes were as fair
> As other dames, now black with black despair,
> And in respect of their complexions changed. (137–41)

The script, music, costume, setting and venue, create a local, politicised geography, a playing space in which issues of colonial power, gender and female self-presentation can be questioned. Britannia, 'Ruled by a sun' in the person of James I, is '*A world divided from the world*' (219). It is out of touch with continental traditions of female performance and influence, like those in which Anna's mother and sisters lived. When the daughters of Niger are invited ashore, each pair of masquers presents fans, but rather than conventionally signifying feminine modesty, each works like an emblem book to teach spectators about the women performers from overseas. Alongside typical associations between female exoticism and fertility, the figures of Glycyte (Sweetness) and Malacia (Delicacy) presented a cloud full of rain symbolising education, an image that mirrored the roof of the banqueting house. The Daughters of Niger were, in fact, teaching the Jacobean court a new performance tradition, while purportedly learning the traditions of Britannia. Possibly their blackened faces alluded to a masque of blackness at the court of Anna's brother, Christian IV of Denmark, in 1596.[45]

The Masque of Blackness employs a spatial dynamic of advancement and retirement in order to cautiously promote Anna's innovative style of self-presentation. The daughters of Niger withdraw to the sea having been prescribed baths in the 'wholesome dew called rosmarine' to refine their complexions (309), probably an allusion to rosemary water as a skin cure. The final song and movements acknowledge the decline of the Elizabethan cult of Diana, the moon: 'our waters know / To ebb, that late did flow'. At the same time, 'with a forward grace', as inexorable as the tide, they confidently signal the entry of a new mode of performance for women in court (324–8).

The companion piece, *The Masque of Beauty* (1608), uses landscape more deliberately to advance female self-determination. The masque's setting, its venue, and the dynamic between the two are clearly sites in which Anna competes politically with James. The garden scene worked in conjunction with the Banqueting House and the royal spectators to promote an image of self-contained government by the transformed daughters of Niger.[46] Their floating island is a garden with a grove 'of grown trees laden with golden fruit', arbours holding the musicians, the ground plot set out as a large maze, and two fountains of pleasure and youth at the front (236–45). The masquers' dances recreated the formal knot patterns that dominated the gardens of their own great houses along the banks of the Thames in Kent and Essex. The script directs Thomas Giles, the choreographer, to take the nymphs 'in those curious *Squares* and *Rounds*', that flow 'betwixt the grounds / Of fruitfull *Kent*, and *Essex* faire' (302–4).

The masque brings an idealised version of the formal country house garden into the palace at Whitehall to advertise the Queen's power to restore the kingdom to its pre-lapsarian state. In *The Masque of Beauty*'s fictional setting, as in Lady Rachel Fane's pastoral entertainments, the seasons coexist in harmony. Temperies figures the fruits of harmonious co-operation: 'On her head a gyrland of flowers, Corne, Vine-leaves, and Olive branches, enterwoven' (206–7). The Mother Nature metaphor was particularly appropriate since, in the years between *Blackness* and *Beauty*, Anna had given birth to Princesses Mary and Sophie. With the presence of the beautiful masquers 'th' *Elyisan* fields are here', declares the final song (407–10).

The court venue changes the significance of the garden setting. With royal and noble performers and spectators, it becomes a geographic embodiment of the State. The on-stage island microcosm alludes to the macrocosm of the island-kingdom. Splendour's iconography is explicitly nationalistic, combining the majesty of the red and white roses, the Tudor past and the unity of England and Scotland. Kenneth Olwig's ingenious discussion of the Stuart masque as a symbol of the changing relationship between the monarch, the State and the geography of early modern Britain helps us to understand *The Masque of Beauty*. In masques, Olwig argues, 'the authority of the state is represented in terms of a spatial structure, or "body geographical" in which the body of the state becomes one with the landscape'. In *Beauty*, the performers in the garden represent the 'members' of the king's symbolic body, the body politic, and symbolise a new 'body geographical', under the centralised power of Stuart government. The monarch seems to hold absolute power in this new abstraction of the geographical state, since it moves in front of him, rather than he having to move through the kingdom on progress, as Elizabeth had done.[47]

The women masquers apparently have little agency as material 'members', moving under the surveillance of the king's controlling eye. Like the Greek *choros,* from which Plato's term *chora* derives, they represent the landscape as a feminine, bodily receptacle through which the state is produced for the male regent. As Olwig points out, however, James's body natural had been reduced to no more than 'an eye in a disembodied head located in a system of coordinate lines', the perspectives that framed bodies on the court stage. As a passive, dismembered head of state, James was in danger of being upstaged by the moving body politic made up of the Queen and her masquers.[48] The *Masque of Beauty* proposes that power is, in fact, located just as much with the Queen and that body politic, as with the King.

Royal competition for power was embedded in the material circumstances of the production. The masque, presented at court on 10 January, staged a highly politicised dialogue between a fictional setting and the venue in which it was performed. The King's newly built banqueting house was a static example of beauty, while the Queen's masque was a living one. As was commonly the case, *The Masque of Beauty* was an exhibition of state power to foreign ambassadors, and differences between the King and Queen over which ambassador should be given precedence prompted the French ambassador to claim that the King was not master in his own house. James had ordered the new wooden banqueting hall to be painted, marbled and gilded to appear like stone. What attracted the ambassador's attention, however, were the moving elements of the spectacle. He reported 'the stage machinery was a miracle' and credited Queen Anna, not James: 'it is evident the mind of her Majesty, the authoress of the whole, is gifted no less highly than her person'.[49]

The design of the masque relocates power from the King's chair of State to the body politic of the Queen's court in the setting. The island is a microcosm of the royal banqueting house, '*divided into eight* squares, *and distinguish'd by so many* Ionick pilasters' (166–7). This echoed the eight Ionic and Doric pillars on each side of Whitehall's banqueting house, newly decorated like the stage set. The island's own 'seate of state' (165), facing that of James in performance, was a Throne of Beauty on which Anna, as 'Harmonia', and her masquers sat. Most importantly, a '*translucent* Pillar' (169) at the centre 'seem'd to be a Mine of light' that reflected on the women's jewels and garments (254). In romance tradition, the palace of light is a trope for wisdom and peaceful government.[50] Its prominence as a feature of the setting locates these political virtues in

Anna's feminine world of imagination and feeling. James needs to embrace that world in order to rule effectively, the masque counsels.

In contrast to the painted pomp of the Banqueting House Anna's symbols of majestic harmony were embodied by living actors. In the Banqueting House, James's throne was watched over by 'boyes of Elme Tymber to hang over the roof' gilded *putti*, or cherubs with two rows of lights.[51] On stage, Anna's throne of beauty was guarded with 'a multitude of *Cupids* (chosen out of the best, and most ingenuous youth of the *Kingdome*, noble and others)' (230–3). *Beauty* shows that the King's role as head of State is only two-dimensional without the living bodies of the court and the support of the next generation to give it substance. As Harmonia, ruling over the fruitful garden, Anna is the mother of an organic kingdom, controlling the fruitful regeneration of a loyal population though love.

In addition to its national political agenda, *The Masque of Beauty* challenges two-dimensional views of female beauty and virtue. The masque refutes two misogynist ideas: the first, that beautiful women in public spheres like the court, or the garden of love, are naturally wanton; the second that their superficial beauty conceals a vacuous mind and soul. A song observes 'It were no politie of Court' to let 'So many *Loves* in armed', but the reply explains that women's virtue makes love a binding force that creates the paradise enjoyed on the island (349–63). A second reply criticises those claiming women have no soul. Rather, the masque counters, women are the souls of men and of the united kingdom: 'So they do move each heart and eye / With the *world's soul*, true harmony' (372–3). It is perhaps not surprising that the masques of *Blackness* and *Beauty* make more extensive use of visual dimensions than *Vision* at Hampton Court, given their venue. They set living female bodies against the two-dimensional images of splendour in the Banqueting House, and promoted Anna's Court as the lifeblood of the healthy State.

The fact that Anna's own masquing performances took place outside her own household, on male territory, with the King as prime consumer, inevitably complicates their spectacular display of queenly autonomy. Gary Waller has argued that court performance necessarily contains any representation of female agency. Taking part in a masque, like entering the court itself, offers only an illusion of power to the otherwise powerless female subject. While the dazzling costumes and scenery command attention and perhaps awe from the spectators, the women who appear are products of an exclusively male gaze. 'To be chosen to play a role in the spectacular theater of the court is to be disclosed as the court's creation, and so individually exploitable and expendable.'[52] Those who took part in the Queen's masques were sharply aware that any agency they enjoyed as masque performers was held only under erasure. Part I of Lady Mary Wroth's *Urania*, for example, presents the dangers of courtly performance very vividly in the episode where Pamphilia and her friends are lured into a round, pillared building like the House of Fame, 'as magnificent a Theater as Art could frame'. The Theatre, complete with a throne, marble seats, and sumptuous embroidered cushions presents a spectacle of richness that is irresistible to women. Once they ascend the throne, they find themselves in a masque:

Instantly the sweetest Musicke and most inchanting harmony of voices, so overruled their sences as they thought no more of any thing but went up and sate downe in the chayres. The gate was instantly lock'd againe, and so was all thought in them shut up for their coming forth thence, till the man most loving and most beloved used his force, who should release them.[53]

For Wroth's noblewomen, the courtly Theatre is a prison. Walter Montague's observations about the court's glittering surfaces or 'flattering glasses', quoted at the opening of the chapter, recognise the same visibility trap. Nevertheless, Waller's reading of court performance for women seems over pessimistic, imagining the court's creative control in exclusively masculine terms. In the masques of *Blackness* and *Beauty*, Anna and her ladies creatively negotiate places of authority for themselves from within the courtly framework, and in doing so they implicitly challenge the very framework that strives to objectify them. *The Masque of Queens*, performed on Twelfth Night 1608, addresses the commodifying culture of the court by presenting performances of female independence in a range of confined spaces. In the setting, Jonson's allusions to Chaucer's House of Fame and the figures of the poets who adorn its walls explicitly foreground the male constructions of women within which the Queens are held.[54]

The masque develops the revolutionary return to Elizabeth signalled in *Twelve Goddesses* and *Blackness*. Its antemasque demonises female power exaggeratedly in the male performance of eleven witches and their Dame. They, like the blackened daughters of Niger, are the products of misogynist ignorance, suspicion, credulity, and bitterness. The setting of a smoking, '*ugly hell*' mouth, from which they enter gives concrete form to the prejudiced discourse that constructs them (21). The masque's idealisations of womanhood supersede the demonic figures to 'make Nature fight / Within her self' (132–3). However, the opposition is not so simple. The witches come to 'overthrow the glory of this night' (98), but if James himself is the 'glory' around which the masquing occasion is built, ironically, the queenly figures carry out the witches' purpose in the main masque. As Peter Holbrook observes, *The Masque of Queens* is 'a bid for transfer of power from King to Queen' in a wider political struggle over foreign policy.[55] Its antemasque, specially requested by the Queen, may hint at her darker purpose. The hags' invocation conjures another setting: the '*glorious and magnificent building figuring the House of Fame*', in which the powerful Queens appear, is produced '*in the heat*' of the witches' grotesque dance (325). Like the hell-mouth, this setting symbolically represents the restrictive discursive framework through which women are produced. Although an idealisation of female virtue and honour is not misogynistic, it is equally restrictive. Jones's design makes its phallo-centric nature explicit: '*for the lower columns, he chose the statues of excellent poets, as Homer, Virgil, Lucan etc. as being the substantial supporters of Fame*' while the upper columns featured '*great heroes which those poets had celebrated*' (624–7).

The Queens resist attempts to contain them within the dominant representational codes of the House setting and the Banqueting Hall venue. The House inverts the classical architectural model of the caryatid by placing the living bodies of the masquers above the static male statues as McManus has pointed out.[56] The Queens do not keep their places in reverence to James as Albion, the son of Neptune (as they had promised to in *Blackness*). Heroic Virtue verbally acknowledges him as the patron who welcomes them 'Unto your court' (407), but the Queens are top girls 'crowned the choice / Of woman-kind' (376) who implicitly resist his patronising embrace. Barbara Lewalski observes their independent status as queens regnant (Berenice, Amalasunta, Candace, Vodicea), fearless military leaders (Artemisia, Hysicratea, Camilla, Thomyris, Zenobia), and Amazonian feminist warriors (Valsca, Penthesilia).[57] Amalasunta is 'rather an example than a second' (580), while Valasca leads the women of Bohemia to slaughter their 'barbarous husbands and lords' and establish female rule (589–93).[58]

The female masquers' movements were undoubtedly constrained by the male-constructed architecture of the scenery and the '*triumphant chariots*' (645) in which they were drawn about the banqueting hall. Unlike Shakespeare's Cleopatra the queens are not represented by male substitutes who will 'boy' their 'greatness'. Physical enclosure in the House of Fame and the chariots advertises the restriction of those spaces and the whole culture of narrow representation fostered in the Banqueting House. The unspoken, autonomous identities of the queens hover like a subversive consciousness through which the living bodies of the masquers transcend the male structures. Most significantly, Anna exceeds male-constructed images of woman by appearing, for the first time in a masque, in her own person as 'Bel-Anna', a queen in whom the other famous women all 'do live!' (676). She and the ruling queens form an independent body politic.

Anna's body politic is more actively integrated into the kingdom in *Tethys Festival* by Samuel Daniel, performed at the Banqueting House in 1610 to celebrate the investiture of Henry as Prince of Wales.[59] The design of the masque, a feminised fictional world into which Henry is integrated as a performer, symbolically advertises Anna's maternal control of the kingdom. Anna and her ladies appeared as Tethys, 'Queene of the Ocean', and the nymphs of some of the country's principal rivers, on tall, moving structures, highly ornamented in silver and gold. The nymphs sat in niches with the Queen on a throne at the centre and Princess Elizabeth (as the Nymph of Thames) at her feet (59–84). Unlike the House of Fame, the throne was an artful representation of natural magnificence, in keeping with the masque's conceit. It featured '*a round bowl of silver in the manner of a fountain*', a golden globe with holes '*out of which issued abundance of water*' and a frieze of fishes and tritons. Daniel's text proclaims, '*there was no place in this great aquatic throne that was not filled with the sprinckling of these two naturall seeming waters*' (257–8). The tableau of living water emanating from the regions and flowing to the sea under the Queen's command, represents the vital relationship between the monarchy and the landed nobility. The State was founded on a model of mutual support where 'the Nobility depend upon the Crown, and the Crown is upheld by the Nobility' as Margaret Cavendish recognised. In *Scenes from The Presence,* she pointed out that Noblemen's houses are 'superintendent Courts', whose function was to 'shew the Honour and Magnificence of the Kingdom'.[60] In *Tethys Festival*, women make the system work: the Queen summons the nymphs, played by the noblewomen of the most important aristocratic families whose country houses stood by the rivers: the Countesses of Arundel (Nymph of Arun), Derby (Nymph of Derwent), Essex (Nymph of Lee), Dorset (Nymph of Ayr), Montgomery (Nymph of Severn), Viscountess Haddington (Nymph of Rother), and Lady Elizabeth Gray (Nymph of Medway).

The masque was not to showcase Anna's favourites (Jane Drummond, her first gentlewoman, did not take part in any masque). Instead it was cast with a deliberately political message in mind. *Tethys Festival* summons the powers of hospitality, support, nurturance that sustain the monarchy at a local level. The masquers' movement across the Hall was a spatial demonstration of how noblewomen fed the nation. The nymphs march up *'with winding meanders like a River'* to a *'Tree of Victory'* at the State throne to offer flowers and wishes of 'everlasting spring' to James (304–22). Anna, still in role as Tethys, sits beneath the tree symbolising the country's natural resources giving life to the State, while the nymphs enact harmony between the different regions of the kingdom, through dance, song and accompanying lute music:

> Our motions, sounds and words,
> Tuned to accords,
> Must show the well-set parts
> Of our affections and our hearts. (336–9)

The meaning of renewal in *Tethys Festival* is celebrated in a final spectacle featuring Prince Charles and six young noblemen. The transfer of power and performance from the women to the next generation of men implicitly bypasses James in favour of the Princes, extending Anna's earlier determination to exercise her maternal authority and bring Henry with her from Scotland to England in May 1603.

A song warns spectators that, since bright glory passes, 'Take it sudden as it flies / Though you take it not to hold' (357–8). Women's majesty is no more substantial than a performance in the court of the Stuart kings. At the same time, combined with the natural symbolism of the rivers, the nymphs also suggest the fluidity of any power. The energising water of life which their performance brings to the Court cannot be controlled by James, even if the Queen and her ladies are transformed safely back to themselves in a 'garden of the spring addressed to Jove' (404).

The subversive suggestion of *Tethys Festival,* that Britain's real potency comes not from James's glorious court but the country surrounding it, was repeated on a local level in honour of one of his rare progress visits into his kingdom. *The Visit of the Nine Goddesses* (1620–1), performed by ladies at Sir John Croftes's house, Little Saxham, is, according to McGee, 'a pastoral of a King's power and a father's potency'.[61] The entertainment expresses a clear preference for the country over 'Courts of great excesse' (12) as a healthy environment for God's deputy. Doubts about the value of royal venues, which are sung by Apollo, echo Elizabeth's translation of the women's chorus from *Hercules Oetaeus*. The classical gods would not have come down to earth

If pallaces, if princes courts
If only rich & royall sportes,
If some curious guilded chamber,
If perfumes of muske & Amber
Were a pleasure
Or a treasure.　　　　　(16–21)

Each goddess offers an alternative form of worship connected to nature. The most obvious are gifts relating to land and sea: Flora brings perpetual 'frutefull Springe summers Prime' (104) for James's honour, and Ceres promises 'feildes with plenty': a land that will 'pay tribute' every year to the King – presumably in the form of taxes (129–30). Other goddesses use rural location at Little Saxham to promote the absolutist ideology by which James rules as part of nature. Juno gives a 'scepter of command', proclaiming 'all shall freely it obay' (65–7), for example, and 'Natura' promises protection to the King. Venus broadens her scope beyond individual passion (with a possible allusion to the rumoured liaison between James and Cicelly Crofts, who may have played the part), to predict perfect fealty from anyone who is blessed by James's love. References to the King's human body and his body politic coexist in the masque's flattering but heavily politicised image of the geographical body. Patriarchal power is reasserted with Pan's final lines, blessing James and Sir John Croftes, his host, as the 'good shepheards' (144). This leads McGee to argue that the masque 'represents no new departure' (p. 378). It does go a stage further than *The Vision of the Twelve Goddesses*, however.

By Anna's death in 1619, female performance in visual and kinetic modes had been irreversibly established on the court stage. Settings and movement featuring women were invariably a self-conscious production of theatrical space designed to promote her queenly agenda. To some extent though, Anna and her ladies were always imprisoned as silent objects of the court gaze. In the specular exchange between fictional representation and court life, their fragile identities as simulacra of powerful beings invited the reproduction of ideals of female behaviour in court: as impressive but shadowy, and above all, silent figures. The entertainment given by the women in Sir John Croftes's household broke the circuit of silence. Perhaps as a consequence of moving out into the country, the goddesses are released from the invisible gags and graceful ventriloquism that had bound them in Anna's *Vision of the Twelve Goddesses* or *Tethys Festival*. They speak a prescribed message but their voices advertise female creativity behind the natural forces that sustain King and country. The female performer's voice further empowered the feminist production of space in entertainments by Queen Henrietta Maria.

FRAMING BEAUTY AND PLANTING VOICES: HENRIETTA MARIA'S COURT DRAMA

Given Henrietta Maria's innovative step in promoting court drama spoken by women, it is ironic, but extremely telling, that her protégé Walter Montague continued to describe the Court in precisely the terms that she appeared to be rejecting. In the *Miscellanea Spiritualia, or Devout Exercises*, dedicated to the Queen, he pointed out that the Court was 'a spectacle to the World, to Angels and to Men' (A3). As discussed above, his idea that its 'lusters and splendours' should function as an 'opticke glass' through which the sublime magnificence of Heaven could be apprehended on earth, relied on a culture of visibility (pp. 88–9). Beauty, even moral beauty, was a dangerous trope for women to promote.

Henrietta Maria's masques and drama are characterised by a struggle against the confinement of the mirror or picture frame (and the objectification of woman which it brings), and an enthusiastic adoption of the spectacular possibilities of court theatre. The Queen placed herself and her female courtiers in ever more extravagant visual frameworks but did so in ways which energised the two-dimensional representations of woman. As Montague's text implies, her religious aesthetic was the key by which she unlocked the glass coffin from within: investing images of female beauty with divine authority and animating them as living flesh.

In the cult of platonic love fostered by Henrietta Maria, the ideal *honnête* woman pursued piety, chastity and compassion but also had a duty to engage actively in society, encouraging these virtues in others by her own attractive behaviour. Beauty and love were especially important goals.[62] The tension between sensual beauty and spiritual abstraction was openly acknowledged in Montague's play, *The Shepherds' Paradise* (1632), in which the Queen and her ladies performed all the speaking roles. The play implicitly defends the production's lavish spectacle by mocking the priest's spiritual focus as a betrayal of the spirit of courtly *honnêteté*.[63] Martiro is teased for worshipping a love 'whose purity & rarity makes it imperceptible' (2762). Prince Basilino's view that 'beauty & enjoying are incompassible' (516) is quickly corrected by the more sensible Agenor, who points out 'unles you could refine your selfe into an Idea, abstracted from your flesh: you not only loose your memory, but all your sences, to retain this new opinion' (519–21).

Margaret Cavendish's play *The Presence* (1668) further satirises the cult of *honnêteté* at Henrietta Maria's court.[64] 'The Court is the Sphere of Beauty' in the play, producing vain figures like Lady Self-conceit (p. 32) alongside spirited women like the Lady Quick-Wit, 'a Lady of excellent

Presence' (p. 16) and Lady Wagtail, a 'metled Lass indeed' (p. 15). The play's comic scenes explore the advantages and dangers of this culture of visibility for women. The romantic plot highlights the political limitations of courtly platonic idealism. The Princess's love of 'an Idea she met with in a Dream in the Region of her Brain', transforms into passion for a common sailor (p. 7). Later transformations bring on a Persian Princess and a Persian Prince to the romantic satisfaction of all. Masque culture, which promoted the royal fantasy of uniting the nation under absolute rule, is gently mocked by Cavendish's 'impossible' romance. Its image of cross-class and cross-gendered love, with twins like *Twelfth Night*, is the stuff of dreams. *The Presence*, whose very title is ironic, anticipates Baudrillard's self-referential world of simulacra, implicitly suggesting that the self-sustaining fantasy of the masque is no more substantial or effective than Cavendish's play-world in which an imagined 'idea' is re-cast to bring comic resolution. *The Presence* can be read as a retrospective analysis of the Caroline court's elitist isolation from the kingdom, which ultimately led to civil war. The play's very structure reproduces fragmentation: the material effects of the civil war years, dramatised in the fortunes of Lord Loyalty, and Mr Underward, are excised from *The Presence* to marginal *Scenes*.

The perceived distance between the Court and the kingdom during Charles I's reign inevitably influenced the rural settings of Henrietta Maria's entertainments. The notion of 'country' was increasingly identified with the party of political activists opposed to the 'party of the court'. Henrietta Maria's pastorals must be seen in relation to that fragmentation. They followed the strategy initiated by Anna of Denmark, of using artistic representations of the landscape to negotiate the triangular relationship between the monarch, the consort and the country. Whereas the rural settings of Anna's masques functioned in the context of a newly united nation State, Henrietta Maria's were presented in a context of fragmentation: a highly charged politicisation of the countryside against the Court.

Given this context, Henrietta Maria's first dramatic offering was less than diplomatic. *L'Artenice* (1626), a French play by Racan, created an impression of the Queen's court as introverted, self-absorbed and distanced from the English kingdom. Its demand for French-speaking performers was both a symptom and a cause of the ongoing conflict between the King and Queen over who should be appointed to Henrietta Maria's household. Charles had tried to use the Privy Council to replace her French ladies-in-waiting with English noblewomen, specifically the Marchioness of Hamilton (Buckingham's niece), the Countess of

Denbigh (Buckingham's sister), and the Countess of Carlisle (Bucking-ham's mistress). Henrietta Maria's refusal to dismiss her French gentle-women, and, instead, to rehearse a French play with them, probably provoked Charles to cancel the Christmas performance. She later pro-tested that all she wanted was the same authority over her servants as Queen Anna, his mother, had held over hers.[65] The production of *L'Artenice*, which eventually took place on 21 February, vaunted such independent authority.

In addition to the French script, the settings were provocative. Racan's pastoral, based on the conventions in *Il Pastor Fido*, was famous for its localised depictions of the Seine basin and of French village life.[66] The scenery for Henrietta Maria's production at Somerset House evoked the text's precise, welcoming setting of 'des deux bords de la Seine, / Qui serrant en ses bras ces beaux champs plantureux / Fait connoistre à chacun l'amour qu'elle a pour eux' [the two banks of the Seine / Who holds in her arms these beautiful fertile fields / Making known to everyone the love she has for them].[67] Scene changes specifying 'La Seine', 'une bois' and 'une village pastoral' are marked in French in the Harvard copy of the play.[68] The romantic plot blazoned the Queen's nationalistic mood. Artenice, warned in a dream that she must marry only a native of her district, despairs of her love for Alcidor and retires to a convent. This plot line mirrored the Queen's determined maintenance of her French Catholic household. Its challenge to British national identity is probably what provoked objections to the production. Henrietta Maria's acting was commended, but, as the Venetian Ambassador reported, 'it did not give complete satisfaction because the English objected to the first part (*attione*) being declaimed by the queen'.[69] Not only was the Queen speaking on stage, she was speaking in French, in a fictional recreation of her homeland rather than the land over which she ruled.

The production of *L'Artenice* seems to have provoked a xenophobic reaction in which religious as well as national identities were at stake. The performance on 21 February was followed by a series of religious disputes at nearby Durham House. The Bishop of Durham had crowded his household into 'the worst and basest Roomes' to allow the French Ambassador comfortable lodgings in the time of plague, but the Ambas-sador turned the house into a centre for Catholic sympathies On 22 February, the Court at Whitehall informed the King 'there is a great Liberty taken by diverse of his Subjects, which resort to the hearing of Masse at Durham House'. The Bishop issued a warrant for Constables to arrest and commit them to prison. On Sunday 25, members of the

French Ambassador's household 'tooke upon them with their swords in their hands to carry the English Papists by strong hands through the Watch' and struck the officers, who retaliated.[70] The Anglican Bishop and Catholic Ambassador exchanged heated words during the ensuing brawl. Tensions between King and Queen over Henrietta Maria's determination to maintain a French, Catholic household, made this more than a local dispute about ownership of domestic space. Its international repercussions obliged Charles I to write to Louis XIII.

L'Artenice blatantly celebrates France as homeland (the hero despairs at a painful self-exile from his country (2791) and the discovery that he is a foundling, and native to the region, produces a happy ending). The Somerset House venue emphasised the script's introverted spatial politics. The production was effectively the inverse of royal progresses undertaken by Elizabeth and, to a lesser extent, Anna. Racan's 1625 epilogue nostalgically evokes the French pastoral scene:

> Cét agreeable pre, cette fertile plaine
> Qui paroient a l'envy les rives de a Seine,
> Ces jardins ou la grace estalloit ses apas
> Alors que tant de fleurs y naissoient sous vos pas.
>   (Eglogue, 69–72)

> [This pleasant meadow, this fertile plain
> Which lovingly line the banks of the Seine,
> These gardens where grace sows her charms
> While so many flowers are born there from your steps].

In the Somerset House production these lines were pronounced in Henrietta Maria's determinedly French household on the banks of the Thames, making the imposition of its setting on an English venue all the more provocative. *Artenice* implicitly presented the Queen colonising Somerset House and its environs, appropriating and rewriting a piece of England through the performance of a French pastoral script. The production suggested that a little corner of France and its rich culture could be recreated within the walls of an English palace.

The pastoral setting of *Chloridia* (1631), performed in the Banqueting Hall at Whitehall, expressed the Queen's royal persona, her relations to the King, court and country, in more positive terms five years later.[71] Cupid and 'Love's rebellious war' (170) are banished to hell, along with wintry tempests, to be succeeded by 'enamoured Spring' (164) in the masque of Chloris. A renewal of love across the land was an apt reminder of the improved marital relations between Charles and Henrietta Maria after the death of Buckingham in 1628, and the birth of Charles in 1630. The proscenium arch, decorated with the word 'Chloridia' in a garland of flowers literally inscribed woman's name on the recreative process (14–15). The King and Queen's next child, Mary, would just have been conceived when the masque was performed on 22 February, making its conceit of Chloris sowing seeds (and making Juno pregnant after touching her with a herb), especially appropriate.

As Chloris, the Queen led a dance of English masquers across the hall. Her contact with the earth allows it to bloom, her feet making 'various flowers to grow' (181), as the ladies with floral headdresses follow her towards the State. Rivers wonder at her creative powers: 'Whether she were the root, / Or they did take th'impression from her foot'. This trope echoes the lines from Racan's play (quoted above) and the pastoral poem he wrote for Henrietta's mother Marie De Medicis: 'N' espargnez points les fleurs / Il en revient assez sous les pas de Marie'.[72] In this production the land is English and the procession enacted the Queen's closeness to her spouse and kingdom as 'the top of paramours' (246). Her inclusive love was indicated through the casting. Ladies of English noble families from across the county, with a range of Catholic and Protestant religious allegiances, played the flowery nymphs. They included the first English-women that Henrietta had appointed as her maids of Honour in 1626–7, the Countess of Carlisle and Sophia Carew from a West Country courtier family. The Countess of Newport, Mrs Olivia Porter, and Anne Weston signalled the Queen's alliances to the Buckingham family; the Countess of Berkshire and Lady Howard represented the powerful Howard dynasty. Lady Catherine Strange was a countrywoman from France, but part of the Huguenot family, so her inclusion advertised Henrietta Maria embracing the Protestant element of her population.

Having left behind the French script of *L'Artenice,* Henrietta Maria did not speak in *Chloridia,* of course. The masque self-consciously advertises the multi-dimensional effects she relied on to promote her message of loyalty. Her Fame, personified on a hill with a trumpet, as in the cover to Brathwait's *The English Gentlewoman* (1631), is sustained by the figures of Poetry, History, Architecture and Sculpture. The effect goes one stage further than the House of Fame in Anna's masque where the women performers were integrated into the scenery. Here, the physical distance between the Queen and the spectacle highlights her seeming inability to speak for herself, or fashion her own reputation. The masque itself offered clear evidence to the contrary, of course, and in Aurelian Townshend's

Tempe Restored (1632), Henrietta Maria was to challenge the English masque structure by introducing female singers in the persons of Madame Coniack, who played Circe, and Mrs Shepherd, who sang the role of Harmony.

Spatially, *Tempe Restored* alienates female bodies and voices by containing them in separate frames; as Townshend tellingly observed, '*these shows are nothing but pictures with light and motion.*'[73] Melinda Gough's excellent essay has argued that the masque's parallel use of dance and song draws on French *ballets de cour,* in which Henrietta Maria participated, and the employment of virtuoso female singers in continental courtly entertainments. Women's vocal performance is first demonised in Madam Coniack's Circe who appears outside a '*sumptuous palace*' on the side of a '*fruitful hill*' (45) to signify 'desire in general' (298). It is re-legitimitated through Harmony's song in the main masque presented in a feminised landscape of '*nature and art*' (45). Gough reads Harmony as the perfect complement to Henrietta Maria's silent dancing as Divine Beauty, her song vocalising the music of the spheres that the Queen and her masquers performed kinetically. Henrietta Maria appears at a distance '*in an oriental sky*' (171) but uses Mrs Shepherd's Harmony to ventriloquise or figuratively throw her voice down to earth.[74] Continental traditions give ample evidence of complementary performance types[75] but the model of harmonious complementarity does not fully explain the spatial fragmentation or conflicts which energise *Tempe Restored,* including those between male and female performers over the territory of the court stage at the moment when Circe tells Pallas 'Man-maid begone!' (628).

Sophie Tomlinson is surely right to suggest that the theatrical vibrancy of Madame Coniack's performance threatened to enchant the court and undermine the triumph of Divine Beauty and Heroic Virtue in the main masque.[76] *Tempe Restored* exemplifies the struggle in Henrietta Maria's court entertainments between the celebration of stunning female beauty as the object of admiring gazes and the emergence of vibrant female voices. Henrietta Maria was the Snow White of the masque; her gorgeous costume was designed, Jones said, 'so that corporeal beauty, consisting in symmetry, colour and certain inexplicable graces, shining in the Queen's majesty, may draw us to the contemplation of the beauty of the soul, unto which it hath analogy' (336–9). Jones was certainly trying to fulfil the spirit and letter of Du Bosc and Montague's idea that the glittering court was a means through which to perceive divine beauty. The problem was that instead of presenting a Queen who was more than she appeared, the masque offered one who was less. When Mrs Shepherd sang 'Not as myself, but as the brightest star / That shines in heaven, come to reign this day. . .', the Queen was not yet visible (145–6) and the masque advertised the detachment of voice and image. The fragmented persona, though magnificent in all its parts, probably did not focus audience attention so fixedly as the passionate figure of Circe, whose costume, movements and voice worked in concert to present a complete woman. Henrietta Maria's close artistic control of her entertainments suggests that this effect was not accidental. I would argue that *Tempe Restored* was her engagement with the madwoman in the attic; her means of confronting the violent polar fragmentation of woman into silent beauty or roaring witch. Her own entertainments struggled to resolve the dichotomy, most immediately in Walter Montague's lengthy play *The Shepherds Paradise* (1632), where she took up an English voice.

The settings of *The Shepherds Paradise* are crucial catalysts for the emergence of women's speech. These fictional places are, in turn, playing spaces through which the emergence of female voices at court can be realised. Henrietta Maria played the protagonist Bellessa 'as well for her recreation as for the exercise of her Englishe' as John Pory noted.[77] The play's pastoral setting is not an expansive territory of State, as in the masques, but a place where individual feelings can be explored. Prince Moramonte and Queen Bellessa realise their mutual love via a convoluted journey through a psychological landscape of love, like that in Wroth's *Love's Victory*. Montague's play uses the classic imagery of the garden as *locus amoenus*. Genorio warns his friend against entering 'into such a Laborinth, as 'tis uncerteine whether every step will carry you backward or forward toward your end, since wee know not where to finde her' (1091).

Bellessa's path through the labyrinth is to find a voice to express her love. The play seems to allude back to the female voices of *Tempe Restored* when she admits that her thoughts need to 'take the aire a little to refresh themselves', and decides to sing, hoping that Love will carry them to Moramonte:

> Presse me noe more kind love, I will confesse
> And tell you all, nay rather more than lesse. . .
> . . . thus you're strong enough to make me speake.
> Held by the virgin shame you'l be too weake,
> *I find that thus,* [ie through song] I *may be safely free.* (2986–92)

The declaration is pressed out of her and the lyric form protects her modesty with the illusion of impersonal performance. It is a first stage of articulation, moving a little further than the practice of throwing one's voice in the masque.

Retreat into a wood allows Bellessa's feeling voice to emerge. In *Love's Victory* Musella hid to hear her beloved speak first, but here the gradual drawing out of Bellessa's voice is prioritised. She withdraws to 'loves Cabonett', where she can declare her feelings privately, and for this a special scene was constructed.[78] The set, entitled 'Loves Cabinett, a relieve' can be taken literally in this case: the green space relieves the protagonist of her emotional burdens. The natural surroundings, which are in harmony with each other, are a place of innocence 'for in your veynes runnes water & not bloud' (3303). The leaves offer 'a Curtaine drawne before thee' (3320–1) to preserve modesty; the site allows for reflection and expression. Even more actively than Wroth's heroines, discussed in the last chapter, Bellessa establishes a cooperative relationship with the setting, regarding nature as an animate force coexisting with her own desires. The set design recreates the interaction by superimposing images of nature and womanhood. Spectators look through an architectural frame, an archway supported by caryatid figures, to trees and a rock, and to the open cabinet with more caryatids at the centre or vanishing point. When Moramonte arrives, Bellessa asks him to declare his love and displaces her own in the echo. This is not as conservative as it sounds since the echo is not a reflection of his words but a distinctive, natural voice. She tells him 'it is my voice', infused into the forest 'that it might not have so much modesty to hold it back' (3374–7). A natural setting staged within a palace venue materialises woman's escape from the frameworks of social decorum to speak what she feels not what she ought to say. Entertainments like *The Shepherds Paradise* offered a demarcated space for female expression, a 'loves Cabonett' in the Court.

The final stage of Bellessa's self-articulation is enabled by confiding in Fidamira (3476), and by the discovery of a new identity. She promises Moramante 'I retract all that I said, as Bellessa, but 'tis to say more as Saphira' (3591–2). At the end of a role of over 500 lines, the promise of a stronger voice for Henrietta Maria beyond the confines of the play and her fictional identity as shepherdess, would have carried considerable weight.[79] A wider community of women also find voices in *The Shepherds Paradise*. Sarah Poynting shows that the play reversed the usual balance of casting in court masques by assigning the majority of speaking roles to untitled women closest to the Queen, who could perhaps be pressured into learning the lines, and take the risk of public censure by performing in a play.[80] Performance showcased the unmarried maids in a court that was the chief marriage market in England, but it showcased them as women with voices.

The shepherds' paradise setting also rewrites the image of divinely appointed patriarchal government so often idealised in Stuart masques. There are no divine figures in the fictional world; it is ruled by a matriarchal government in which the queen is elected 'every yeare by the plurality of the sisters voyces' (476–7). The all-female election is a satiric inversion of the situation in early modern England, where the myth of women's emotional rather than rational nature was often cited as a reason for their exclusion from the parliamentary process. In the shepherds' paradise men are excluded from voting because they are guided too much by passion for their own particular beloveds, whereas women are able to judge objectively (874–6). Bellessa must swear to 'keepe the honour & the Regall due: / withough exacting any thing that's new' (719–20). The paradise is both conservative and radical: a royalist regime that has traditionally been centred on a community of women. Its history of 'instituted regality' (796–7) looks back to memories of Elizabeth, the Virgin Queen, and Fidamira's succession predicts a symbolic return to Elizabethan female rule.

A prologue of divine spectators implicitly co-opts the approval of King Charles and the court to *The Shepherds Paradise*'s radical feminist agenda. It announces that the gods have come to witness the spectacle: 'Each one to put himselfe into a starre: / And thus in Gallantry each brings a light, / And waits with it, a servant to this night' (13–16). A design shows masquers sitting in two tiers within a grotto. They may have carried candles to the stage, as Poynting has proposed.[81] As 'servant[s] to this night' they occupy a very different position to god-like authority of the monarch in masques. Jupiter – implicitly King Charles – views the fictional Paradise as 'his propper place' (23–5). To do so, of course, would mean accepting its values. Like Anna of Denmark before her (in *Hymen's Triumph*), Henrietta Maria's production draws power from its Somerset House venue. By inviting Charles into her own theatre, a performance space on her own territory, Henrietta Maria implicitly expected him to accept the rules of her household.

The proto-feminist ideals of the shepherds' paradise depend crucially on its location, on the levels of setting, performance venue, and court environment. Votorio explains 'the peace & setlednes of this place is secur'd by natures Inclosure of it, on all sides by impregnanblenes, as if it was meant for Chastity only to make a plantation here' (846–8). The tropes of the cloister (discussed further in chapter 4), the enclosed garden of chastity and the *hortus conclusus*, were demonstrated on many levels in the play's performance. The paradise of women's government and public, vocal self-expression depend on the distinctive culture of the Queen's Court. Access is controlled so 'that noe brother or sister shall ever goe out of the lymmits of the kingdome but by a finall dismission' (754). This recalls Henrietta Maria's coterie, where the promotion of *honnêteté* enabled her ladies to intervene vocally in the exercise of pleasure and politics. Like the setting, the play was itself a bounded territory, of course, a playing space safely walled by the limits of fiction and therefore a privileged arena for the expression of entertaining and progressive ideas. Agenor defines the trip to the shepherds' paradise as 'a Deviation into Noviltyes which guide sad thoughts, the best by a diversion of them' (483).

The generic boundaries of *The Shepherds Paradise* were given material form in a purpose-built, enclosed theatre at Somerset House. Records for the paved court theatre show a 'roome' of 76 by 36 feet, (23×11m) using the East and West walls of the courtyard, and walled in with wood at the north and south. This was probably the court to the east of the main courtyard. Somewhat ironically, the rural paradise and its venue were covered with a pine roof to protect the performance from bad weather, as the French ambassador reported.[82] Degrees of seating were erected for the spectators and, for the performers, a raked stage of 24′ 10″ (7.5m) high, 25′ 4″ (7.7m) deep and 34 feet (10m) wide.[83] The large wings used to create the perspective scenery meant the acting area on stage would only have been small. Orrell notes 'its very structure would propel the performers down onto the level floor of the house, in close contact with the audience and particularly with the state, leaving Jones's scenic picture as a decoration in three dimensions, neatly framed within its border'.[84] Spatially, the architecture projected the female actors, their ideas and voices, out from the fictive setting and into the court venue, within the enclosed zone of the temporary theatre. The theatre must have been a place of wonder like the shepherds' paradise 'where curiosity is fed, faster then it can swallow' (787–8) as Moramante says.

In textual and theatrical terms, the shepherds' paradise paradoxically represents illusions of democracy within the palace of an absolutist court. The playing space superimposes a communist utopian setting onto the exclusive courtyard venue at Somerset House, since the laws of the Paradise decree that 'There is noe propriety of any thing among the Society; but a Community of all which the world calls riches or possessions' (750–1). The construction of the theatre, costing £314. 16s 11d, blatantly contradicted the democratic ideals voiced on its stage. Mr Beaulieu's only comment about the play is telling: 'This night, our queen hath acted her costly pastoral in Somerset House.'[85] *The Shepherds Paradise* made little attempt to connect the Court with the kingdom. Indeed, its skewed geographical politics were part of the performance. Orrell notes that the different prospects painted by Jones for the play all have horizons at quite different levels, and from nowhere in the auditorium would they blend consistently with the raked stage and the painted wings.[86] In order for a State to win the consent of the population, its ideology needs to work expansively, binding local customs and links to the land on the part of small communities to those national projects produced from a geographically fixed point of government.[87] *The Shepherds Paradise* created a unique set of local customs from a geographically and culturally fixed point of government (the Queen's court), and then promoted these to a select group of courtly spectators. Such exclusive pastoral landscaping undoubtedly helped to provoke Parliament's revolution on behalf of the country. In spite of the play's disastrous national politics, problems with length and the comprehensibility of the performers, at a local level of venue and setting *The Shepherds Paradise* did validate women's voices.

Throughout the period, women's dramatic performances at Court were attempts to cross boundaries. The extrovert progresses of Elizabeth and the staging of rural scenes in palaces were dramatic modes designed to bridge the distance between the Court and the country. Indoor and outdoor venues constituted the monarch very differently, the former offering deeply embedded material reflections of regal power, the latter often displacing the monarch into unknown geographical and political territory. For the Stuart consorts, drama was a bridge to negotiate relationships between the centre of power (the State) and the Queen's court, by appropriating princes' palace venues or establishing separate ones at Somerset House. The Queens drew on a continental tradition of female performance that was new to England, so their dramatic activities crossed boundaries of propriety as well as custom.

Henrietta Maria's cultivation of a French précieuse culture created barriers between her court and the kingdom that her drama often intensified rather than annihilating. The conflation of woman with the land was a difficult trope to control, but, as Anna of Denmark had shown, its representation within the heightened theatre of the court forged symbolic relationships between queen and country that implicitly bypassed the reigning king. Henrietta Maria was the most adventurous of a tiny elite of royal and noble women who adopted the progress, the masque and eventually the play to express themselves in the most powerful theatre in the kingdom. Their privileged position often makes their performances appear introverted. Nevertheless, court entertainments were still attempts to annihilate barriers between the ideal of female autonomy and the realities of physical spaces and cultural traditions. Queen Henrietta Maria's struggle to escape from a court of objectifying 'flattering glasses, and mirrours' was one shared by most women, and is still shared by those at the forefront of the national media, our contemporary equivalent of the Banqueting House. Her own artistic progress in and out of the spectacle of masques and the verbal liberty of a play demonstrated unequivocally that the Court was a site where women produced space in ways that could legitimate the female voice and shatter the fragile simulacra that conspired to enclose them as mirrors of male desire.

CHAPTER 4

Sororities

This chapter investigates the different dramatic opportunities offered by places that were specifically dedicated to the needs of female communities: convents, academies, and beyond them separatist households and circles. The convent and the female academy were places formally separated from the everyday world for the purpose of protecting and educating sororities: women grouped architecturally, culturally and emotionally in enclaves of gender similitude. The female academy frequently drew on the strong educational model provided by women's religious houses. In Thomas Becon's 1559 dialogue *The Catechism*, for example, the Son argues for the establishment of girls' schools with 'learned matrons made rulers of the same', to follow a tradition of 'monasteries of solitary women, whom we heretofore called nuns'.[1] Over a hundred years later, in *A Serious Proposal to the Ladies* (1694 and 1697), Mary Astell famously recommended the foundation of 'a *Monastery* or if you will a *Religious Retirement*', with a double purpose: 'being not only a Retreat from the World for those who desire that advantage', but also an institution 'to Expel that cloud of Ignorance which Custom has involv'd us in, to furnish our minds with a stock of solid and useful Knowledge, that the Souls of women may no longer be the only unadorned and neglected things'.[2]

Both Becon and Astell, writing from post-Reformation England, view the female monastery from the position of loss of course. Its disappearance in material terms seems to have increased its imaginative appeal, as can be seen in drama by women that recreates the all-female playing space in secular or quasi-religious terms. The convent and the women's house of learning are often superimposed in terms of setting, venue, educational and monastic discourse, within a sub-genre of women's drama that is explicitly didactic. This chapter begins by identifying some broad characteristics of the sororal community to suggest its enduring appeal to women dramatists. It then examines early examples of convent drama and the nature of performance in consecrated playing spaces. From these attempts to place women's liturgical drama in the material contexts of church and convent, the discussion moves on to consider imaginative recreations of the convent in seventeenth-century women's drama.

The 'house of women' is a particular type of chronotope, to use Bakhtin's term to define a site where time and place meet. Its horizontal synchronic plane unites generations of women through a common gender and *modus vivendi* within the walls of the house. In diachronic terms it is unlike the aristocratic country house or the court palaces. Although God and Christ are the supreme authorities in a medieval or early modern women's house, its architecture, furnishings and paintings do not display the traces of centuries or generations of patriarchal dynasty. Instead, its diachronic axis of descent is matrilineal: pupils or religious devotees looked back to the past and forward to a future history of female saints, abbesses, sisters and pupils.[3] The bounded enclave of a sorority thus offered different opportunities for drama than the sites of home, garden and court investigated so far. It created female 'companies': company as a source of shared experience, education and visions, and playing companies of female performers. In many cases, the primary audiences were also female.

The examples of sorority offered by religious houses thus 'created fertile ground for the growth of a separate feminine sensibility and strengthened the bonds of sisterhood', as Jo MacNamara observes. This had far-reaching consequences beyond the religious dimension. 'Sisters in arms', as McNamara titles them, 'have broken new paths for women in a hostile and forbidden world' by laying the foundations of female autonomy through their own professions to God and their church.[4] Female autonomy and sisterly co-operation were intrinsic to women's religious houses. Fox's *Benedictine Rule for Women* (1517) stated 'Noon in the monastery shall followe their owne wylle,' but that all were franchised subjects, called to counsel the Abbess at meetings in the chapterhouse.[5] Nunneries also offered inspiring examples of female authority that challenged the exclusive masculine prerogative to power. The Abbesses of Shaftesbury, Barking, and Wilton, for example, were all heads of Benedictine institutions of ancient foundation and held the rank of baroness.[6] The Abbess 'is to beare Christs person in the Monastery', as Benedictine nun Alexia Gray remarked in 1632.[7] Although Abbesses and senior nuns were not ordained and were subject to the authority of local bishops, they frequently occupied higher status positions than the unbeneficed priests who were employed to fulfil sacramental duties.

Convents and female academies challenged the social order as environments in which bonds between women could be maintained into maturity,
in contrast to society's norm of dissolving them in favour of heterosexual
marriage. Women who entered religious institutions re-formed their individual identities as part of a community of women via a symbolic wedding
to Christ. Vowing chaste love to God within a group of like-minded
women represented a potential threat to compulsory domestic heterosexu-
ality, as Valerie Traub has argued. It transformed chastity from being a
guarantee of patriarchal ownership (ensuring the legitimacy of children),
into a primary affective same-sex bond in an alternative sociality.[8] Religious celebrations of sisterhood invariably subvert the marital structures
that underpin patriarchy. For example, in the dialogue *The English Nvnne*
(1642), Cosmophila (lover of the world) comes to recall her sister Celia
from the convent to be an heiress-bride, only to be converted herself.
Celia rejoices 'O happy houre! We are now *Sisters* in a double manner,
Before by Nature, now by grace, before by Generation of Parents, now by
regeneration of God.'[9] For women, enclosure offered utopian liberation
from the conventional roles limiting female behaviour and authority. Lady
Mary Roper Lovel left her children to join the Brussels Benedictines in
1608, explaining to Robert Cecil that she sought 'securitie of my soule' in a
state of life 'seperated [sic] from the miseries and dangers of the world'.[10]

Membership of a sisterhood was fostered through spatial practice. The
convent was a chronotope with its own sense of time and space. Nuns
reoriented themselves temporally by observing the *horarium* or monastic
timetable; and spatially, by being enclosed within buildings whose material culture probably helped to construct collective identities. Ceremonies
and rituals were an essential part of the nuns' religious *habitus*. The
imitation of these rituals in early women's drama can usefully be read as
a means to re-invoke the sense of collective, sisterly identity that they were
designed to foster in their original venues. Representations of imagined
female communities in drama are a tangible manifestation of a shared
desire for such alliances, a desire that is utopian: the search for a home
beyond patriarchy. Women's plays frequently invoke a sororal community in idealistic terms. For example, Lady Happy in Margaret Cavendish's *The Convent of Pleasure* (1668) proclaims 'I mean to live incloistered
with all the delights and pleasures that are allowable and lawful.'[11] Paradoxically, the very thing that makes pleasure lawful and permissible – the
fact that it is shared between women – also makes it most threatening: it
creates a self-sustaining, autonomous sorority that has no need of men.

Playing spaces (settings and venues) that celebrated sororal communities were invariably subversive forms of early women's drama.

The short liturgical dramas produced by Abbesses in medieval England were taken from a corpus of approved practice, in contrast to the plays, verse and music of exceptional figures like Hrostvitha of Gandersheim and Hildegard of Bingen,[12] Dunbar Ogden has identified twenty-three music dramas performed by nuns from across Europe, from the twelfth century to 1600, which 'answer a need for dramatic expression by women and for the education of women'.[13] By examining interpolations into the regular patterns of liturgy at Wilton and Barking, we can glimpse a female-centred convent drama. In the Wilton and Barking scripts for the *Visitatio Sepulcri* (a dramatisation of the three Maries' visit to Christ's tomb), the Maries were personated by nuns. Here, and at Origny, France, the singers undertook a purification ritual, something not found in any of the 680 churches where men played the Maries.[14] The Latin text from St Edith's Wilton (later home to Mary Sidney Herbert), describes the *cantrices* washing their hands and covering their heads with white veils: 'Dum cantatur tertia lectio levent tres cantrices et lavent manus suas, et absconso velamine, candidum velum capitibus suis imponant in similitudine mulierum.'[15] It is impossible to say whether the washing ritual was visible to members of the congregation; its most important function appears to have been for the participants. Was special purification needed by women who became actors, as these cloistered women did? Perhaps the English prejudice against female performance may explain why we do not find more Easter plays in English convents, as opposed to the French or German houses.

In religious drama performed by nuns, ritual and art combine in the service of God so the performer's work is not an end in itself. The personation of a role by a nun was, in all senses, part of a service, and thus had a different quality from women's performances in the household, the garden, or the royal court. The significance of enactment probably related as much to the individual performer as to those who saw it. Taking a role could be a form of spiritual learning. From her experience of working with dancers, Maggie Kast argues that performing in a church creates 'an experience of increased intimacy with the sacred' for participants.[16] For sisters in a religious order in the medieval and early modern periods, the playing spaces created by drama probably gave opportunities to transform their familiarity with the fabric and liturgy of the Church into strikingly personal emotional experiences of God.

The Wilton *Visitatio* text enacts an intimacy between the female body and the sacred. It prioritises the humanity of the Maries and the singers in contrast to the priest's more spiritual role as an *angelus* [angel] who also sings as Christ appearing to Mary Magdalen (81). Lines that emphasise the central importance of the human body in sacred expressions of Christianity serve to foreground the presence of the choristers' bodies as first witnesses to the risen Christ and beneficiaries of the salvation he brings:

Adest Jhesus carne innovatus,
visu pulchro nimisque amabilis,
salutans seminans purificans animas
Pedes eius strinxerunt venerantes eis pia oscula prebuerunt. (64–7)

[Jesus is present, renewed in flesh,
A beautiful sight of loveliness beyond measure
The pure spirit animates the seed
The worshipping women grasped his feet and bestowed
pious kisses on them.]

In the subsequent action, including the kissing of a cloth passed into the congregation ('osculetotur postea omnis et populus', 68–9), the Maries are apostolic figures mediating between the priest personating the figure of Christ, and the congregation.

We know nothing about St Edith's Abbey as the performance venue, but in the case of the Easter liturgical dramas produced at Barking, sparse evidence allows us to reconstruct a conjectural plan (Figure 7) and to speculate on how the Abbey church, as playing space, might have magnified the effects of the script. The *Depositio, Elevatio* and *Visitatio Sepulchri* produced by Katherine of Sutton (Abbess 1363–76) were explicitly didactic; designed, with the unanimous agreement of the sisters, to educate the spiritually-lethargic population under the Abbey's pastoral care by re-awakening their emotional engagement with the sacred: 'quoniam populorum concursus temporibus illis videbatur deucione frigessere, et torpor humanus maxime accrescens'.[17] The church congregation is somewhat different from audiences in the venues considered thus far because, like the singers, its members were there as participants. They were part of the body of the Church celebrating the ritual enacted through the performance. Katherine of Sutton's aim to promote spiritual engagement was conventional; what the texts did went beyond convention. The three scenes build up a central dramatic and spiritual role for the sisters of the monastic

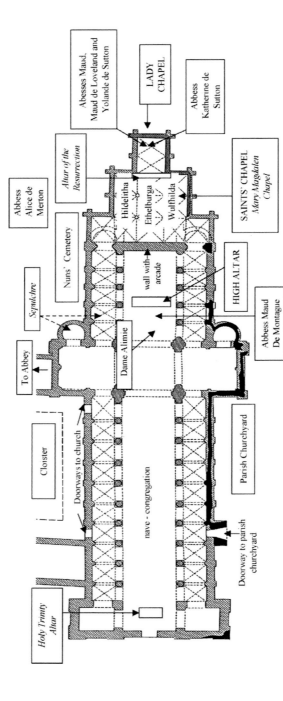

Figure 7. Conjectural Plan of Barking Abbey with burials of Abbesses and possible stage sites (in italics), based on Arthur C. Clapham's excavations and Philip Judge's sketch [*By permission of Roberta Gilchrist*].

community. The congregation's participation had the power to legitimate a female-centred interpretation of the Passion.

The Abbey church venue made an important contribution to the drama's promotion of female spirituality because it gave architectural form to Barking Abbey's strong interest in its own female-centred history.[18] Its six special saints included three former Abbesses, Ethelburga, Hildelitha, Wulfhilda, and two former nuns, Saints Tortith and Edith. Its calendar specialised in celebrating virgins, virgin martyrs, and its own female leaders.[19] Archeological research has shown that in the thirteenth century the east end of the Abbey church was altered and extended, probably with the aim of honouring these revered foremothers. Evidence (summarised in Figure 7) suggests that a new chapel with three aisles provided a special resting place for the remains of Saint Ethelburga and Saints Hildelitha and Wulfhilda. Beyond this was a Chapel of our Lady of Salvation, with a tiled floor, a step and an altar. Records of 1420 indicate that the Abbesses and social elite associated with the Abbey were buried here. Katherine of Sutton was buried in the Salvation chapel along with three former abbesses: Maud (c. 1200), daughter of Henry II, Maud de Loveland (c. 1276), and Yolande de Sutton (d. 1341).[20]

As the plan shows, the location of the two chapels put women at the 'holy' end of the church, creating a place that conflated the sacred and the feminine, an ideal playing space for the convent's drama. Consecrated venues such as the Abbey church are already a 'stage for enacting myth through ritual', as Thomas Barrie argues. In terms of Bakhtin's diachronic axis, a church's altars, chapels, aisles, pulpit and the rails and screens which divide up the space are deeply marked by layers of meaning that have accumulated through years and years of use in worship.[21] By producing and participating in liturgical drama, women intervened in the making of meanings within the church, both physical and institutional.

We have very little information about the ritual arrangements of Barking Abbey church, making it impossible to locate the performance with certainty. The Latin scripts (sadly with no music), indicate four specific sites which are conjecturally marked in italics on the plan: a Mary Magdalen chapel large enough to accommodate all the convent including male clerics; a Holy Trinity altar; a high altar; and a sepulchre large enough for a priest to enter, in which the image of Christ's body is placed. The latter is hung with a gold carpet and clean white linen ('locum tapetum palleo auriculari quoque et lintheis nitidissimis decenter ornatum', p. 164) and may have been a portable structure.

In England, Easter sepulchres seem to have been at the north side of the chancel near the aumbrey (the cupboard for sacred vessels), thus forging a spatial connection between the sacrament and the Easter sepulchre ceremonies.[22] At Barking this position would have been particularly apt for the *depositio* drama (where the crucifix is laid in the tomb), since the nuns' own cemetery was located beyond the outside wall at the north side of the chancel,[23] following a vision of St Ethelburga in which a light resembling a sheet (lintheum) came down on the sisters and then moved to the south of the monastery.[24] On Good Friday, after the sepulchre was prepared, the Barking nuns visited St Ethelburga's shrine to recite psalms. The sepulchre setting with its shining white linen seems to recall her miraculous vision.

The Easter ceremonies surrounding the scripted drama help to incorporate each sister in the Passion story to be enacted. After the priests brought down the crucifix, the nuns prostrated themselves by it in a Creeping of the Cross ceremony led by the Abbess.[25] Individual physical action creates a moment of intimacy with the sacred, empathetically connecting each sister with the *Visitatio* scene in which the Maries later grasp and kiss the feet of the resurrected Christ. The Abbess directs the priests representing the persons of Joseph and Nicodemus to take the washed crucifix to the Easter sepulchre setting.[26] In both the *Depositio* and the *Elevatio Hostiae*, the mixture of male and female voices gives the impression that experience of the Passion is something shared equally by both sexes. The priests raising the cross and singing are answered by a female 'cantrix' (instead of the usual male 'cantor'), who leads the choir of nuns.

The *Elevatio* drama elaborates the harrowing of hell ritual as a spatial enactment of sharing worship and education between men and women. The Abbess leads the convent, including the clerics, to the Magdalen Chapel where they are confined behind the closed doors to represent the spirits of the Old Testament Patriarchs ('figurants animas sanctorum Patrum') trapped in hell. A priest personating the figure of Christ knocks three times on the door of the Saint Mary Magdalen chapel and it opens ('tercia pulsacione ostium aperiat', p. 165) to release the prisoners. Members of the convent move out into the body of the church, each priest or clerk carrying an illuminated candle. We do not know which was the Mary Magdalen chapel in Barking's conventual church. The two apsidal chapels extending to the east of the north and south transepts are only twelve feet six in diameter, so may not have been large enough to accommodate the whole convent. Another possible venue was the unnamed saints' chapel behind the high altar, particularly associated with the abbey's own history because of the three women buried there who were the founding mothers of the convent's spiritual identity (see Figure 7). Possibly the nuns processed here with the Abbess and priests, and then moved out through the middle of the choir stalls to the 'downstage' sepulchre ('per medium chori ad Sepulchrum', p. 166). The saints' chapel was hidden from the congregation by a large wall at the east end of the presbytery, probably carried up in the form of an open arcade through which voices could be heard. Sung from this enclosure, the drama would have promoted a special sense of intimacy between the enactment of salvation and the Abbey's own past.

Nuns and priests are joined as the body of the Church through movement. They process to the sepulchre, from which the Host is raised, and finally to the altar of the Holy Trinity in imitation of Christ's disciples journeying to Galilee. If the Holy Trinity altar was at the west end of the church, a traditional locus for Galilee,[27] then the movement authorises male and female disciples to move amongst the 'populus' (see Figure 7). Barking's *Visitatio Sepulchri,* which followed immediately, expands the Abbess's presumed agenda of foregrounding nuns as spiritual disciples and active educators in the parish.

The Barking *Visitatio* focuses attention on women as mediators of the Resurrection message: divinely chosen because they are more emotionally attuned to receive the truth and to convey it to the congregation. St Augustine's reasoning, that this was why Mary Magdalen was first to meet the risen Christ, was enacted in performances with female singers.[28] At Barking, the purification ritual where the singers change into white surplices and veils took place in the Mary Magdalen Chapel, probably recalling that Saint's conversion from sinner to penitent, and the ceremonial professions of the convent sisters past and present.[29] Each Mary sings some individual lines in the *Visitatio,* thus providing individual points of access to the story's emotional dimensions for listeners. The representation of Christ's appearance to the women cleverly combines emotional, physical immediacy and sacred venue (the altar), in ways that empower the nun performers as spiritual leaders, roles normally reserved for male clergy. The cleric presenting the 'Persona' of Christ first appears at the left-hand side of the altar, telling Magdalen not to touch the resurrected body, and thus seeming to follow the tradition that read *noli me tangere* as a prohibition against women's teaching, preaching, and performing sacramental duties. When the 'Persona' vanishes and reappears on the right of the altar, however, the three Maries kiss his hands and feet: 'Tunc ille humi prostrate teneant pedes eius et deosculentur' (p. 383). This recalls the ceremony of the Creeping of the Cross.

A complex interaction between types of celebration operates at the altar site. Boundaries between performance and reality are deliberately eliminated as the presencing of Christ's original sacrifice is realised in the consecration of the host, a living act, not a mimetic performance. As Margaret Pappano argues, the physicality of touch also crosses boundaries between real and dramatic action, blurring differences between the fictional Maries' contact with the body of Christ, the nuns' touching of the priest representing Christ's 'Persona', and the celebrant's touching of the Host.[30] While it is crucial to remember that the nuns are not able to consecrate the elements, their presence creates a striking proximity between women's bodies, the sacred history of Resurrection, and the creation of the Real Presence.

The 1420 interment records give details of 'l'auteur de la Resurexion', an altar which would seem a likely place of performance. We do not know the location of the altar but it had strong female associations since Sybil de Felton, who succeeded Katherine of Sutton as Abbess, was buried in front of it between her mother and Abbess Anne de Vere, whose grave was near Saint Hildelitha's.[31] If, as seems likely, St Hildelitha's grave and the altar of the resurrection were in the Saints' chapel, the dramatic moment of resurrection would have been visually concealed from the congregation. The enclosed playing space would have emphasised the convent's authority as a separate place of intensified spirituality.

A stage direction 'Finites hijs versibus, tunc Mariae stantes super gradua ante altare' (p. 383) indicates that after joyfully acknowledging Christ, the Maries stand on the steps before the altar and face the congregation to sing their celebratory '*Alleluia*', answered by the choir. If the turn from the altar was intended to aid visual as well as oral projection, the nuns may have moved in front of the wall after their verses, or the Maries scene may have been sung near the High Altar. The 'haut auteur' seems to have been located near to the sacristy with an archway in front, as records for the burials of Dame Alimie and Abbess Maud Montague suggest (see Figure 7).[32]

Whatever the exact position of the altar, women are invested with a privileged power to communicate the Gospel in the dramatised *Visitatio*. The nuns who sing the biblical characters mimetically tell the good news mid-way between the altar and the congregation ('anter altare uertentes se ad populum', p. 383), so, within the playing space, they become primary mediators of the divine message. Mary Magdalen as 'apostola apostolorum', apostle to the apostles, promotes a cherished educational tradition at the Benedictine Abbey.[33] The nun singing Magdalen is authorised, in that moment of performance, to teach the male priests and clergy. Cast as the disciples 'in figuram Disciplinorum Christi', they appeal to her for the truth: '*Dic nobis Maria*' (p. 383). By using female singers for the Maries, this production realises the Bible's account of a sisterhood as the first disciples and the people with first direct access to the truth of resurrection. In performance, the moment serves as a divinely sanctioned reminder of women's rights and duties to educate others, including men, in the public domain beyond the household. It authorises the nuns' acting and the convent's public production. Fittingly, the Abbess mediates between the represented world of the drama and the wider congregation of sisters by granting the peace ('abatissa eas iubeat exire ad quiescendum', p. 384) at the conclusion. The Barking scripts' dramatic vivifications of women's spiritual roles seem to have been effective since they were performed into the sixteenth century.

PLAYING SPACES ABROAD: CONTINENTAL CONVENT DRAMA

The dissolution of monasteries in England literally dis-placed religious orders of women, removing them from the architectural structures that played such an important part in their lives. For examples of a continuing tradition of convent theatre in the early modern period, we must turn to the continent. Elissa Weaver's study of convent drama in early modern Italy outlines a thriving dramatic culture. The *sacre rappresentazioni*, of which the accomplished Florentine dramatist Antonia Pulci (née Tanini) was a pioneer, were a logical development from liturgical drama.[34] Examination of Pulci's *Play of Saint Domitilla* (1483) and *Play of Saint Guglielma* (ante quem 1488), much reprinted in the sixteenth and seventeenth centuries, shows how religious drama made distinctive use of setting and performance venue to examine the convent's relationship to the world beyond its walls.[35] Antonia married a businessman and writer, Bernardo Pulci, but seems to have had close connections with convent life in Florence through her sisters. Antonia and her husband probably attended the profession of Suor Annalena Tanini at the Murate, and Antonia became an Augustinian tertiary after Bernardo's death in 1488. She bequeathed money to found the convent of Santa Maria della Misericordia.[36]

Saint Domitilla's distinguishing spatial feature is the crossing of boundaries. Its scenes take place on thresholds which function as sites of individual choice between secular and religious lives. Bakhtin's chronotopic reading of the borderline site is useful to understand Pulci's deployment of the threshold as a place and a moment of physical, mental and spiritual transformation. The action opens at the threshold of Domitilla's childhood home and her adult life, with the heroine poised to marry the Roman Patrician Aurelian or dedicate herself to Christ 'in company with virgins chosen, if / You choose to take the straight and narrow way' (86–8). The script sets up a dialogue between secular and religious houses, chronotopes that coexist in the playing space. Bakhtin argues that such dialogue exists outside the world represented, in the 'world of the author, of the performer, and the world of listeners and readers', the creative playing space. Pulci's central character functions as the locus for the dialogue created by the text.[37]

Domitilla's choice of the veil is, contrary to superficial perceptions, the more active option for women. The spiritual life is a journey to new horizons, while the sufferings of marriage, which the heroine recalls from her mother's experiences (153–4), are claustrophobic. In addition to a husband's jealously possessive nature (and its unspoken corollary, enclosure), one has to think about maternal confinement, 'the pangs of childbirth and the woes / So grievous when the children are brought forth' (167–76). Religious life is 'true repose' (199) while worldly existence is a frantic and unsatisfying search for peace, symbolised in the fate of Aurelian who dances himself to death. The paradox between actively journeying to Christ and not needing to move physically is cleverly resolved by a scene-dissolve. Domitilla's house transforms invisibly into a convent as the Pope intones 'I consecrate you, give to you this veil / That is sent to you from Heaven by your spouse.'[38] Spoken in the convent, these words enact the ritual which every spectator and performer had personally experienced, creating a communal bond between the fictional character and the nuns. If, as Weaver suggests, the play was composed for the convent ceremonies of clothing or profession, perhaps for one of Antonia's sisters, the boundaries between fictional performance and convent life, or stage and venue, would have been especially porous.[39]

When Domitilla is exiled to the island of Pontus, and thus physically separated from the fictional convent 'like a woman lost' [una cosa smarrita], physical displacement inaugurates another exploration of thresholds between worldly and spiritual realms (562–8). Domitilla's faith allows her to recreate the convent on the island by converting women sent by Aurelian to retrieve her. Her miraculous cure of blind and mute servants removes the women's 'veil of ignorance' (167) and replaces it with the veils of nuns, who then proceed to convert their husbands-to-be to monastic life. Domitilla's prayers, like the Pope's words of consecration, dissolve a worldly setting into the religious venue. This scene of revealing and re-veiling forms the play's dramatic climax, appropriately, given the probable occasion of performance. *Saint Domitilla* seizes upon the educational opportunities offered by the profession ceremony in order to reach members of the outside community who attended such occasions, as did Antonia and her husband. Proclaiming the value of monastic life was as important as celebrating the particular saint in this play.

Saint Guglielma is more concerned with the world outside the walls than *Domitilla*, demonstrating Saundra Weddle's point that the actions, objects and people who occupy interior spaces, like the enclosed convent, cannot be defined simply or exclusively as 'private'. The permeability of convent walls in early modern Florence, she argues, reveals a 'contradic-tion whereby the ideology of the enclosure was simultaneously main-tained by the ruling class and the Church, and circumvented by nuns, their families, and their patrons'.[40] The play produces theatrical space as a porous dialogue between the convent and the worldly community. It opens in an English court setting but journeys beyond to follow the disas-trous consequences of an arranged marriage to the King of Hungary that overbears the heroine's wish to profess as a nun. When the King takes a 'sacred pilgrimage' (203) to Jerusalem she suffers the unwanted attentions of his brother. Nuns watching this could not fail to notice the warning against admitting men to the convent or the impropriety of speaking to them alone in the parlour.

To escape scandal and the threat of execution, Guglielma flees to a wasteland, a setting that materialises her lack of a home in either the Court or the convent. Surprisingly, when divinely guided to a 'very fitting place' (517), she will not be confined in the nunnery. Instead, she chooses a position at the threshold as its gatekeeper, defining herself as a worldly sinner and outsider. From this position, Guglielma uses her powers of intercession to cure the sinful, including her leprous brother-in-law and the King. The play presents an eloquent argument that those who live within the convent's secure religious embrace should move beyond its walls to promote Christian ideals in the world.

This was Pulci's position as an Augustinian tertiary. The heroine of *Saint Guglielma* remains a woman of the world whose Christian charity and forgiveness successfully reforms her husband. The play speaks clearly to its audience of nuns and lay women who 'wander in this erring wood' (835), emphasising the common humanity of all and pointing out that the walls of the convent should be a porous membrane, not an absolute boundary set up to falsely differentiate divine purity from hopeless sin.

An ideal performance space would have been at the grate, the liminal space through which members of the wider community could see and hear the nuns' performance and the nuns, likewise, could see and speak to the lay sisters. The official restriction of audiences to those inside the convent walls, designed to protect the purity of the enclosed women, was often breached in practice. Women and even some men attended performances of convent plays.[41]

Pulci's human-centred drama (including the addition of an extensive role for Saul's widow in her play of David and Saul) paved the way for a broader tradition of convent theatre in Italy, with male and female authored scripts and some elaborate staging, as Weaver's fascinating study *Convent Theatre* shows. Some plays superimposed setting and venue to speak directly to the shared experience of those in the playing space. For example, Maria Costanza Ubaldini's *Rappresentazione dell'evangelica parabola delle deci vergine,* based on the parable of the wise and foolish virgins, takes women on and off stage on a journey through the temptations to the moment of profession. The play's climax exploits synchronic and diachronic forms of sorority created by the convent in order to invoke a powerfully magnetic dialogue between the world of the setting and that of the performance venue. The virgins witness a wedding between a long-haired bride and bridegroom, figuring themselves and Christ, and the whole play is accompanied by a Choir of nuns carrying lamps to illuminate the stage.[42] The profession of vows unites the nuns (fictional characters and spectators) spatially – in their membership of the convent – and across time. It is shared by all the sisters at the performance, so the play bonds the convent's women on and off stage as a company. Those entering the Order see themselves welcomed like the bride character whose hair would be cut like their own; those already professed celebrate their own enlightenment in union with Christ, looking back to the moment of their own profession and forward to that of sisters-to-be.

The tradition of convent drama can be extended beyond early modern Italy to France and Spain, where figures like Saints Thérèse of Lisieux and Teresa of Avila encouraged the performance of plays.[43] Perhaps the most remarkable extension of the convent farce is *El festejo de Los empenos de una casa* [Festival of the trials of a noble house], by the nun Sor Juana Ines de La Cruz, which satirises the values of the Spanish baroque court at which it was performed in Mexico City in 1668.[44] In the earlier, European context, the lack of dramatic activity in English convents on the continent is perhaps surprising. Schools set up under Mary Ward's missionary order, *The Institute of the Blessed Virgin Mary,* apparently encouraged dramatic productions in line with the Jesuit system of education which they were designed to parallel,[45] but all the other English houses were contemplative orders. This alone does not adequately explain the difference. A crucial factor seems to have been the insular nature of the English houses. Claire Walker has shown that English convents allied themselves through prayer, correspondence and patronage to their homeland rather than the immediate communities of their geographical locations.[46] Physical enclosure fostered a strong sense of national religious identity, and English nuns of noble birth often carried a heavy burden as symbols of the spiritual purity of their families. The convent's example of uncompromised chastity, holiness, and prayer for the motherland, was a powerful inspiration for the full restoration of Catholicism to those at home who had no material place in which to centre their faith. A dedication to Elizabeth Tydesley, the Abbess of the Poor Clares in Gravelines, regarded them as beacons to 'our poore countrie', because

although yee and other virgins of other orders of religion . . . can not serve God at home in religious houses by reason of the difficulties of the time, yet doe yee in number dayly increase . . . yee make your houses shine as though they were of yvorie.[47]

Until Henrietta Maria controversially laid the foundation stone of her Roman Catholic chapel in 1632, Catholic Englishwomen could only build such spectacular architectural declarations of their faith through their imaginations. The convent became an idealised fictive space. The palaces of light inhabited by women in the masques sponsored by Anna of Denmark and Henrietta Maria can be read, on one level, as theatrical recreations of a separate, all-female space like the convent. From here, women's relationships to the central institutions of power, concentrated at Court, could be defined in new ways.

'WHERE VIRGINS STILL SHALL MEET': HOUSES OF CHASTE SISTERHOOD REVIVED

On 4 May 1617, Anna of Denmark presided over *Cupid's Banishment*, an entertainment presented by the pupils of Ladies Hall and scripted by their Master, Robert White.[48] We have no records of the school, but its site, between the Globe Inn and Watergate at Deptford, meant that it was conveniently placed to bring a production to the Queen's Court at Greenwich. Greenwich Palace was a female-centred retreat for the Queen in 1617. James gave it to Anna in 1614; two years later she commissioned an

Italian-style building in the aristocratic tradition of 'secret' garden retreats, as if to typify Greenwich's geographical remove from Whitehall. Paula Henderson reminds us that the Queen's House (though not completed until after Anna's death), 'says much about practices of secrecy, privacy and pleasure in the period'.[49]

Cupid's Banishment can be best understood as a celebration of strategic retreat, drawing on the sororal traditions of convent theatre and the Catholic Queen's political withdrawal from Whitehall in 1617. Anna had tried and failed to win regency over the country while James was on progress to Scotland. Perhaps apprehensive about Anna's Catholicism, he had appointed the Archbishop of Canterbury and Lord Bacon, a staunch Protestant, as effective governors in his absence. Anna and Prince Charles were nominated to the council, yet the Venetian ambassador noted, on 30 March, 'I do not believe she will ever go there, as she proposes to pass the whole time out of London, and the prince will do much the same.'[50] *Cupid's Banishment* constructed Anna as a heavenly queen; placing her in the 'seat of state' she had been denied in Whitehall and addressing her as the 'Gracious and great Sovereigness' of a court where 'female worth' would be valued (1–3). As Clare McManus has shown, it can be read in secular terms as an attempt to relocate the structures of the patriarchal court in a female one.[51] Its feminist educational purpose may, indeed, have been what its producer, Lucy Russell, the Protestant Countess of Bedford, most wished to promote. In addition to complimenting the Queen, and teaching the performers, its celebration of a female-governed 'Academy' (27) may have been directed specifically to Prince Charles, who was in Greenwich when it was performed.

The version of courtly education offered at Ladies' Hall does not look forward to the dame schools but across to English convents on the Continent.[52] The Benedictine house at Liège, for example, advertised a curriculum in which young ladies could learn 'all qualities befitting their sex, as writing, reading, needle-work, French, Musick'.[53] Spatially, the distinguishing feature of convent education is the introverted woman-centred perspective created by enclosure. *Cupid's Banishment* offers a dramatic recreation of that enclosure. In its playing space, the Ladies' eloquence (from Ann Watkins's speech as Fortune), their dancing, embroidery, and letters (in the terpsichorean formation of the names of the royal family) are displayed primarily to entertain and delight other women. The exclusive occasion of performance undoubtedly added to the sense of a sororal chronotope, a women's house of learning. Entry to *Cupid's Banishment* was by invitation only; as in convent drama, access was ultimately controlled by two powerful women. Within the venue, it was the dominant gazes of the Queen and her primary lady-in-waiting that determined the young ladies' actions. The Queen's name was first in the dances spelling out royal names. Anna is offered embroidered gifts celebrating her royal identity by her god-daughters (302ff). The acorn (for Anna) and rosemary (for Regina), are chronotopic: looking forward to the growth of a new generation of independent women, and memorialising Anna's example.

Cupid's Banishment adapts the celebration of profession found in convents in order to promote female autonomy and community. Robert White describes it as 'a sport our little ladies can use on Candlemas night'. Candlemas, the purification of the Virgin, was celebrated on 2 February, often with convent drama. The performance of *Cupid's Banishment* on 4 May looks like a deliberately artificial recreation of convent festivity amid a pagan, classical setting. White's dedication to Lucy Russell explains that the masque enacts 'a form of uniting chaste hearts', that will not easily be understood: 'What should Hymen have to do where Diana is? Or why should there be a marriage solemnised by the Queen of Chastity?' (p. 83). Anyone with knowledge of the convent ritual in which the nun becomes a queenly bride of Christ would easily solve the paradox. White's disdainful jibe at the ignorant critic 'whose hungry ears feeds still on other men's provision, and perchance his teeth on other men's tables' probably refers to the Archbishop of Canterbury or Bacon, the Lord Keeper. The masque appropriates the monastic aim of rejecting worldly love for a divine, chaste match, as a route to freedom. At Diana's command, Hymen 'clad in all purity' (150) crowns a King and a Queen-bride clothed in silver to show the '*revels did wholly tend to Chastity*'. Cupid's attempt to join the symbolic wedding by dressing in white is hopeless. He is literally banished from the playing space by the 'sacred sisters' (280), who are 'attired all in white tinsie to show their defiance to CUPID' (285). The Ladies of the Hall, costumed as dryads and armed with darts, crown Cupid with Actaeon's horns and chase him off stage. *Cupid's Banishment* thus produces the chaste sisterhood's exclusive spatial ownership of fictional setting and venue as the main feature of its plot.

There are elements of *Cupid's Banishment* that would certainly be out of place in a convent: specifically a level of classical and emblematic allusion through Diana and Fortune, a Bacchanalian toast, and extravagant costumes, including naked arms for the wood nymphs. These draw on an alternative, more eroticised dimension of Diana's court of chaste nymphs, going back to early modern retellings of Ovid's Calisto story, in which Jupiter disguises himself as Diana to seduce her virgin-follower. Valerie Traub uses this myth to trace the perversion of chaste femme love in seventeenth-century England and her arguments illuminate our understanding of the entertainment. She observes that the fetishisation of chastity between women is an anxious reaction both to a series of erotic practices that elude conventional definition, and to the threat posed by an institutionalised community of women.[54] Chaste sisterhood is certainly threatening in *Cupid's Banishment*. Diana appears in an eroticised pastoral setting: within a mount that opens to reveal *'her arbour adorned with flowers encompassed round with her nymphs'*. The over-anxious stage-directions for the Queen-Bride insist *'their revels did wholly tend to Chastity, being a sport the goddess and her nymphs did use in bowers and retired places without any prejudice to virginity or scandal to any entire vow'* (195). The nymphs' sport, including the performance itself, does not threaten in the ways an act of heterosexual flirtation or rape would. Nevertheless, its re-location of pleasure in 'retired places' peopled only by women is challenging. It reconstructs women's chastity as exclusive autonomy and women's pleasure as a political alternative to marriage. *Cupid's Banishment*'s relocation of festivity and authority to the Queen's Court, via a female academy, was politically astute in the light of Anna's retirement to Greenwich in 1617. The Epilogue unites the virgin performers and the 'stars of women' watching (380) as a self-contained community. Its expansion of religious sorority to foreground pleasure and social politics was a pattern developed by Henrietta Maria and Margaret Cavendish.

The fusion of courtly and monastic culture became much more explicit under the aegis of Henrietta Maria and the cult of *honnêteté* she fostered. Du Bosc's *Compleat Woman*, translated by one of her courtiers Walter Montague, argued that hermits should 'come to studie perfection in the Court, and to take example of austeritie even in the place of pleasures. We have no need this day to seeke in Cloysters the precepts of vertue. It is enough to be a good Courtier, to be devout.'[55] Following Henrietta Maria's example of Marian devotion, religious communities acquired semi-official status, a local habitation and a name. According to Father Cyprien, one of Anna's Capuchin priests, 'the brothers and sisters of the confraternity of the Rosary met, confessed, and communicated regularly'.[56]

Margaret Cavendish's play *The Presence* (1688) comically satirises the religious culture of Henrietta Maria's household. Lady Bashful, 'fitter for a Nunnery, then a Court' (p. 37), is a semi-autobiographical portrait of Cavendish's own inability to engage actively in court life. Maids of

Honour take an oath of service to a Princess who 'keeps her Chamber',[57] and, in retirement, they enjoy considerable liberty as 'Mistresses of themselves' (p. 57). The play rehearses typical arguments about the advantages of religious life that transform the cloistered setting into a place of 'Freedom' (p. 57). The Maids follow a doctrine of Platonic love and 'live so happily in the Court' that 'they hate to think of Marriage' (p. 58). Pleasure does not come from sisterly affection, however. Chaste sisterhood is comically undercut in scenes where Lady Supple and Madam Liberty swap places in the bath and the bed to be entertained by Mr Amorous and Mr Break-jest (p. 70). The platonic *préciosité* of Henrietta Maria's court was similarly compromised when her lady-in-waiting Eleanor Villliers became pregnant in 1635.

Allusions to communal religious life permeated Henrietta Maria's drama, most obviously in the enclosed 'cloister' of *The Shepherds Paradise* by Montague (who converted to Catholicism in 1635). Its all-female democracy of 'sisters voyces' resembles the practice of convents where nuns elected their Abbess and gave their valued opinions on issues pertaining to their government. The play's pastoral setting that associated chaste sisterhood with the Diana/Calisto myth, also invited more radical interpretations of the play's same-sex alliances. William Prynne's slander of the Queen and her acting company as 'notorious whores' may be a reaction to the female community promoted by the play and the production, rather than simply a criticism of women's performances *per se*. *The Shepherds Paradise* literally presented (or made present) exclusive female–female desire because heterosexual romance was played between women actors in the *hortus conclusus* created by its pastoral setting and Somerset House venue. Government is also located in female hands since the men cannot vote. The Queen's presentation of a sorority that challenged the heart of England's social and political fabric was bound to create a furore. Pastoral images of chaste sisterhood in masques posed similar challenges.

Images of Roman Catholicism were deeply entwined in Henrietta Maria's court masques as Erica Veevers has argued.[58] *The Temple of Love* and *Luminalia* recreate the Queen and her ladies as an elite sorority inspired by the Virgin Mary's example, and imitating her role as a mediator or co-redeemer on a national level. Alice Wood has perceptively analysed the Virgin Mary's importance in the drama of the Trinity through which human salvation is played out and understood. Using Irigaray to read the Virgin as an essential, active mediator between the Godhead and humanity, she argues that 'Mary and the Spirit are portrayed as a kind of theological Bonnie and Clyde, stealing divinity from the law and institutions, even apparently from under the nose of the Godhead', by a mutual identification or indwelling.[59] This is an appropriate description of the Marian role adopted by Henrietta Maria and her ladies in the court entertainments. Elaborate masque scenery representing the heavens and its glorious light, represented a sisterhood of masquers in direct collusion with ethereal divinity, in effect appropriating divine radiance from the law and institutions represented by the King and Court in the lower body of the banqueting hall. This was part of the Queen's wider project to build Catholic aestheticism into the material culture of the Court.

The Temple of Love (1634), scripted by Davenant, celebrated the foundation of a chapel for the Capuchins at Somerset House. Henrietta Maria laid the foundation stone on 26 September 1632 before an audience of more than two thousand people. From its beginning, the chapel had a distinctively theatrical quality. The site was 'tastefully fitted up in the form of a church' with tapestries for walls, flowers strewn on the floor, and an altar at which Mass was said.[60] *The Temple of Love*'s central architectural motif: 'the Temple of Chaste Love should be re-established in this Island', proclaims a counter-Reformation restoration of monastic life with an obvious allusion to the new building that was nearing completion.[61] The setting brings the Capuchin temple into the Banqueting House at Whitehall. As with *Cupid's Banishment,* however, the masque goes beyond a concern with the spiritual and makes extensive use of exotic spectacle, seeming to revisit elements of *Blackness* and *Beauty* danced by Queen Anna. *The Temple of Love* reverses the gender-order of the transformations in Jonson's masques, making the Greek Poets, the Persian knights, and implicitly Charles I, the subjects of conversion. Indamora, the Indian Queen played by Henrietta Maria, is the agent of change.

Indamora's cult of platonic love is misunderstood by the Poets, who see it as 'dull imaginary pleasures of / Their souls' (p. 293). The exotic settings crowned by the Queen's appearance in 'a rich seat', against 'a great skallop shell' flatly contradict their views. Henrietta Maria and her masquers in costumes of 'Isabella colour and wachet' (p. 300), interweave divine and material beauty, materialising the masque's definition of chaste love.[62] Only this sisterly group have the power to restore 'Love's true temple'. It is a sacred space 'where noble virgins still shall meet, / And breath their orizons, more sweet / Than is the spring's ungather'd flower' (p. 300). Several of the masquers representing these 'noble virgins' were Catholic and one, Lady Thimelby, had strong connections to monastic orders on the continent.[63] The silent presence of Sappho hints at an alternative reading to the expressions of fervour, but lesbian possibilities implicit in the virgin sisterhood's power to restore true love are superseded by their dances with the Persian knights and the Queen taking a seat beside the King.

The chaste sisterhood's conversion of the State is produced through movement. The procession of the Queen and her ladies across the Banqueting House carry additional religious significance because of a strong similarity between the architecture of the perspective stage and the basilical model used for building Counter-Reformation churches.[64] By leaving the perspective scene to 'descend into the room' (p. 301), they symbolically step down from the 'holy' end of the church to convert the 'congregation' of spectators, including the King. The female masquers transform the stranger knights to chaste lovers through the structured patterns of dance. Significantly Indamora and her ladies disembark from the sea scene to the dry land of the Hall in their original state. Each brings her identity (religious as well as cultural) to Britain intact, unlike the daughters of Niger who have to be washed white by the monarch.

When Henrietta Maria moves to the King's side, a change of scene literally converts the State to the 'true Temple of Chaste Love' (p. 302). The setting's material restoration of a lost temple is an appropriate fictional equivalent of the Queen's triumph in establishing the Capuchin chapel in England. Father Cyprien claimed she had 'planted the cross upon the mount of Somerset House, the first place from which heresy hurled it when the religion was changed in this unhappy kingdom'.[65] Chaste Love's final song recasts the earlier rural scene in spiritual terms: The State's influence will now 'fructify each barren heart / And give eternal *growth to love*' (p. 304). The 'great *Chorus*' of performers who process to the State behind the figure of Chaste Love are also effectively converts to Catholicism (p. 304). Male masquers included devout Catholics such as Weston and men ripe for conversion like the Duke of Lennox.

Catholic aesthetics and courtly entertainment were even more closely interwoven in Henrietta Maria's 1638 Shrovetide masque *Luminalia*. It can best be read, as Erica Veevers points out, as a response to the Puritan criticism that followed the opening of the Capuchin Chapel in December, 1636, and the increasingly extrovert celebration of Catholic festivals and conversions in Henrietta Maria's court.[66] Father Cyprien's account of the Chapel's opening could easily be of a masque. The altar was raised like a stage and connected to the nave of the chapel with steps 'in theatrical form' (311). Curtains obscured a scene above, displaying a dove to represent the Holy Spirit, two hundred archangels, seraphim and cherubim 'painted and placed according to the rules of perspective', with the Holy Sacrament at the vanishing point. (311–12). When Mass began, the curtains drew back to reveal a combination of painting, light, and music:

The music, composed of excellent voices, set up an anthem, the harmony of which having no other outlet but between the clouds and the figures of Angels, it seemed as if the whole Paradise was full of music, and as if the Angels themselves were the musicians, those who sung being in fact concealed and not seen by anybody: thus the eye and ear found at the same time gratification in this contrivance of piety and skill. (p. 313)

Light was the main feature of the spectacle, the candles making the place 'appear all on fire' (p. 312).

Luminalia or the Festivall of Light Personated at a Masque at Court by the Queenes Majestie and her Ladies (1637) was also presented in a new building.[67] It was the Queen's first masque in the wooden banqueting house, constructed to prevent the Rubens ceiling in the permanent banqueting house from damage by candles. In November 1637 Sir John Finett reported 'Wee have a stately building toward in Whytehall', noting that it extended 'in length toward the hall and gard chamber about a hundred and ten foot, in bredth: ten or twelve foot into the first court'; and, significantly 'about five and forty into that of the preaching place'.[68] In *Luminalia*, the new banqueting house became Henrietta Maria's preaching place; the masque constructed it as a courtly parallel to her Chapel. Puritan detractors later referred to it as 'the Queen's Dancing Barn'.[69]

Luminalia's central conceit, 'consisting of darknesse and light' (A1), has obvious connections with the Catholic celebration of the Virgin as Queen of light and spiritual enlightenment. James Yoch has argued that the masque's '*avant garde* technical expertise' is also political since 'light was one of the most important elements of the political theology'.[70] 'The garden of *Britanides*' invokes the spiritual dimensions of the garden setting as prelapsarian *hortus conclusus* to stage a pattern of cultural and spiritual restoration (A1v) under the protection of the King and Queen. Antemasques set in 'The City of Sleep' give a flashback to a nightmarish regime ruled by the '*dreadfull Queen*' (p. 5) of Night, recalling the dark and dangerous years of Elizabeth I's England when Catholic recusants and priests were subject to fines, torture, execution. The antemasque–masque structure of *Luminalia* was probably informed Father Cyprien's view that such persecution 'renders the memory of Queen Elizabeth infamous, execrable', and 'gives a wonderful lustre to the piety and zeal of Queen Henrietta Maria'. His brief account of 'the pitiable state of Catholics' before Henrietta Maria's arrival suggests a strong historical awareness at her Court.[71] Perhaps spectators would have recognised the figure of Queen Elizabeth in Night's 'purple robe', 'her browne haire loose, and a golden Scepter in her hand' (p. 4). The urban setting figures the dangers of losing faith in a Protestant darkness. Sleep and its associated hypnotic and distracting qualities dance through a claustrophobic darkened city.

In contrast, the prelapsarian garden of the main masque is a Counter-reformation haven in which the King and Queen's virtues give freedom to the 'Prophetick Priests' who had been 'constrained either to live in disguises, or hide their heads in caves' (p. 2). Aurora promises a 'terrestrial Beautie, in whom intellectual and corporeall brightness are joyn'd' (p. 13), and Henrietta Maria appeared as a sun queen against 'a bright skie' to warm the national garden, drawing on the Catholic celebration of the Virgin Mary. Her ladies, in silver embroidered costumes 'cut in starre-like beames of white' (p. 18), created a sororal group around the Queen, enhancing the masque's Marian imagery which would have been especially obvious four days after Candelmas when it was performed. Francis Lenton's celebratory encomiastic verses *Great Britains Beauties* defined each masquer within a Marian tradition of female religious community.[72] Henrietta Maria is an ideal person to lead her companions, a 'Sacred Queene' (DI),

> From whose celestiall light, & virtuous mind
> These Ladies (All) the milk-white Path doe find,
> (By your example) unto virtues height,
> At which they ayme, with labour, and delight. (A2v)

The challenging nature of the female community is hinted at in the acrostic for the Countess of Lennox, which observes that 'women (though but weak) can mickle do' (B2v).

The venue would have emphasised *Luminalia's* effects. The decoration of the new banqueting house had rows of twenty windows to let in daylight and its ceiling was decked with velarium of about 4,624 feet in blue cloth, the colour of the Virgin.[73] In *Luminalia*, as in *The Temple of Love,* the Queen's proselytism is enacted spatially as the Queen and ladies descend from the heavens and dance, concluding with Henrietta Maria 'seated under the state by the King'. Movement across the Banqueting House floor secures the political future of English Catholics and liberates the glorious spectacle of a final setting, 'a heaven full of Deities or second causes' (p. 19).

The masquers' confident extrovert movements reflected the endeavours of Catholic noblewomen to sponsor the re-foundation of religious houses for women in England during Henrietta Maria and Charles's reign. The Poor Clares of Gravelines had sent a filiation to Dublin in 1625 which lasted until 1649. In 1639, Franciscan nuns of Nieuport sent three sisters to England 'for the setting up of a Seminary in our native soyle of England, of Yong Gentlewomen', which survived until 1650. In the 1640s Katherine Manners (Duchess of Buckingham), obtained permission to sponsor a Benedictine filiation to Ireland.[74]

In addition to these concrete re-foundations, Henrietta Maria's reinventions of the convent in her household and on stage inspired the creation of fictive women's houses as settings in drama. Unsurprisingly, the women of the Cavendish family found these settings politically appealing from royalist and feminist perspectives. Jane Cavendish and Elizabeth Brackley's *Pastorall*, for example, draws on the courtly, Marian cult of chaste sisterhood to legitimate a wholly unconventional rejection of heterosexual courtship and marriage (as discussed in chapter 2). The preservation of sisterly bonds holds particular poignancy for the authors in the light of Elizabeth's marriage to John Egerton and the sisters' imminent separation.[75] The nunnery scenes of their play *The Concealed Fancies* (1645) are informed by a similar desire to sustain the empowering aspects of sisterhood. The settings draw on the pre-Reformation history of their home Welbeck Abbey, whose monastic buildings, including the whole of the south cloister range, remained.[76] In a domestic performance of *The Concealed Fancies*, the venue would have 'doubled' the effect of the setting. The lost monastic space is re-invoked amid Civil War trauma in politically conservative ways to share a royalist communion of loss. The nunnery's gender politics are more radical: Welbeck Abbey gives material shape to the sisters' decision to reject wifely subjection in favour of a religious life of relative freedom. Their self-enclosure frustrates the goals of all the men in the main plot. The continued popularity of the convent as a subversive, utopian female community is seen in plays by Cavendish and Brackley's step-mother, Margaret.

MARGARET CAVENDISH'S CONVENTS AND ACADEMIES

Several of Margaret Cavendish's plays bring the traditions of the academy and convent together in ways that problematise the all-female community as utopian space. The overlap of convent and academy is not surprising given Cavendish's cultural environment. The Cavendish household, her married home, provided a school of learning in which William and his brother Charles encouraged research into philosophy, politics, science as well as writing. A monastic presence was always close by. Antwerp, where William and Margaret lived from 1648–60, was home to a Jesuit college and a Benedictine order for women. The material remains of abbey buildings were integrated into their English homes. Like Welbeck, Newcastle House in Clerkenwell, London, was a converted nunnery. The cloisters of St Mary's were still in place, and in 1668 Margaret succeeded in securing this property as part of her jointure.[77]

In *Youth's Glory and Death's Banquet* (1662) monastic or educational discourse converts household settings into two separatist spaces that give contrasting perspectives on women's enclosure.[78] The uneducated Lady Innocence is trapped within the physical and mental cloister of wifely identity. Lady Sanspareille's physical enclosure is counterpointed by an education that opens doors to a life beyond the household. The play 'represents a radical moment in the history of women's education', as Annette Kramer rightly observes.[79] Like the deserted homekeepers analysed in chapter 1, Lady Innocence is 'enclosed' in ignorance and passivity. She cannot resist the withdrawal of her husband's love or adequately defend herself against accusations of infidelity and theft (p. 165). Cavendish's monastic allusions heighten the self-destructive effects of this cultural fashioning. Innocence is cruelly catechised by her master, Lord de L'Amour, when she is believed guilty:

LADY INNOCENCE	I am too strict a Votary to truth to tell a lye.
LORD DE L'AMOUR	I should be glad you were vowed one of her Order.
LADY INNOCENCE	I am so, and have taken the habit of sincerity upon me.
LORD DE L'AMOUR	Tell me truly, do you never use to lye? . . . I hear to my great grief you have many faults, pray mend them . . .
LADY INNOCENCE	I shall desire to know them.
LORD DE L'AMOUR	Examine yourself, and you will find them.
LADY INNOCENCE	I shall condemn, and sacrifice them on the Altar of Repentance and crave for mercy and forgiveness.
LORD DE L'AMOUR	Pray do so. (p. 153)

Cavendish's dialogue converts a domestic scene into a private confessional. It recreates the patriarch of the household as a suspicious and unforgiving holy father whose manner is anything but loving. The play makes it clear that a life of passive retirement may not be at all comfortable. Lady Innocence's lonely suicide is the pathetic consequence of her determination to follow a life of solitude and melancholy contemplation.

Lady Sanspareille's death takes place after an oration against marriage, for which she is costumed like a bride in the tradition of professing sisters. Her father's grief makes it easy to read the play as a tragedy of incestuous passion dramatising a daughter's difficulty in leaving her father's house. However, Sir Thomas Father-Love's educational programme, like the convent, offers intellectual means to transcend the roles of daughter, bride and housewife. This plot shows that even isolated withdrawal and education can have limited benefits. Without the sorority, however, there is nowhere for Lady Sanspareille to go after her rejection of marriage. Perhaps her tragic demise is Cavendish's comment on the loss of convent culture for Protestant women. The play seeks to open alternatives to marriage in the secular, public world through Lady Sanspareille's orations. From a golden-railed platform, she argues that women's voices should be 'the chief Pillar or upholder of Monarchical States and Common-wealths', and should, likewise, be protected by them (p. 155).

The onstage setting promotes the permeability of boundaries between an enclosed female space and the world beyond. The Queen of Attention, a member of the coterie audience invited by Sanspareille's father, comments 'I wonder not that you let her speak in publick' (p. 155). Sanspareille's discourse transforms the household platform into a pulpit, university lectern, and legal bench. The setting probably mirrors the conditions of reading or production in the Cavendish household, commenting metatheatrically on the political potential of domestic performance: women may appear to be enclosed within walls, but by acting as orators in a range of fictional public venues, they can effectively transform the private space, destroying the myth that women cannot speak on learned subjects. The two playing spaces, on and off the stage, raise the possibility of extending fictional speeches into the real world. Lady Sanspareille advocates the educational value of theatre:

Stages and Publick Theaters, were first ordained and built for the education of noble youth . . . Theaters were not only schools to learn or practise in, but publick patterns to take example from. Thus Theaters were profitable, both to the Actors and Spectators; for as these Theaters were publick Schools, where noble principles were taught, so it was the dressing rooms of vertue, where the Actors, as her Servants did help to set her forth. (p. 126)

Sanspareille's words construct both setting and venue as a school. Spectators and actors in any production of *Youth's Glory and Death's Banquet*
learn through their experiences of the play. Lady Sanspareille teaches that
churches, royal thrones, and judges' benches are 'but glorious Theaters' in
which each powerful man 'acts their parts' (p. 127). She appreciates that
any site of authority is arbitrary, so why shouldn't a woman hold it just as
much as a man? Her radical ideas are enacted by the actress speaking, and
passed on to all those listening, opening the door to much stronger female
participation in the theatres of power.

In contrast to this extrovert, educational impulse, Lady Sanspareille's
utopian visions draw on a monastic tradition of contemplative retreat.
Unlike Lady Contemplation, Cavendish's other recluse, Lady Sanspareille
does not create sociable fantasies. She is more like a medieval mystic,
inventing a landscape of learning informed by a moral sensibility. She
traces a psychological journey where introverted self-reflection leads to a
spiritual resting place with 'Landskips of perfection; green Meddows of
hopes wherein grows sweet Primroses of Joy', animated by desire and a
'Sun of Fervency' (p. 143). Cavendish's pastoral utopia is a very long way
from the Ovidian tradition of Diana's chaste sisterhood, or the divinely
inspired coteries in Henrietta Maria's drama. What is most striking about
Lady Sanspareille's fantasy landscape, a garden where the Muses and poets
and live in peace, is the sense of isolation:

The Muses, as all other Femals takes a delight to enjoy their lovers alone, that
makes them separate themsevels from other Company, and poets, as all lovers to
loveth solitude . . . the Muses lovers of the Poets oftimes chooseth a solitary life,
as being a Paradise for Innocent delight, wherein the Senses lyes on soft banks of
repose, whilst the mind with a sober, and serious peace, walkes in the silent
shades of contemplation . . . about this paradise, which paradise is a solitary life,
the calm smooth River of safety flowes, which Winds or Circles in the life, from
suffering, or acting injury, or wrong. And from this River of safety, runs many
streams of pleasures . . . And in this solitary life 3 Trees doth grow, Peace, Rest,
and Silence, are they names, the fruits they bare is plenty, ease and quiet. (p. 149)

Sanspareille's paradise is a literary version of the medieval mystic's garden
of contemplation. It is an imaginary space in all senses of the word, not yet
realisable on earth. Likewise, Fame's palace is a utopian dream for women.
Lady Sanspareille recognises that it can be built on many different situations (p.151), but her attempts to plant firm foundations are unrealisable at
the moment of the play. Her name indicates her isolation: she is unique.
Without a supportive sisterhood of writers and feminist thinkers, her

solitary visions of female autonomy remain in the realms of the imagination. The Epilogue seeks a feminist network of spectators: 'now let's hear
what you say,' it urges (p. 180). Men's voices would further the cause by
expressing approval, women's voices would realise it. Unless the play can
form a bridge between the utopian chronotope of Lady Sanspareille's vision
and that of the play's audience or readership, it will remain entombed in
the separatist realm of fiction.

A more optimistic vision of female education appears in Cavendish's
The Female Academy (1662), where Lady Sanspareille's lonely mysticism is
replaced by female company. Spatially, the Academy imitates the enclosed
structure of the convent: its members can be seen and heard only behind a
'large open Grate' (p. 653). The play creates a female community of
performers and a separate female community of spectators: men watch
from a grate at one side of the room while lay women watch from the
other end. The walls of the female academy are an explicit challenge to
conventional spatial arrangements between the sexes designed to perpetuate status differences. As Daphne Spavin has argued, the enclosures
created by grammar schools, universities or the Inns of Court perpetuated
the fiction of male superiority by providing exclusive access to valued
knowledge for men and reducing it for women.[80] Astell's *Serious Proposal
to the Ladies* tellingly pointed out 'I know not how the men will resent it
to have their enclosure broke down, and women invited to taste of that
tree of knowledge they have so long unjustly monopolised' (p. 121). In
Cavendish's play, the female academy does more than breach the educational enclosure; it rejects it entirely. The ladies 'take no notice of the
Academy of Men, nor seem to consider what the men say' (p. 671), their
reason being that many 'young Novices' have been badly instructed by
'foolish, cautionary, formal Tutors or Educators' (p. 673). By reversing
conventional spatial practice, the play creates comedy: the men are
reduced to infantile behaviour, trying to disrupt the women's education
by blowing their own trumpets 'uncivilly and discourteously at their
Grate and Gates' (p. 679).

Spatial segregation creates an atmosphere in which women's rights
to learning can be voiced more confidently than in *Youth's Glory*. The
senior Matron encourages the first Lady Speaker to take possession of
the chair confidently, not 'like a Robber' who has no right (p. 654). The
Academy's rigorous control of its own space nurtures distinctive female
knowledge and resources. Like the convent chronotope, its diachronic axis
is structured on matriarchal lines. The Matron refers to a female geneal-
ogy of learning, headed by Nature, mother of the 'Lady *Wit*', who, in

turn, has 'nine Daughters, very beautifull Ladies, namely the Nine Muses'. The Muses entertain male admirers but 'have vowed single lives', at their Mother's Court in a magnificent palace (p. 654). Cavendish's attractive picture of chaste sisterhood probably draws on her impressions of Henrietta Maria's household coterie.

The Academy prizes Mother wit rather than the traditional repositories of wisdom in the councils of kings and princes (p. 657). Truth is clearly located in the female academy while sophistry dominates the rival male school. The men's arguments against the female academy are obviously prejudiced and lack reason or logic: they complain that the women will dedicate themselves to virginity. This is not the academy's real threat. A Matron points out 'these Ladies have not vowed Virginity, [n]or are they incloystred; for an Academy is not a Cloyster, but a School' teaching them how 'to be good Wives when they are married' (p. 679). It is not separation but education that is dangerous. *The Female Academy* drama-tises the subversive potential of sororal communities to encourage secular as well as religious conversions: transforming women from victims of subjection to autonomous, articulate, speaking and thinking subjects. Cavendish's commitment to all-female education is gently satirised in Susanna Centlivre's play *The Basset-Table* (1705). Valeria, an aspiring natural philosopher, is told 'you should bestow your Fortune in founding a College for the Study of Philosophy, where none but Women should be admitted'.[81]

Cavendish interrogates the idea of sororal community more trenchantly in *The Convent of Pleasure* (1688). At a superficial level, the text recreates a lost tradition of didactic convent drama. It charts a process of education for the Princess, for performers, and for the onstage and offstage audi-ences. As in many Italian spiritual comedies, aptly-named male characters, including Monsieur Take-Pleasure and Monsieur Facil, are set up for mockery. The first play-within-the-play presented by the convent's sisters rehearses the traditional anti-marriage arguments appropriated so vigor-ously by monastic discourse, and articulated by the Flemish nun who triumphantly declared 'I was out of danger of ever being in the Slavery of Marriage for which I had so great an aversion and there was no other way to avoid it, but in embracing the State of Religion.'[82]

Scenes illustrating the miseries of marriage in *The Convent of Pleasure* echo the warnings of earlier convent drama, such as those given to the heroine of Antonia Pulci's *Domitilla* (lines 161-8). Cavendish could not have read convent plays in the original Italian but the dramatic recreation of their ideas in *The Convent of Pleasure* demonstrates her awareness of a well-publicised monastic discourse. *The English Nvnne*, for example, advised its young female readership that 'the accustomed miseries of a married lyfe, and of having issue, ought much rather to sway with women, for their forbearance of marriage' (A4). The situations it details are dramatised with unsentimental brevity by the sisters in Cavendish's *Convent of Pleasure*, in scenes cataloguing wives' physical and sexual abuse, the dangers of childbirth, and the difficulties of raising children. The all-female company rehearses a shared set of values about men. It comes as no surprise when the last victimised lady declares: 'I must prevent my own ruin, and the sweet virtuous lady's by going into a nunnery; wherefore, I'll put myself in one tonight. There will I live, and serve the Gods on high, and leave this wicked world and vanity' (p. 273). The Epilogue bridges the threshold between the metatheatrical play world and the onstage convent venue in her summary of a shared belief system: 'Marriage is a curse we find / Especially to women kind' (p. 273).

Aside from that shared vision, however, the convent of pleasure is founded on very different principles from that of its religious predecessors. Indeed, Lady Happy pointedly rejects the monastic ideals of modesty, humility, self-deprivation and physical suffering on the grounds that, with these, 'the soul can have but little will to worship' (p. 259). The alternative she offers is, at first glance, very attractive: 'a place of freedom, not to vex the senses, but to please them' (p. 260), a philosophy that closely echoes Roman Catholicism's emphasis on sensual appeal as a gateway to spiritual inspiration, and Henrietta Maria's own religious aesthetics. As a memorial of the Queen's elite coterie, however, the play is highly critical. Cavendish spares no pains to outline the material luxuries to be provided in the seasonal programme of furnishings and sensual delights of the gardens (pp. 264–5), but sets these in disturbing opposition to the lay-women's painful experiences of lack in the anti-marriage play. Ironically, the pleasures enjoyed by the sisters in the convent, including those of performance and spectatorship, depend structurally on the suffering of other women who are outside its protective walls. In performance, the anti-marriage play is often darkly comic. The laughter it produces is elitist and selfish. Cavendish questions the integrity of the socially privileged female company and the foundations of its woman-centred utopia.

The play goes on to interrogate the legitimacy of a sorority founded exclusively on pleasure. Unlike the Lady who vows to 'serve the Gods on high' the sisters in the play do not use the cloister to further their spiritual, meditative, or intellectual lives. Lady Happy admits the finite quality of the convent's aims in her vow to 'Live with delight, and with it die' (p. 261). Whether she voices Margaret Cavendish's own beliefs, or whether the play offers a criticism of the worldly preoccupations of Henrietta Maria's court is impossible to determine. In either case, *The Convent of Pleasure* explores how an enclosed sorority operates in a spiritual vacuum. Importantly, membership of the convent of pleasure differs markedly from Henrietta Maria's coteries. The pastoral haven in *The Shepherds Paradise* admitted both men and women, as did the arch-confraternity of the rosary in her court. In *The Convent of Pleasure* (and *The Female Academy*), however, the walls are apparently a non-permeable barrier between an enclosed group of women and the men outside. Judith Peacock argues that Cavendish's depiction of alternative female environments like the convent and the academy, where 'women conduct their own lives, without interference from men or indeed society, would have been considered deeply disturbing by the audiences of the 1660s' and may, in fact, have restricted the plays to the 'closet', or the enclosed venue of private performance.[83]

Cavendish's play engages with what Valerie Traub identifies as a growing anxiety about chaste sisterhoods in the later part of the seventeenth century.[84] Male paranoia fetishises the alternative erotic pleasures that convents could offer in texts like 'Upon Appleton House' by Cavendish's contemporary Andrew Marvell.[85] Marvell's poem was written in 1651 for General Thomas Fairfax, to whom Jane and Frances Cavendish had appealed when they were besieged. Since we do not know of any manuscript copies in circulation before its publication in 1681 it is impossible to trace a route whereby Margaret might have known it when she wrote *The Convent of Pleasure*. There are, however, interesting parallels between the poem's account of William Fairfax's forced entry to seize his beloved from the abbey at Nun Appleton and the end of Cavendish's play. In Marvell's poem 'Young Fairfax through the wall does rise', spies Isobel Thwaites amid the 'relics false', bears her away by force of arms 'And to the nuns bequeaths her tears.'[86] Patsy Griffin argues that Marvell's poem implicitly defends the Protestant appropriation of religious houses, something that would apply equally well to the Cavendish context at Welbeck and Clerkenwell.[87]

Unlike Marvell's conquering hero, the Prince/Princess in Cavendish's play does not enter the convent with a sword. He succeeds in dressing mentally as well as physically to become one of the female company, bettering the superficial performances of Courtly and Presumption in Cavendish and Brackley's *The Concealed Fancies* (see chapter 1). He surrenders his worldly identity with his clothes, accepting the communal lifestyle advocated by Lady Happy like a novice hoping to take vows. Only his reaction to the anti-marriage play and Lady Happy's reprimand 'I fear you will become an apostate' (p. 273), give a clue about his eventual dissolution of the sisterhood. As critics have argued, the text offers opportunities to explore a range of different kinds of sexual attraction. This is one case in which uncertainty over where, if at all, *The Convent of Pleasure* was to be performed, can serve the play's meaning. Cavendish's failure to designate professional stage, closet performance, or reading as the arena for her play keeps the gender of the actor playing the Princess indeterminate, and the protagonists' sexual orientations fluid. The convent's performances can thus offer a range of pleasures to spectators or readers.

However, the ambiguously gendered Princess brings problems as well as pleasures to Lady Happy and the female community. Changes of setting where '*the scene is changed*' to a pastoral (p. 275) or '*The Scene is opened*' for a sea masque (p. 280) function as physical markers of an altered perspective s/he brings. Cavendish uses the Princess to dramatise the perversion of chaste femme–femme love by increasingly anxious early modern commentators. The pastoral starring Lady Happy and the Princess re-presents a version of the classic story of illusory same-sex desire in Ovid's Calisto, but offers a prefatory dialogue that registers deep anxiety about its lesbian possibilities. Lady Happy's belief that she will be punished for loving another woman makes it clear that kisses and embraces 'amongst us woman-kind' are no longer perceived as innocent (274). The presence of a 'masculine mind' or viewpoint on 'female embraces' (p. 275) pollutes the possibility of utopian pastoral unity where they can 'join as one body and soul, or Heav'nly spirit' (p. 278). Lady Happy and the Princess 'go in' to this patriarchal ideological landscape by entering a rural scene with '*a Maypole in the middle*' (p. 275).

The insidious invasion of masculine authority through art rather than force of arms is expanded as the Prince(ss) colonises the settings of the convent's theatrical productions. In the sea masque, s/he dominates the female community as Neptune, declaring 'I am the King of All the Seas / All wat'ry creatures do me please,' a trident signifying masculine 'power and command' (p. 280). The entertainment is based on Neptune's address in John Ogilby's triumphal entertainment for the restoration of Charles II. Ogilby's entertainment praises Charles as 'Neptuno Britannico' (the British Neptune), in the same terms:

You are our *Neptune*, every Port, and Bay
Your Chambers; the whole Sea is Your High-way
Though sev'ral Nations Boast their Strength on Land,
Yet you Alone the Wat'ry World command.[88]

The reproduction of Ogilby's restoration script in the convent and *The Convent of Pleasure*, constitutes a second colonisation of the female playing space at a theatrical level. It anticipates the Prince's apostasy and the imminent restoration of patriarchy.

Nevertheless, by surreptitiously joining the female company, the Prince has learned to see and perhaps feel things differently. Like Marvell, Cavendish depicts the dissolution of the convent as a heterosexual comic resolution of the plot but with adroit irony. Madam Mediator is the character most distressed and weeps like Marvell's nuns. Lady Happy and the Princess stand together when news of the male infiltrator is announced while the other nuns '*skip from each other as though afraid of each other*' (p. 283). Is their fear excited by the proximity of a man or the intrusive heterosexual gaze that would censor their embraces 'of female kind' (p. 275)? Either way, these sisters in arms show that the company of women is still attractive as a mark of security or of desire. Cavendish scrutinises the idea of the convent critically; its exclusivity (in terms of class and gender) is rendered problematic. Nevertheless, the play's denouement keenly registers the loss of a place in which fears and pleasures can be shared just between women.

Perhaps because chaste sororities were increasingly perceived as threatening towards the end of the seventeenth century, the convent endured as a place of otherness in the female literary and dramatic imagination. 'The Royal Nun', a late seventeenth-century fragment of performance text in the Catholic Tixall manuscript, serves as a final illustrative example of its appeal. Based on the story of St Pulcheria (339–414), who vowed virginity and persuaded her sisters to do the same, 'The Royal Nun' opens with a chorus of virgins welcoming a novice.[89] They lead her with excitement: 'Her holy birth-day now begin; / In humble weeds, but cleane array' (p. 166). Pulcheria asks her sister Marina to leave the Court and join the religious community, surrendering her 'costly robes' for 'poore attire' and her 'golden bed' for humble 'matts'. Marina must adopt the convent *horarium* with its regime of 'broken slumbers', fasting, prayer and penitence (p. 167). She stands on the threshold, recognising that 'the gate to blisse doth open stand', yet finding it difficult to bid the world adieu.

The date of the fragment and the type of performance it came from are impossible to determine, although a version of it appears in Nathaniel Lee's play *Theodosius* (1680), staged at the time of the Exclusion Crisis. The power of sisterly affection in the Tixall fragment is rendered more acute in the context of relationships between the women who wrote and collected poetry in the family manuscripts: Gertrude Aston Thimelby, Lady Aston, and a religious sisterhood on the continent. Winefred Thimelby, sister to Lady Aston and sister-in-law to Gertrude, was professed at Louvain in 1635, aged sixteen, and elected prioress in 1668. According to her brother, she had desired to be a nun since childhood. In a letter to Herbert Aston, Winefred reports a visit from her niece Katherine, known as 'Keat', and her widowed sister-in-law, Gertrude (Herbert's sister). They were at St Monica's in the late 1650s and Winefrid hoped they would profess to enjoy 'continuance of that peace the world cannot give'.[90] In a later letter, she reports the ceremony of Gertrude's profession on Michaelmas Day, where she changes her mourning clothes to become a bride of Christ:

Our dear sister hath now changed murning into whight attire. Oh had you sen the solemnity I am confident yr hart wod not have contained all the ioy, but shed sum att yr eyes. Keat was the bearer of her crowne; was itt not fitt she shuld, who meanes to duble itt, in the last and lasting nuptiall feast? No less then heaven can dim the splendor of this glorius day. All thinges wear so compleatly acted, by both bride and bridmayde, that my brother Ned and I wear not a lettle goodly.[91]

This is an alternative family celebration, the moment of monastic self-definition alluded to in the *Visitatio* plays, Italian convent dramas, and *Cupid's Banishment.* What makes the celebration different is that the bridegroom is physically absent, leaving the stage to a company of women. Given the tone of Winefrid's letters, it is possible that 'The Royal Nun' may have formed part of Gertrude and Katherine Aston's thinking process and perhaps their rehearsal of a future as convent sisters. Like the conversion of Cosmophila in *The English Nvnne* or the solidarity in *The Female Academy,* the manuscripts describe a powerful theatre of sisterhood. Traub has suggested a cultural occlusion of the expressions of love between women in the Tixall letters,[92] and its displacement into a fictional setting may help to explain the passionate tone of 'The Royal Nun'. Marina, believing she has 'heaven in view', asks the Chorus of Virgins to 'hast to take me in / For ever locke Religions dore / Secure me from the charmes of sinne / And let me see the world no more' (p. 168).

Over a hundred years after the dissolution of the monasteries in England, the convent still held its appeal to women. Throughout the period, it represented possibility rather than restriction. Its enclosed walls separated it from the everyday world in ways which opened doors to female education, and to a different kind of identity, a sense of self that did not depend on one's relationship to a worldly family. Religious discourse, settings and venues lent additional authority to the scripted words spoken by women. Some scripts, like the liturgical drama of Wilton and Barking, worked within the boundaries set by traditional spaces. Others, such as the Cavendish women's entertainments, departed so far from their religious beginnings to evade even the divine paternal authority under which they were founded. The convent and the academy's separation from societal norms made them automatic playing spaces for the exploration of utopian alternatives. Perhaps their most appealing quality was the emotional and political sense of sisterhood they fostered. Here were places where interests and values born of a common experience could be shared across generations; where sisterly feelings could be prioritised. Here were houses where a room of one's own was replaced by the company of women.

CHAPTER 5

Cities

The city caters for the two opposite impulses in human life: movement and settlement,[1] and is thus constituted on oppositional models that offer very different places to women. Unlike the rural landscape or the garden, the governing dynamic of city spaces is not the relationships between human beings and nature. The buildings, streets, squares and monuments – traditionally a man-made panorama – make travelling through urban space primarily a social orientation. The cosmological urban model, related to settlement, saw the ideal city as an extension of the classical, masculine body, neatly divided into elements with distinctive functions and locations that contribute to the successful operation of the whole.[2] Robert Burton's *Historical Remarques and Obvervations of the Ancient and Present State of London* (1681), for example, defined London in a tradition of Roman writers who, 'to magnify the City of *Rome*, drew its Original from Gods and Demy-Gods':

> *The noble Seat of Kings it is;*
> *For State and Royalty.*
> *Of All the Realm, the Fence, the Heart*
> *The Life, the Light, the Eye.*[3]

This is a model of the city as 'place': an environment in which everything has a proper position. Woman is not completely absent; she is displayed as the decorative figurehead of the city as Augusta or Britannia, controlled by the god-like gaze of the governor, the body to his head. The organisation of space in this model prioritises a superior, phallocentric gaze. It can only be properly perceived from above, as in a map, from the totalising quasi-divine perspective that eliminates the realities of everyday early modern spatial practice.[4]

The city in these terms bears many similarities to the patriarchal household examined in chapter 1. Its legal constitution, male-authored buildings and institutions were, in most cases, closed places for women. *The Case of the City of London* (1692), for example, defined the old City in exclusively masculine terms. 'The City of *London* is a Body Politic', composed of Freemen with 'Power to make Bye-Laws for their own better Government and Advantage', it declared. Those who were not 'Members of the said Body' were 'nevertheless Bound' to its constitution as residents. Rigid cultural and physical boundaries in London's formal shape were means to organise an urban population that had no automatic ties of kinship or feudal loyalty. In effect, this meant the exclusion or containment of women who represented all the 'physical, mental and political pollutions' that would compromise the rational organisation of the city as a unified and autonomous masculine subject.[5] How could woman identify with this model of the city? Like the household of chapter 1, London does not appear to offer a home to early modern women.

Nevertheless, Lady Meanwell in Elizabeth Polwhele's play *The Froelicks* (*c.* 1671) declares 'There is no Elysium but this London', and goes on to observe that only fools 'forsake this soul-charming city for the dirty, melancholy country'.[6] Madam Malateste in Cavendish's *The Unnatural Tragedy* (1668) agrees with her, telling the Steward of her husband's estate 'I would have you take me a fine house in the City: for I intend to live there, and not in this dull place.'[7] Although Cavendish spent most of her time at her husband's country estates when the couple returned to England, she managed to secure possession of the Newcastle town house in Clerkenwell as part of her jointure in 1667, the year before the play was published.[8] Madam Malateste's outspoken desires for the novelty of the metropolis perhaps echo those of the author. Cavendish's visits to London, attired ostentatiously in black and silver for a ride in Hyde Park, or attending a meeting of the Royal Society in a long train to observe its activities, are just one example of the increasingly visible and active part of women in post-Restoration London. The varied autobiographies of Mary Carleton show that the streets of the capital which had famously made Dick Whittington's fortune were also a transformative arena for women. Carleton, a shoemaker's daughter, used the city as a stage to refashion herself as a German Princess. At the end of *The Wittie Combat* (1663), a dramatisation of her story, she confidently told the audience 'The World's a Cheat, and we that move in it / In our degrees do exercise our Wit' (F2v).[9]

The enthusiasm of these female voices points to the existence of another London. In opposition to the masculine city cosmos stands what might be termed a feminine urban model related to movement and disorder. Early modern writers recognised that London was dangerously deformed in architectural and spatial terms, more like Bakhtin's image of the grotesque body than the classical, masculine idea. The ancient walled City was an asymmetric mass of narrow and chaotically winding streets; there was no governing design to the architecture, and the resulting stylistic chaos was grotesque. John Evelyn's *Character of England* (1659) suggested that London's spatial irregularity produced social and spiritual disorder, complaining that 'the *Buildings* . . . are as deformed as the minds & confusions of the people', the Magistrate having no power to command uniformity in building, religious worship, or regulation of dress codes so that 'it is not an easy matter to distinguish the *Ladie* from the *Chambermaid*'.[10]

The feminine model of the city, opposed to fixed architectural 'place', offers a useful starting point to explore how early modern women accommodated themselves in urban space. Donatella Mazzoleni argues that the secondary city exists alongside and in opposition to its partner, 'born out of the representation of the communicative relationship between an inside and an outside, in the body and beyond the body, and as a production of doubles of and separate from the body' (p. 296). This is the lived, material reality of the city as experienced by the multiple, autonomous bodies of the people who make up the unofficial civic body. Their individual spatial practices fragment urban space in innumerable pathways. De Certeau usefully likens this to walking through the city, a process which 'creates a mobile organicity in the environment' as the individual actualises possibilities from an ensemble offered by his or her locations. In the same way that a speech act actively operates on the constructed order or discourse from which it is drawn, a walk through the city (which de Certeau compares to an extended rhetorical performance), fashions or transforms the environment in which it, literally, 'takes' place:

The long poem of walking manipulates spatial organizations, no matter how panoptic they may be; it is neither foreign to them (it can only take place within them) nor in conformity with them (it does not receive its identity from them). It creates shadows and ambiguities within them. (p. 101)

In contrast to a clearly defined masculine *polis*, the mysterious city, full of secret passageways and unexpected openings is, like the female grotesque body, a leaky vessel. In post-Restoration London, as in other times and places, women's movement through the city could be a dangerous business, but the very existence of such routes created spaces in which women could devise and operate their own versions of urban life. Writing and performing drama were ways of establishing a local authority in the city.

Women's drama engages with the paradoxical character of urban space. Conservative *polis* and radical grotesque elements are juxtaposed with either fruitful or destructive effects depending on the chemistry of any given cultural site. Mazzoleni defines the more productive combination as a 'culture of cities', and the refusal to integrate as a 'culture of metropolises':

> In this possibility of symmetrical opposition between cosmic and grotesque, one sees how, in 'the culture of cities', the Apollonian and Dionysiac are poles of a dialectic, of a game which is therefore *dramatic*, and which can be re-composed at a superior level, while the 'culture of metropolises' seems instead to be asymmetric, non-dialectic, *tragic*. (p. 296)

Early women's drama enters actively into this equation. Female responses to the city change it spatially and socially, and the city's own changes in terms of architecture and culture, likewise, change the way female identity is constituted. Re-forming the city through drama is a means to alter the ways women perceive themselves. Women's drama *per se* engages the urban space according to the 'culture of cities': it recomposes masculine architecture at a superior level of performance to encourage fruitful, liberating movement and security for both men and women. However, city settings within the plays often stage a tragic opposition between existing structures and oppositional energies, where no cooperative dialogue exists. Although most of the plays discussed in this chapter are comedies, the dramatists sometimes raise awareness of a tragic subtext caused by the refusal of rigid masculine civic structures to accommodate women's needs, desires or voices.

RESHAPING COURT AND CITY

Charles II's triumphal return constructed London as a royal national theatre. Elaborate processions, complete with purpose-built archways and ceremonial handing over of keys, were staged in the streets to celebrate the Restoration of the Monarchy.[11] In the King, the capital had recovered '*the Heart / The Life, the Light, the Eye*' of its cosmological body. Indeed, Robert Burton described the capital as 'the Chamber of the King, the Chiefest Emporium or Town of Trade in the World'.[12] It is easy to read post-Restoration London in Mumford's terms as a 'command performance' (p. 387), a proliferation of the royal household beyond the walls of its palaces into the parks, pleasure gardens and theatres of urban space. The theatres were an integral part of this masculine civic body.

Some of London's most important public arenas had been planned by theatre designers. Inigo Jones's vision of the Court's expansion into the city had been staged before the Civil War. In Davenant's *Salmacida Spolia* (1640), the last masque performed at the Caroline Court, Jones's designs for the climax of the masque placed Charles and Henrietta Maria in front of a city scene with

magnificent buildings composed of several selected pieces of architecture. In the furthest part was a bridge over a river, where many people, coaches, horses, and such like were seen to pass to and fro. Beyond this on the shore were buildings in prospective, which, shooting far from the eye, showed as the suburbs of a great city.[13]

Here, the monarchy endeavoured to incorporate a reduced version of the city into its own exclusive courtly performance space, an action that seems characteristic of the introverted absolutism that led to revolution. After the Restoration, Charles II's more extrovert policy resulted in the creation of a theatrical duopoly. The King's and the Duke's Companies, managed by Thomas Killigrew and Sir William Davenant, officially marked out public theatre as part of a royal and aristocratic domain controlled by men. Charles decreed that 'there shall be no more places of representation nor companies of actors of plays' in the City or its liberties.[14]

In spite of this authoritarian, masculine façade women did find room to manoeuvre in the Restoration playhouses. The theatres' location in the relatively new, fashionable area of Town created opportunities for innovation, as did the improvised quality of the first buildings. Killigrew's King's Company started playing at Gibbon's Tennis Court, Vere Street, in November 1660, while Davenant's Duke's Company began performances at Salisbury Court Playhouse and then at Lisle's Tennis Court, Lincoln's Inn Fields, from June 1661. Two major innovations were the employment of actresses and the use of perspective scenery. Davenant's decision to fit out the tennis court conversion with facilities for scenic effects was so successful that, in competition, Killigrew was obliged to build a better-equipped Theatre Royal in Bridges Street, which opened in 1663. Later theatres built at Dorset Garden (1671) and Drury Lane (1674) had more elaborate interior decoration and facilities for scenic effects. Professional actresses had to find a place within these venues.

Although perspective scenery was a continuation of court masque tradition in which women had participated, commercial theatre was a completely different experience for female performers, who had previously been restricted to the private venues of homes, gardens, courts and convents, albeit with large and important audiences. Entering the market can remove the unique set of attributes associated with a location, as geographer Robert Slack has recognised. Once commercialised, a place takes on the generic qualities and accessibility of its competitors, becoming like them and yet differentiating itself from them in the market.[15] Whereas before, women's theatre had made deft use of the unique set of attributes found in each of their performance locations, the professional stage and its self-selecting audience presented a much more anonymous venue for their work. Actresses were immediately thrust into the pressures and pleasures of working in competitive theatre in order to earn their livings. Female playwrights were much slower to respond to the opportunities offered by the Duke's and King's Companies, even though the incorporation of women performers appeared to have brought professional theatre a long way from the pre-war exclusivity of the King's Men, Queen's Men or Prince's Men.

By the end of the century, Charles Gildon's updated version of Langbaine's *Lives and Characters of the English Dramatic Poets* (1699) was able to declare that 'this Poetick Age' was a time of opportunity in drama, 'when all Sexes and Degrees venture on the Sock or Buskins', but this was not the case in the first ten years after the Restoration.[16] Why wasn't a woman's play produced by either the King's or the Duke's Company until 1669? Katherine Philips's *Pompey* appeared at the Smock Alley, Dublin in 1663, but London had to wait until 1669 until her translation of Corneille's *Horace* was transferred from Court to the King's Theatre Royal.[17] This was followed by Boothby's *Marcelia* (late summer 1669), and, at the Duke's, two plays by Elizabeth Polwhele and Behn's first play *The Jealous Bridegroom* (1670). As proprietor of the Duke's Company from 1668, Lady Davenant does not seem to have taken a central administrative role, although the presence of a female figurehead may have encouraged women playwrights. There is a bigger, geographical context for the emergence of women's drama.

The Great Fire that swept through London in 1666 completely destroyed the city's pretensions to be a neatly-ordered *polis* structured by the totalising gaze of its ruling monarch. Cynthia Wall has argued that the Fire produced a literature of chaos in which the loss of physical landmarks also unmoored the foundations of social class, faith, and language itself. Behind the many topographical details crammed into narrative accounts of the Fire lies a horror of the void. The Fire's widespread destruction of streets demolished and distorted the traditional boundaries of the city.[18] The Duke's venue at Lincoln's Inn Fields and the Theatre Royal were not destroyed, but the Great Fire literally made space for women's drama on the public stage.

Wall shows that the literary response to the Fire combined a rhetoric of loss and re-definitions of urban space. To fill the void, writers looked back to the past and forward to rebuilding. Schemes proposed by Evelyn and Newcourt attempted to reorganise London along classical, geometric lines to re-establish social order. The urgent actualities of rebuilding defied these principles by recreating the disorderly pattern of the old City streets.[19] The conservative, even nostalgic principles of reconstruction, undertaken in a haphazard fashion as householders hurried to rebuild on the ruins of their homes, ironically produced a more grotesquely disordered urban body than before. At this point, probably more than any other, London exemplified the paradoxical human foundations of cities: movement and settlement. Women dramatists' desire to move freely through the city and settle there was ideally served by such an environment. Their plays of 1668–70 followed the pattern Wall observes in other literature: combining a rhetorics of loss and a female redefinition of urban space.

The earliest post-Restoration plays by women all contain metatheatrical scenes referring back to the privileged site of private household performance. Elizabeth Polwhele's tragedy *The Faithfull Virgins* (*c.* 1669) stages a masque within a royal palace; her comedy *The Frolicks* (1671) ends with a household masque; Frances Boothby's *Marcelia* (1669) alludes to a royal masque and presents an entertainment offered to the Lady Perilla at her home, by her suitor. Why should women who had just laid claim to the public stage look back to the exclusive performance arenas to which their dramatic activities had previously been restricted? Critics have attempted to explain a similar discrepancy between commercial theatre and nostalgic representations of private performance in Shakespeare's plays, attributing this to an idealisation of a failed patronage system or as symptomatic of deep insecurity on Shakespeare's part.[20] In the case of women dramatists, allusions to court performance look far more pragmatic. Female playwrights did not look back in a rose-tinted way to the freedoms of private performance that their few foremothers enjoyed. The Court was their future as well as their past. In addition to the links of patronage between the theatre companies and the royal household, post-Restoration London saw the popularisation of aristocratic style amongst an emerging *beau monde,* an urban social elite who could afford to attend the playhouses. As Hume has argued, theatregoing was not a popular pastime in the broad social sense. The regular audiences for the first examples of women's professional drama were the wealthiest five per cent of the population.[21] Writers must have been acutely aware that allusions to the Court would be appealing to royal, noble and socially aspiring spectators.

Re-presenting the Court in a theatre venue like Lincoln's Inn Fields changed the dynamic between the worlds of the stage and spectators that operated in banqueting house or palace performances. The city venues interrupted the narcissistic circuit of reproduction outlined in chapter 3, whereby fictional performance and heightened courtly style existed in a mutual gaze that sustained an illusion of power. The city's gaze, albeit that of a social elite, intervened to observe the Court from a perspective of difference rather than sameness. When royal or aristocratic spectators attended the theatre (an integral part of their expansion into the capital), this new climate inevitably altered the Court's view of itself. The plays staged there were a product and producer of new interactions between the Court and the city. Examples of an early and a late play show how female dramatists exploited the expanded triangular relationship between city, Court and setting.

Polwhele's *The Faithful Virgins* (1669), performed by the Duke's Theatre Company, utilises the widened gap between representative setting and represented object to develop the critique of royal behaviour (found in some earlier masques), in a specifically gendered way.[22] The masque-within-the-play is deliberately old-fashioned: a morality 'in vertue's prayse' which offers a very pronounced criticism of Charles II's licentious and immoral behaviour (The Duke's Company had an immediate sense of this since their lead comic actress, Moll Davis, had become Charles II's mistress and recently left the Company). At the opening of Act 3 of *The Faithfull Virgins* a gentleman setting up chairs for the masque points out:

> Vertue's disgrac't, we should not use her name
> That would be allamood [*a la mode*], and prize our fame,
> A pitteous, wreatched out of fashion thing,
> Scorn'd now as much by Beggar as by _____. (59v)

Those who seek to imitate the King are warned that their behaviour, though fashionable, is morally reprehensible. The old-fashioned theatre form is the place to tell uncomfortable truths, however politically unwise. The lust of the play's Duke, and by implication Charles II, is critiqued in the unattractive figure of Lechery, while the vices of Ambition, Pride and Flattery are thinly disguised caricatures of the royal mistresses, particularly

Lady Castlemaine. An angel places Spurned Chastity at the feet of the play's Duchess Isabella, who implicitly represents Catherine, Charles II's Catholic Queen. Isabella is told that the Duke 'must have mistresses and often change' while she, 'a scorn'd wife Must as a Cypher stand' (52v–53). Such plain speaking attracted the attention of Sir Henry Herbert who censored five of the lines. Nevertheless, an obvious indictment of the royal household is allowed to remain in the masque's conclusion, which point-edly remarks that Chastity is absent since 'a deadly ague has tane hold of her / And she is now so weak she cannot live' (64r).

The metatheatrical effects created by the masque-within-the-play ad-vertise the illusory nature of courtly authority. *The Faithfull Virgins* daringly promotes the authority of a female citizen to criticise the behav-iour of her monarch. Its sympathetic allusions to Queen Catherine initiate a wider critique of the abuse of women, glamourised at Court. Charles II's affairs with actresses Moll Davis and Nell Gwyn were accompanied by endowments of property, status and affection. These women were icons for an intimacy between court and city that increasingly erased boundaries between the two. As Cynthia Lowenthal remarks, 'onstage and sometimes off, common women *enacted* the aristocratic imperatives supposedly denied them by their nonaristocratic status'.[23] The fear of performance as a threat to social authenticity continued to the end of the century. In Centlivre's *The Basset Table* (1701), for example, the apothecary's wife Mrs Sago admires Lady Reveller so much that she 'endeavours to mimick her in every Thing. Not a Suit of Clothes, or a Top-knot, that is not exactly the same with her's.'[24]

The erosion of boundaries between Court and city was a geographical reality. The fashionable royal parks of St James, Spring Gardens, and Hyde Park were spatial examples of a new social hybridity. In 1660 the parks had been opened to the public as a parading ground of the nobility and gentry, offering 'a retreat into the *known,* the secure, green spaces of uninterrupted social life', as Wall claims.[25] By the end of the century, the invasion of those traditional retreats by people from the Town and the City eager to imitate courtly style made them anything but conserva-tive in social terms. In *A Petition of the Ladies of the Court* (1692), for example, the Ladies appeal to the House of Lords to 'repair those Breaches in the Ancient and commendable Fences wherein their Glories were formerly Circumscribed'. The ladies in the pamphlet (if indeed it is by women) complain that their exclusive right to courtly magnificence is now being challenged by '*The Pride and Luxury of the City Dames*'.[26]

A second boundary has been breached: between the City and the social elite (represented by the amalgam of Town and Court). The attempts of female citizens to move into zones culturally ring-fenced for their social superiors, and the anxiety of that elite, is a source of comedy in plays by Centlivre and Pix. In Centlivre's *The Beau's Duel* (1701), for example, the snobbish Ogle claims that when a Merchant's wife or 'City Animal' wanted an affair with him he 'left her to the Brutes of her own Corporation, for I will have nothing to do with the Body Politic'.[27] Mary Pix's *The Beau Defeated* (1700) satirises the aristocratic pretensions of the '*City Dames*' complained of in the Petition.[28] It was performed at Lincoln's Inn Fields to which the rebel actors, under Betterton's direction, had removed. The play opens with the aptly-named Mrs. Rich complaining that she has been insulted by a Duchess who forced her coach to reverse in the street, and then told her '"Hold thy peace, Citizen"' (p. 163). The following exchange with Betty the maid draws directly on sentiments of the *Petition*:

BETTY   A very impertinent duchess. What! Madam, your person shining all o'er with jewels, your new gilt coach, you dappled Flanders with long tails, your coachman with cocking whiskers like a Swiss Guard, your six footmen covered with lace more than any on a Lord Mayor's day? I say, could not all this imprint some respect in the duchess?

MRS RICH   Not at all. And this beggarly duchess, at the end of an old coach, drawn by two miserable starved jades, made her tattered footmen insult me. (p. 163)

The street is a public stage on which competition for the higher reputation is fiercely channelled. The Ladies in the *Petition* complained about similar 'outvyings' by city dames whose 'bold Usurpations' of courtly style upstage the appearance of court ladies at public occasions:

'tis become Impossible for the foresaid Ladies . . . to appear with that Magnificence they ought on the moste Solemn and Festival Days (when the Honour and Grandeur of the Majesties should be most apparent) in Habits equal to the City Dames, when they are, or account themselves but meanly clad.

The city dames are 'so shiningly and magnificently Habited' that their dress appears to be a deliberate defiance of courtly superiority.[29]

Mrs Rich's conduct in the play, which is just of this type, is the result and symptom of relocation. We are told that she has moved house '*from behind the Exchange, at the Citizens' Folly, into Covent Garden*' (p. 209).

Relocating herself in the first square of town houses developed for aristocracy and the nobility is an attempt to re-place herself culturally. A verse pamphlet, *The Renowned City of London Suveyed and Illustrated* (1670), had praised the spectacular splendour of such palatial residences 'where the port / Of every brave built house doth seem a Court'.[30] In *The Beau Defeated* Mrs Rich comically assumes the style of the Court, declaring 'I will appear in state' at her at-home. Mr Rich, her sensible brother-in-law, tells her 'this behaviour does not become ye; . . . you'll one day repent of your ridiculous way of living, and carriage' (p. 183). Possibly Mr Rich's criticism of his sister's defection referred to the theatrical politics of the time, since the co-operative of actors who had broken away from Christopher Rich's company in Drury Lane were, by 1700, experiencing serious financial problems.[31] Mrs Rich's carriage, not just her coach, is the source of much humour. She claims that to recognise her late husband's citizen family as kin would be socially demeaning and insists that her maid Betty adopts a more modish French name, ironically 'De la Bette' (of the brute). Her behaviour exemplifies the social pretensions complained of by the Court Lady Petitioners, where city dames dare 'almost to compare even with the Queen her self' (p. 1).

Real court figures are absent in the play. Pix's model for the truly noble in spirit is the quiet, reasonable Lady Landsworth, a Yorkshire widow. The highly affected Sir John Roverhead and Lady Bassett are exposed as disguised servants. Pix could not, of course, have presented anything but a mimicry of nobility on the public stage. By the 1690s, however, mimicry was a dangerous subversion of aristocratic authenticity. Theatres were geographically and culturally central to the *beau monde* in which courtiers and actors performed in close proximity. The *Petition of the Ladies of the Court* complains that balls and plays 'permit not a particular Examination of the Conditions of All Persons who at such Times and Places do appear', making the outward imitation of nobility by 'affected Puppets' all the more pernicious (p. 2). By not granting the Court a place in the city setting, except as a mimicry of itself, Pix cleverly – and diplomatically – preserves its superior anonymity and avoids the risk of offending any courtly spectators. Simultaneously, and more radically, the play implies true nobility, determined by modest, civil, humane behaviour, is not dependent on birth or courtly context. Courtiers who conduct themselves thus in the theatre are 'invisible': part of the larger genteel city audience, and indistinguishable from those who are, technically, their social inferiors. *The Beau Defeated* quietly suggests that the city incorporates the best of courtly virtue, and may be the best place to nurture sensitive civility.

PLAYING WITH(IN) FRAMES: MAKING WOMEN VISIBLE

It has often been argued that the public dimension of the city offers the attraction of anonymity but Judith Garber rightly points out that 'anonymity has a complex and deeply paradoxical relationship to the search for identity in the city'. This is certainly true of versions of post-Restoration London represented on stage by women playwrights. Heroines in Polwhele's *The Frolicks* (1671), Behn's *The Town Fopp* (1676), or Ariadne's *She Ventures and He Wins* (1695), for example, dress up as men to move about the city anonymously but their final goal is always the establishment of their own, female identity. In Centlivre's *The Beau's Duel* (1702), Bellmein explains that his beloved's 'desire to be unknown herself' led them to communicate freely (p. 67) by codenames. However, Emilia and Clarinda discover the dangers of anonymity. They must assert their own identities to claim their lovers. A similar pattern operates in the case of women as a political group. Judith Garber observes that a group's manipulation of urban space is intrinsically bound up with a wish to replace the quest for anonymity with 'a desire for legitimation and acceptance or group identity'.[32] In drama, women characters, performers and writers manipulate city spaces to develop a group identity, a political presence for women. The move from invisibility to visibility and the control of visibility are key factors in this process.

The appearance of female actors on the public stage made women visible in London and in society at large. Restoration theatre literally brought the female body back from abstraction; plays by women use theatre's double reality levels to raise awareness of the spatial abstraction and domination of women, and to reinstate the living unity of the female body through the presence of female actors. Juliet Blair has pointed out that an actress is not just an individual, 'that the normal distinctions between "private" and "public" are neither incumbent upon nor possible' for her. She is a repository of, and vehicle for the expression of, a vast range of different female experiences. These are drawn from the roles she has played or plays, and from the reactions of female spectators to those roles, which the actor registers and incorporates into her experience. Each individual woman who appears on the post-Restoration stage is therefore 'a host of informants on women'.[33] Her visibility in a city setting on the public stage thus encompasses the 'private' lives and experiences of other women in cities across time and space. The London venues for post-Restoration theatre naturally made the actress a political and emotional focus for the views of women in the city. The public forum in which she appeared was a privileged arena in which to represent those views and experiences.

Visibility was not just a privilege for the female actor; it was a responsibility and a potential trap. As commercial enterprises, the theatres operated in the vast circulation of trade that grew up around the City, a flamboyant sign of high capitalism. Lefebvre notes that such a regime tends to rigidly demarcate space and pulverise individuals by fragmenting the living unity of the body. 'This is especially true of the female body, as transformed into exchange value, into a sign of a commodity and indeed into a commodity per se.'[34] Throughout the period, women dramatists are aware that their plays and the bodies of the women who enact them are objects offered in exchange for the purchase of tickets. Ariadne's *She Ventures and He Wins* (1695) summarises the situation in an epilogue written and performed by a man, 'I'm much afraid a woman's like a play, / You'd have 'em new and pretty every day.'[35]

The appearance of actresses and perspective scenery enabled a range of new stage effects that playwrights were quick to exploit. On one hand, the proscenium arch and the use of flat scenery produced framing effects that culminated in the introduction of perspective begun with the English publication of Serlio's *Architettura* (1611) and carried into court theatre designs by Inigo Jones and John Webb. Early visitors to Davenant's theatre at Lincoln's Inn Fields and the Theatre Royal in Bridges Street, which opened on 7 May 1663, were impressed by the use of scenery. In 1663 Monsieur de Monconys reported 'The scene changes and the machines are most ingeniously thought out and executed', while Samuel Sorbière remarked 'the scenic area is quite open with many scene changes and perspective views'.[36] The Duke's Playhouse at Dorset Garden, which opened on 9 November 1671, was equipped with a forestage, an ornate proscenium arch and a large upstage area with the facilities to use wings and shutters to stage perspective scenes.[37]

As with court stages, perspective scenery in the Restoration theatres used pairs of receding wings following the geometry of a vanishing point and shutters across the breadth of the stage, also in perspective. The design concept privileged the sightlines of a principal spectator (usually the monarch), who sat at the centre point of the auditorium. As such, it was a clear example of the abstraction of space in the early modern period. Edward S. Casey points out that with the advent of perspective, space is 'no longer situated in the physical world but in the subjectivity of the human mind that formally shapes the world'.[38] This had been the guiding principle behind Jones's and Webb's designs for court masques. Restoration theatres brought the royal perspective into the city.

However, London's theatres were no more willing to limit their designs to a quasi-divine monolithic view of the stage than its citizens had been to accept the redrawing of the their chaotic City streets in geometric patterns. Colin Visser has demonstrated that the proscenium walls and the stage areas in front were frequently integral to a play's scenic geography. The areas downstage of the frame, in close proximity with the audience, need not represent a neutral space. Doors and balconies in the proscenium walls meant they could be the location for interiors or exteriors of house settings, the balconies looking out onto the street or to the private garden in the house's interior.[39] Characters and performers could thus move in and out of the proscenium frame. Women were not automatically trapped within male-constructed tableaux; the pictorial effects were flexible, and could be self-consciously and critically deployed by playwrights and performers.

Straznicky points out that because female dramatists' bodies were not literally on display, they enjoyed a greater freedom to 'play *metaphorically* with bodily self-representation' in prologues and epilogues.[40] Their empathy with female actors' experiences of commodification encouraged them to use that freedom politically, by strategically choreographing the moves of the women who performed their lines. Frances Boothby's *Marcelia* (1669), the first female-authored play performed in London, recognises the dangers of public visibility.[41] Its Prologue tells the audience that Boothby '*prays ye to be gone / You'll croud her Wit to death in such a Throng*' (A3), as if voicing the anxieties of women playwrights transferring from private to public arenas. The male actor who introduces the performance continues to joke teasingly about the author's bodily absence, exiting and re-entering to communicate with Boothby, and receiving two messages from her. She remains a tantalising presence, just off stage but invisible.

In *Marcelia,* Boothby's staging explores the condition of being 'framed' in spatial and metaphorical senses. The villain's actions are accompanied by stage positions that enact the framing effects of his deceitful plots. In the first garden scene, for example (Act 2 Scene 6), the proscenium arch probably separates watchers and watched. Melynet brings Marcelia to walk in the public gardens (a fictional equivalent to the newly-opened Spring Gardens or Mulberry Gardens in London), where she beholds her beloved apparently wooing the Lady Arcasia. She sees them '*walk up and down, and talk softly*, and notes in dismay that they 'are about to leave the Garden by the other gate' (EI). Assuming that at least part of the scene is played upstage of the proscenium to take advantage of the scenery, either Marcelia is physically and culturally 'framed' by the plot as she watches from upstage, or, alternatively, the framing of a carefully choreographed picture of courtship is physically telegraphed as she watches through the proscenium from downstage. The other alternative would be to have each pair of actors occupy one side of the upstage scene, and look across at each other. In this case the audience see that the actions and reactions of each have been framed by the villain.

Subsequent scenes suggest that Boothby understands the commodifying effects of the perspective stage, and can advertise these knowingly, but without the confidence to move her heroines or actresses outside the confining power of the royal, male gaze. The main plot, where a king deserts his betrothed to lust after Marcelia, looks like another critique of Charles II's licentious behaviour. The court scene on the stage of the Theatre Royal, Bridges Street, presents the courtly audience in the auditorium with an image of itself refracted through the lens of the city. The Court is obliged to re-examine itself within the public domain. The King in the play, like Charles II in the playhouse, is the observed of all observers whose purview constructs everyone around him. He vows that the court Ladies' beauty is so powerful 'I fear I shall go off my self a Prisoner' (F2v) but his words immediately imprison them within the gaze of on and offstage audiences. Any sense of women as individuals is pulverised by Lucidore's idea that their 'severall beauties' can be 'compounded' in a pill or love potion (F2v). As the King and Lucidore contemplate the ladies, their appetite for beauty highlights how the actresses are displayed on stage to be consumed by the desiring gazes of the theatre audience.

An area outside the frame of royal dominance and subjection is glimpsed at several occasions in the play. In Act 3 Scene 6 Melynet brings Marcelia to the court to 'see the Mask' (FIv), entering 'at one door, and *Lotharicus* at another privately' (F3v). These are obviously the doors in the proscenium walls, giving the characters an off-centre view of the court scene from the sides of the stage. Their skewed perspective physically disrupts the self-returning gaze of the fictional and factual monarchs that the perspective scenery is designed to privilege. Marcelia dazzles like 'a Sun at mid-night', even though she is not a titled lady, and the King commands 'Bring here that conquering Beauty' (F3v–F4). The audience watch Marcelia's independence collapse as she is gradually but inexorably drawn upstage and into the frame by the King's desire. Her spoken words set up a line of resistance. She tells him 'I know the distance of a Subject, Sir', and insists she will not lose 'the due sense of what your Majesty is, and what I am' (F4). By the end of her next speech, though, she is intimately close to him '*The King talks to her softly, she smiles . . .*' (F4). Stage movement in *Marcelia* reproduces the radical erosion of differences in rank enacted in the theatre. Marcelia's lack of aristocratic birth parallels her with the figure of the actress, and the King's fascination mirrors that of his offstage counterpart. Offstage spectators are only too aware that differences between noblewomen and actresses were collapsing in the wake of the King's desire. Lotharicus's misogynist diatribe 'Woman, what art thou but mans tempting shame' (F4v) is emptied out by the audience's knowledge that Marcelia has been doubly framed by Melynet's ambition and the King's power so that any agency she has is severely compromised. Lotharicus refuses to blame the King, whose 'Name is Sacred' (F4v), thus advertising the male bias of the stage from his side of the proscenium wall.

Boothby does not release the actress from the transfixing power of the male gaze to explore what she might achieve as a desiring subject. In a final scene when Lotharicus is brought to trial for attempting to murder Melynet and the villain's plots are exposed, Boothby repeats the blocking pattern used in Act 3 Scene 6 to present a remarkable opportunity for the heroine to make an independent choice. Upstage the court setting is a double representation as royal household and legal institution. Lotharicus and a guard enter at one proscenium wall door and Marcelia and her brother at the other. Marcelia acknowledges that women have no legal voice and ''tis not fit' for them to come into the courtroom, but begs leave to observe the trial (M1). What looks like conservative exclusion at the beginning of the scene is radically transformed when the King, having unravelled the plots, asks Marcelia to make a free choice between him and Lotharicus. Disappointingly, Marcelia's downstage position does not grant her agency as a desiring subject. She says 'Heav'n leaves me not to an Election free', claiming that 'if I should chuse / I'd be unjust to him I did refuse' (M2v–M3). It is left to the King to curb his desire and surrender her to Lotharicus. In 1669, Boothby can only gesture towards woman's agency beyond the confines of the play, the court and the public stage. The actress is positioned outside the frame but cannot exploit the freedom that playing space gives her.

Later women dramatists manipulate the proscenium arch and forestage area with increasing confidence to critique the commodification of female bodies. In anticipation of Behn's later plays, the actress prologue of

The Forc'd Marriage (1670), appropriates the culture of visibility for herself and women in the audience:

> *Can any see this glorious sight, and say,*
> *A Woman shall not Victor prove to day:*
> *Who is't that to their Beauty wou'd submit*
> *And yet refuse the Fetters of their Wit.*[42]

Behn's increasingly deft use of theatrical effects helps to fulfil a feminist agenda in this competitive commercial arena. She is the supreme exemplar of Catherine Gallagher's well-known thesis that female-authored scripts put into play the identities of actress and playwright as public, paid woman: 'the dramatic masking of the prostitute and the stagey masking of the playwright's interest in money are exactly parallel cases of theatrical unmasking' that reveal 'the playwright is a whore'.[43] In the theatre, the moving, speaking body of the paid actress is the site where the relations between female agency and market forces converge. Behn's use of discovery spaces, balconies, curtains, pictures, most obviously in *The Rover*, brilliantly challenges the framing and fragmentation of woman as marketable object.[44] Indeed, in Act 2, Angellica the whore deftly turns the frame that commodifies her back onto the man she desires, sending Moretta to fetch a mirror so that Willmore can 'surveigh himself', but with her eyes: 'to see what Charms he has – and guess my business'.[45] Women's mastery of the new theatrical medium depends vitally on the performer's ability to look back through the frame at spectators, a process that shifts the play of social energy in the theatre. Although Dorset Garden was perhaps twice the size of the tennis court theatres or those in Bridges Street or Drury Lane, the distance from the front of the stage to the back wall was still probably no more than seventy feet.[46] By gazing back at spectators across the auditorium, the actress energises them into self-examination, including a recognition of their own viewing practices.[47]

Centlivre's *The Beau's Duel*, which was performed at Lincoln's Inn Fields in 1701, shows how far women's drama has moved on from the static picture of female beauty. Betterton's co-operative had turned Lincoln's Inn Fields back into a theatre but financial problems, which reached an all-time low in 1701, meant there was little money for elaborate decorations by the time Centlivre's play was staged.[48] Possibly the smaller theatre with more rudimentary facilities for perspective scenery helped the play's effects. It openly mocks masculine attempts to confine women behind frames in a satiric portrait of the fortune-hunter Ogle, who meets

Captain Bellmein outside Clarinda's house and proceeds to explain his successful courtship of her:

Then if she sees me walking here – as I generally do every Morning, she strait repairs to the Window – Thus do you see – stand you there – Now suppose me the Lady – you look up at my Window, and walk thus, do you see? – Then I run to the Window thus – clap my Arms a-cross thus – and hang my Head thus – turn my Eyes languishing thus – as who shou'd say, if it were the Custom for Women to make the first Addresses, I woul'd now beckon you up. (p. 84)

The comedy of this exchange, in which Ogle directs himself in the woman's part and Bellmein as the wooer, lies in the non-appearance of a real 'Lady'. Ogle claims that when Clarinda sees him walking there, she appears according to his desires at the window, but she is notable only by her absence. The men play out a male fantasy of coy female allurement on their own because the character and the performer who plays her are not interested in the part it offers.

Instead, Clarinda and Emilia are cross-dressing for a very different kind of role play beyond the frame, in Hyde Park, the city's place of recreation. They will, Clarinda tells her cousin, rescue Clarinda (herself) from the clutches of unwanted suitors like Mr Ogle and Sir William Mode, the man her father intends her to marry:

I, my own Knight-Errant, and thou my trusty, Squire, will march *En cavalier*, and deliver the distress'd Damsel, by beating the Giant into a Pigmy; then be our own Heralds, and proclaim our Victory to my Father, and hollow the Coward so loud in his Ears, that we will shame him out of all Thoughts of this Fool. (p. 95)

The heroines bully Mr Ogle and Sir William in the duel of the play's title, which recalls Jonson's *Epicoene*.[49] Careful is determined 'to have you in your feminine Capacity again; for tho' you bully in Breeches, I hope you'll marry in Petticoats' (p. 103). The heroines resume their women's clothes but not the passive feminine stereotype, as Centlivre's final reversal of the framing and containing motif shows.

Clarinda, who has plotted to marry Manly, advertises her autonomy by sending a curtained picture as a present to her supposed mother-in-law. In fact, Plotwell is an accomplice who poses as a sober Quaker to induce Careful to marry her, and then casts off her disguise to reveal herself as a woman of the *beau monde*, to trick him. Plotwell caricatures a woman obsessed by visual culture. She insists that the house be 'lin'd with Looking-Glass' (p. 121), and orders 'Let my Paint, Powder and Patches be ready' at the dressing table (p. 119). Clarinda's picture gift physicalises the strategic framing of men by women in the play. When the curtains are drawn, Toper emerges from the frame in the role of seducing rake and Careful sees this as indisputable evidence of his imminent cuckoldry (pp. 124–5). Framed by the women's plots, he accepts Clarinda's match as the lesser evil.

Barry O'Connor argues that there is a correlation between heroic portraiture and the physical framing effects of the stage in the creation of Restoration heroes but the effect here deconstructs the gallant.[50] Toper is nothing but a decorative tool in the women's plots: put on display briefly only to be discarded (p. 125). The picture frame is a counter-discourse to Plotwell's supposed fascination with her own appearance as the object of a male gaze. By juxtaposing the framing of men and the breaking out of cultural frames by women, *The Beau's Duel* dismantles typically gendered behaviour. Its witty use of theatrical space and city settings reflects women's growing confidence in the professional theatres.

Early plays such as Polwhele's *Faithfull Virgins* or Boothby's *Marcelia* used the proximity of court and city in a clever deployment of the spatial axis created by the stage proscenium. Later scripts play more freely with the appeal of the actress as a spectacle, the permeability of boundaries between court and capital and the flexibility of the Restoration stage. Actresses answer the gaze of spectators to challenge the culture of commodification. Stage settings represent a metropolitan culture where different social classes move in the same fashionable places, putting aristocratic identity under erasure. Frames become fetishised in scenes that move easily in and out of the doors, windows and proscenium arches, to self-consciously question the cultural containment of women.

LABYRINTH AND MAZE: MOVING THROUGH THE CITY

Moving outside to public settings such as streets, parks and playhouses is significant for female characters. We must recognise that, in spite of the dangers, crossing public urban space alone or in groups can bring pleasure and advantages for women. City comedies often promote women's rights to the carnival pleasures and risks of the city. Lucinda, the youngest woman in Mary Pix's *The Beau Defeated*, insists on such rights. She explains that she has only agreed to run away with Sir John Roverhead to enjoy the freedom of the streets:

I run away only for more pleasure, more liberty, etc. I will go every day to the play, or else to the Park; and every time I go to the park, to the lodge, to Chelsea:

in fine where I please, or as I run away with you, I'll run away from you, sue for my own fortune again, and live as I please: what I have heard how ladies with fortunes do. (p. 223)

Lucinda sees London as a future of independence rather than dependence on a nobly born husband. Her words to Sir John outline an urban practice that challenges patriarchal systems outright. Spoken with the confidence of youth, her lines express a vision of what London might hold for women.

The street is political, as Spiro Kostof usefully reminds us. Housefronts with doors and windows that abut the street are endowed with a public presence and, to a lesser extent, so are their female occupants. To move out into the street or to stage it, is to go one step further. The street designates a public domain that takes precedence over individual rights since one cannot build out into it or obstruct it. To occupy the street is therefore to position oneself in the ebb and flow of public, political action. As Kostof observes, the street 'structures community' in several important ways: 'it puts on display the workings of the city and supplies a backdrop for its common rituals'.[51] As a public stage, the street gives women a place to redefine their relationship with the community.

The detailed urban geography of women's plays often relates closely to the public arenas of London which women traversed, participating in its busy commercial and cultural exchanges as consumers, traders, beggars. Lorenzo Magalotti, an Italian visitor to Charles II's court in 1669, noticed

the liberty enjoyed by the ladies in London, who are not prohibited from walking in the streets by night as well as by day, without any attendance. By day they go on foot or in their carriages, either *incognito* with masks, or without, as they think proper . . .
The women of London [he went on to observe] . . . live with all the liberty that the custom of the country authorizes . . . and they go whithersoever they please, either alone, or in company; and those of the lower order frequently go so far as to play ball publicly in the streets.[52]

Women's presence in the city's public places disturbs the classical masculine framework with reminders of the grotesque body, the disorderly element of urban culture. Elizabeth Wilson describes woman as the sphinx in the city, an 'irruption' that symbolises disorder. She points out that, 'almost from the beginning, the presence of women in cities, and particularly in city streets, has been questioned, and the controlling and surveillance aspects of city life have always been directed particularly at women'.[53]

Women's movement through the streets and parks of seventeenth-century London accelerates the disruptive effect of walking in the city outlined by De Certeau. It creates shadows and ambiguities that cloud the clear panoptic vision of the metropolis with precisely positioned boundaries, routes, and places for everyone and everything. If, as De Certeau claims, walking in the city is predicated on the lack of place, women, who are culturally defined as lack, magnify the effects of moving which 'makes the city itself an immense social experience of lacking a place'. One effect of the Great Fire was to detach the names of places in the City from the geographical locations they were supposed to define. In the years that followed, women's plays creatively exploited this lack of fixed place and consequent fluidity of meaning to open up spaces for female agency. Scripted movement across the city functions in a similar way to De Certeau's model of the story. Plays create a fictional field that authorises dangerous and apparently haphazard actions, opening the city as a legitimate theatre for such actions beyond the walls of the playhouse.[54]

In Polwhele's comedy *The Frolicks* (1671), apparently written for the King's Company at Drury Lane, the streets of London are places of sexual equality.[55] Unlike the plays discussed so far, this one is set within the walled City, a territory dominated by the paternal presence of Swallow, a rich lawyer, moneylender and Justice of the Peace. As well as being Clarabell's father, he functions as a symbolic City Father, a representative of law and civic institutions. Clarabell, the spirited heroine, is a street-wise 'fizgig cockney' (2.107), full of energy. In the sub-plot, whose setting is less obvious, the country wife Lady Meanwell exudes an innocent enthusiasm for the delights London has to offer. The play alternates scenes inside houses and public sites of street and tavern. Its swift intercutting suggests theatrical craftswomanship based on a working knowledge of the effects that could be achieved with shutters and scenery offered by the Theatre Royal. Contrasting settings advertise how the female characters are both products and producers of space.

In Act 2, for example, the main plot's tavern scene is played on the forestage. Here, the rake Rightwit attempts to set up a match between his sister Leonora and the rich Sir Gregory or Zany. The clear-sighted Leonora rejects both foolish suitors in a decisive exit that exemplifies her freedom of movement and judgement. By contrast, the following scene 'opens' behind the proscenium to discover Lady Meanwell and her sister Faith talking with suitors in one of Procreate's rooms. Since Procreate is a bawd, the illusion of feminine, indoor security is false; the women are being set up to please the eager sexual appetites of Sir Francis

Makelove and Lord Courtall. A measured dance has the appearance of order in contrast to the drunken singing of the tavern, but, unlike Leonora, Lady Meanwell and Faith have no escape route from its formal patterns and steps.

The play defies conventional spatial categories – women inside, men abroad – suggesting instead that London's open streets are more likely to encourage the honest behaviour proper to both sexes. Lady Meanwell's 'excellent dissimulation' in the pursuit of an affair suggests that private rooms foster female conspiracy and guile (2.436). Clarabell's 'frolic' involves a fairly transparent physical dissimulation: to 'turn boy for an hour or two' by cross-dressing as her cousin Philario (2.543–5). Disguise releases her onto the streets where she and Rightwit are obliged to acknowledge his promiscuity in a comic scene where three whores demand paternity payments and strap their children to his back (4.135–51). Clarabell's free movement from setting to setting is enacted by the movement of the female body across the stage in the venue.

Polwhele celebrates the actress's physical presence in contrast to the abstractions of women that had characterised pre-Restoration professional theatre. She roundly rejects the tradition of boy actors representing women in a comic drag plot with the foolish suitors – Sir Gregory and Zany. Gendered identity is thrown into carnivalesque confusion when they join Clarabell in a dance, 'The Frolics' (3.136), and 'strive which shall woman it the best' (3.156). Polwhele's mockery of female impersonation probably took on extra resonance since Edward Kynaston, the most famous performer of women's roles and 'the prettiest woman in the house' according to Pepys, was a member of the King's Company when *The Frolicks* was written.[56] By tricking and ridiculing the suitors (who are later arrested), Clarabell dismantles the limitations of a male-dominated theatre profession that seeks to represent women only in its own image. Her own cross-dressing, which probably capitalised on the sex appeal of the 'breeches role' in which Nell Gwyn was so popular, was typical of transvestism in the Restoration theatre.[57] Jacqueline Pearson has pointed out that almost a quarter of plays showed female characters played by female actors, disguised as men.[58] In *The Frolicks*, male attire is a mask that gives Clarabell licence to control her erotic power over men. Her movement across the city empowers her to harness the unattractive elements of rakish behaviour that inevitably limit female autonomy. These are personified by Rightwit, whom she out-manoeuvres.

In Act 4 Rightwit is confined to prison by Clarabell's father. She, however, evades any paternal scheme to keep her indoors or imprison

her in a forced marriage. The re-gendering of movement and stasis is
obvious when she visits Rightwit and her cousin Philario:

RIGHTWIT	What the Devil brought thee here?
CLARABELL	Things call'd legs – with a willing mind. I thought a
	woman would have been welcome to you, but
	I perceive you know not what to do with one. Fare
	ye well.
RIGHTWIT	Stay! I can cure thy greensickness yet, as low as the tide is.
CLARABELL (SINGS)	If I were tortur'd with greensickness,
	Dost think I would be cur'd by thee?
	I then too soon might swell in thickness –
	A pox on your remedy!
	The cure may prove worse than the anguish,
	And I of a fresh disease may languish.
	But I'll keep myself from such distemper
	In spite of all that you dare do;
	Although you are free to venter,
	I'll be hang'd if I did not baffle you.
RIGHTWIT	Nay, like enough. Come, prithee let me kiss thee a little.
	'Tis that, I know, thou cam'st for. The holiest of you
	cannot live without it. (4.351–70)

Humour arises from the fact that, in spite of his assertions of sexual
power, Rightwit is behind bars. Clarabell's lines draw pointed attention
to the physical dimensions of the scene and her greater autonomy. Her
'things called legs', which she openly displays, are no longer meaningful as
attractive objects to either her or him; it is the freedom they give her to
come or go as she pleases – and which he obviously lacks - that counts. In
spite of claiming that he can easily cure Clarabell's greensickness with an
appropriate dose of sex, he is certainly not 'free to venture', a fact that
Clarabell fully appreciates when she teasingly suggests that he does not
know what to do with a woman. *The Frolicks* shows the heroine taking
control of the city setting and through it the stage whose male-dominated
values threatened to imprison her. Her final challenge to Rightwit, that
she will marry him only when he gets the good will of her father,
implicitly asks for formal acceptance of women's liberty and equality on
the part of the City Fathers.

The experience of moving across the city, on which Clarabell's success
depends, is linked to the metaphors of a labyrinth and maze. As Elizabeth
Wilson argues, the two metaphors imply two different kinds of journey:
for the wanderer in a labyrinth, the city seems to be without a centre and

the journey an endless, circular route through which discoveries can be made but solutions are unattainable.[59] The *flâneur* who enters a maze, however, does so with a sense of the city holding a secret centre, an answer to the puzzle. For dramatic protagonists of this type, journeying through the city is a quest. Women's drama explores the fun and the risks of moving through a carnivalesque urban space energised by the circulation of diverse social energies. It suggests that experiences of the city are gendered: that its unpredictability makes it more like a labyrinth for male characters and that female characters weave their way through it like a maze. Undoubtedly, the very real dangers of crossing cities for women contribute to their more urgent sense of purpose.

The Rover by Aphra Behn exemplifies different, gendered experiences of the city. The play opens by contrasting the enclosure of the nunnery, as an offstage place of confinement, and the open streets of Naples in which it is set. Carnival time, a season of pleasure, deviation and disruption, gives open expression to the usually subversive elements of urban life. Among these are the primitive instincts of greed and desire, the latter making the city especially dangerous for women. Dramatic performance can magnify the effects of carnival. The holiday space of play-time reminds spectators of the canivalesque potential of the city in both its utopian and nightmarish guises.

Men and women in *The Rover* journey through the streets from a position of lack. Behn configures Naples as a feminine space and pre-empts de Certeau's image of the city as 'an immense social experience of lacking a place' (p. 103). While the men wander the streets in search of various kinds of satisfaction, the women have clear goals. Willmore is a 'wandring Inconstant' (3.1.27–8), the rover in the labyrinth whose business is 'to enjoy myself' (1.2.64). He traverses the city as an opportunist, taking advantage of a variety of encounters with women. His attempted seduction of Florinda in her garden is without sin, he explains, 'because 'twas neither design'd nor premeditated' (3.2.141–2). The garden setting lends some validity to his attempt to construct his libertinism as pre-lapsarian love, a subject that Behn had addressed in her poem 'The Golden Age', but the play constitutes a feminist critique of the emotionally indifferent rake hero.[60] To Willmore, the city's streets are escape routes to new encounters. Faced with the dual claims of Angellica and Hellena, he turns to find 'new Joys, new Charms' (4.472) in the masked Florinda, a third 'likely Wench' who happens to pass by (4.522).

Willmore's opportunism is at home in the labyrinth but other male characters in *The Rover* find it disorientating. The Naples setting is one of mysterious openings, concealed chambers and passages. Even Don Pedro and Antonio, natives to the scene, are surprised by their chance encounters. Their identities, their financial and cultural control are usurped by the disguised Englishmen who wed the heroines. The Englishmen become equally lost. Belvile's failure to recognise Florinda beneath her vizard and grasp the opportunity offered by the encounter is a typical contrast to the improvisatory powers of Willmore, the man who feels at home in the fluid, unstable urban environment.

Blunt, Behn's satiric portrait of an archetypal solid Englishman, is a focus for the anxieties and dangers felt by the male characters. Blunt engages with the feminine city eagerly in following the whore Lucetta. Having been charmed by her rich clothes, jewels and the furnishings of her house (2.1.65), he is horribly surprised when, after undressing to join her in an alcove bed, the bed disappears in the darkness and he falls through a trapdoor into the common sewer. This geographical black hole is a nightmarish metaphor for Lucetta the whore.[61] Behn parallels the elusive quality of woman and the city setting. Blunt's descent into the sewer is not just a loss of status but a complete loss of place. The pimp Philippo jokes 'he knows neither your Name, nor that of the Street where your House is, nay nor the way to his own Lodgings' (3.2.78–9). Blunt desperately seeks 'home' (3.2.105), but finds his lodging invaded by another woman and panics. 'Can I not be safe in my House for you, not in my Chamber, nay, even being naked too' (4.606–8), he wails, reflecting a wider male unease about the city's surprises. His desire for revenge on the feminine city by raping Florinda is unfulfilled, revealing only his inability to distinguish between a whore and a 'Lady of Quality' (5.1.26). Blunt's journey through the city, like the male quest to contain women's behaviour, is an endless, circular route through which discoveries can be made but solutions are unattainable.

In contrast, Hellena's journey through Naples is a quest for the centre of a maze: a husband, or more specifically, 'a handsome proper fellow of my humour' (1.1.33–5). Although she describes it as a 'Ramble' (1.1.168), her engagement with Naples is a journey of exploration directed by desire. Her goal is 'to Love and to be belov'd' (3.1.41). Hellena's disguise as a page does not protect her emotionally from the discovery of Angellica as a rival. When the two women meet on the Molo the setting functions on two levels. Its importance is suggested by the fact that Behn asked the Duke's Company for a specially painted piece of scenery for the Molo, something she had not done before.[62] The Molo is a site of military defence and struggle of course, effectively physicalising the struggle between Hellena and Angellica over Willmore. At another level, the exposed setting gives a material, geographical reality to the raw feelings of the female protagonists. In spite of the rivalry between them, the stage spatially unites them as victims of uncontrolled male lust. Both women are obliged to confront the uncomfortable truth about their hero. Angellica realises 'there's no Faith in any thing he says' (4.455) and Hellena recognises that Willmore may not be lying when he claims not to love her any more than a monkey or a parrot (4.424–5).

Hellena's project to expose Willmore's inconstancy is conceived of spatially; she resolves to 'find his haunts, and plague him every where' (4.556). She navigates her way successfully through the city even though, when she finally makes Willmore agree to marry her, it is uncertain whether their affection will last. Their union is based on a mutual acceptance of inconstancy. Nevertheless, Willmore's view that 'a womans Honour' is her own and cannot be guarded 'when she has a mind to part with it' (5.505) is refreshingly liberal, demolishing the sexual double standard. The carnival does, therefore, end in satisfactory closure for Hellena: she successfully redirects her life and dowry from the nunnery, to become a woman of the world.

Hellena's purposeful course through the maze of Naples is echoed in *The Second Part of the Rover* by the enterprising Ariadne, who vows to reject the rich husbands chosen by her parents and 'please my self in the choice of this Stranger if he is to be had' (2.390), although she finally rejects Willmore's inconstancy.[63] Her determination to choose a husband is realised more successfully in *She Ventures and He Wins* (1695) by 'Ariadne', a young lady titling herself in the tradition of heroines with the skill to lead men out of the labyrinth. In *She Ventures*, Charlotte's 'mad frolick' (p. 111) is educational: she tests her suitor's affections, rewriting the pattern of 1670s comedies where comic closure depends on the sexual success of the libertine. In this plot, a woman weaves a strand of manipulations to lead the emotionally and morally sensitive characters to a happy ending in which both hero and heroine win. Perhaps its feminist rewriting of the comic tradition was the reason for its failure at the box office, resulting in a temporary closure of Lincoln's Inn Fields, even though Mrs Barry had sponsored the production.[64]

Charlotte's extrovert quest contrasts spatially and emotionally with the position of Sir Charles Frankford, her brother, and her cousin Juliana, who are too shy to declare their love for each other. Juliana's shyness leads to retreat. Like the lovers in Wroth's *Love's Victory* and Montague's *The Shepherds' Paradise*, she conceals herself in an arbour in the garden to make a private confession of her passionate feelings. The words of Betty's song, 'Restless in thoughts, disturbed in mind' (p. 123), ventriloquise for Juliana. Sir Charles is concealed and listening, but is still reluctant to believe he could be the object of her love. The enclosed garden setting conveys an impression of suffocating insecurity disguised as proper reserve. Charlotte sensibly recognises that they must 'break that useless piece of modesty, imposed by custom' which 'gives so many of us the pip' (p. 123).

Her own assertive behaviour is needed to draw characters out from themselves and make public demonstrations of their self-worth and their affections. She does this by moving out to public green spaces. In the first scene, she and Juliana are cross-dressed in preparation for a trip to St James's Park. From the Restoration onwards, and increasingly after the Great Fire, London's parks were places that combined novelty and the reassurance of continuity. As places of recreation, like the playhouses, they symbolised adventure and tradition at the same time which made them appealing not just to the court and social elite, but to an increasingly diverse population of London. St James's Park, with its canal, deer, and 'long, straight and spacious walk, intended for the amusement of the Mall,' was an elegant place of play and liberty.[65] Unlike the secluded garden arbour, its public arena is characterised by the paradox of secrecy and sexual openness. The Earl of Rochester's poem 'A Ramble in St James's Parke', for example, describes an 'all-sin-sheltering Grove' in which social differences between 'Great Ladies, Chamber Maydes, and Drudges' are levelled by sex.[66] In the play, it is likewise a public setting that generates private passion. It gives Charlotte space to declare her desire for Lovewell from beneath her disguises as a boy, a masked woman, and finally as an unmasked woman.

The Park's illusion of democratic social inclusiveness is a launch pad for Charlotte's project to win Lovewell on her own merits rather than her fortune. She alienates herself spatially from her identity as a city heiress by moving out to Kensington village and re-casting herself into two *dramatis personae* who return to the city to redeem Lovewell from prison. Geographical movement between places produces freedom to define and redefine one's identity. Charlotte plays the whore-trickster herself and enlists the help of her cousin Bellasira to play the part of heiress. Her ingenious device reverses the fragmentation of female identity found in so many other texts, which deny woman a unified subject position from which to speak. Instead, it enacts the pleasures of doubleness, a fantasy of extending female control through the city by being present in two places at once, to watch and influence behaviour from two different subject positions. In addition, the metatheatrical dimension of doubling engages with prevailing insecurities about authentic aristocratic identity in the metropolis. The paired roles of Bellasira-as-Charlotte and Charlotte-as-deceiver, appearing one after the other to test Lovewell's affections, dramatise an increasingly 'theatricalized' aristocratic self-awareness which was characteristic of the 1690s.[67]

Charlotte's acting can be read as a typically aristocratic attempt to naturalise her nobility and attractions for Lovewell through performance. On the other hand, her wish to suspend her social superiority and 'claim you as my own' (p. 131), is generous since it also liberates Lovewell from the position of fortune hunter. In the enclosed prison scene, he is physically and psychologically freed into a full sense of his own human worth, as well as hers. Charlotte's performance of identities is a feminist and aristocratic fantasy of control. It is, however, beneficent control with a redemptive social function. She uses her authority to help others realise their own potential. Juliana shrewdly points out that 'a woman once vested in authority, though 'tis by no other than her own making, does not willingly part with it' (p. 109). Charlotte's intelligence and flexibility in playing different parts recommends her as an active citizen, a powerful advocate for woman's full participation in city life beyond the walls of the theatre.

In spite of its celebration of physical mobility as a catalyst for self-transformation, *She Ventures and He Wins* shows that geographical re-location is not enough. Members of the Wouldbe family enter St James's Park but are limited by their failure to engage with its vibrant circulation of social energy. The prim city wives, Mistresses Dowdy and Beldam snootily point out that they are 'none of this-end-of-the-town folks' (p. 144). Their refusal to identify with the public space is symptomatic of their own social insecurities. It is not the Wouldbe family's status as citizens but their rigid social affectations that make them the butts of the comedy. The pawn shop on which their superficial nobility is based is a microcosm of the competitive market economy that governs the City: worldly comforts are furnished from the loss of others. As such, it reminds the audience of the nightmare that could consume Lovewell, the gentleman without money.

The Wouldbe family's inverted snobbery is dramatised spatially in introverted domestic scenes. Mistress Dowdy endeavours to keep her husband Squire Wouldbe at her side with the temptation of 'a most lovely buttock of Beef and cabbage' (p. 119). The comforts of home and sentimental affection are suffocating, especially to women. Dowdy, called 'Bunny' by her unfaithful husband, is an earlier version of Alison in *Look Back In Anger*. She is infantilised to the extent of not even having 'sense enough for an intrigue' (p. 157), and the audience are encouraged to share her husband's revulsion at her 'nauseous fondness' (p. 119). The play warns that such gullibility leads only to masochistic suffering, in the tradition of Patient Grissil, a chilling alternative to the active citizenship personified by Charlotte.

A third setting, a public tavern, represents a happy medium between the open park and the claustrophobic private space of the home, and offers a happier image of middle-class life. Freeman and his wife Urania (the object of Wouldbe's unwanted attentions), are just as witty and clever as the noble characters, showing that self-assertion for men and for women is not only the privilege of the elite. The domestic apartments, a kitchen and bedchamber, are governed by Urania, played by Mrs Barry who sponsored the production. Urania directs a plot worthy of Shakespeare's merry wives, in which Squire Wouldbe is treated to humiliating punishments in the kitchen, followed by a hellish descent though a trapdoor as he approaches her bed (p. 128). Like Blunt in *The Rover*, Wouldbe experiences the city beyond his house as a frighteningly unpredictable place. The tavern setting is probably based on Lockets, the Charing Cross inn frequented by the gentry after the theatre. The tavern's utopian image of urban incorporation is an appropriate place for the play's comic denouement. The social diversity of London is represented in microcosm when the noble characters repair there for a celebratory wedding dinner and Wouldbe and Dowdy appear '*wrapped in a blanket*' and '*in a nightgown*' (p. 169). Urania and Freedom know just how to treat each person according to their merits, so the play concludes with an image of overarching middle-class control that complements Charlotte's example of aristocratic command.

THE CITY, CAPITAL AND RISK

As a crossroads of commercial exchange, the City appeals as a place of opportunity. The City, rather than the royal household, was the powerhouse of the capital after the Great Fire. 'Sir Tho[mas] Greshams Statue' at the Royal Exchange 'remaine'd intire, when all those of the Kings since the Conquest were broken to pieces,' commentators noted.[68] *Great Britains glory, or A brief description of the present state, splendor and magnificence of the Royal Exchange* (1672) introduces the City as a glorious landscape: 'Come Reader then, let us joyn hand in hand, / And take a view of this rich Piece of Land.'[69] Like the garden analysed in chapter 2, the Royal Exchange can be read in symbolic and theatrical terms as site of the nation's wealth. It has 'Walks above, and also them below' (p. 6), but instead of containing natural specimens, they are filled with various man-made riches and consumables to satisfy the reader's desires. The commercial garden even has a utopian dimension like the Paradise of its natural equivalent. The Royal Exchange's different architectural elements hang together 'like Sister and like Brother'. They are an architectural example of economic cooperation to the London population who must also 'Live but in Peace, and all joyn hand in hand' (p. 16).

What place does woman hold in London's economy? Although the text's architectural metaphors imply sexual equality, sister and brother engage differently with the commodities of the Exchange. Shops on the upper walk are occupied by 'great Ladies' (p. 17); purchasing power appears to be male. The author offers to take the reader window shopping 'thy mind for to fulfil' (p. 18) with the prospect of 'Gowns and Mantles' worn by the 'Gentry' (p. 18); stays, and 'Rare beauty waters, for your Ladies face' (p. 18); lace edgings; Jewellery and 'knacks' (18). Although male customers are imagined for the caps, girdles, stockings, mourning and wedding dress, it is women's desires that dominate the market: 'Here they are tempted, oftimes o're and o're / To buy such knacks they never saw before' (18). After the Restoration, women's experience of the City, as of the theatre, was dictated by their value or their ability to make use of financial, intellectual and cultural capital. Female-authored plays set under the influence of the City dramatise ingenious pathways through the economy by characters who negotiate successfully between the poles of consumer and consumed object. These texts often bring together the figure of endowed woman (whether daughter, widow or heiress), and those of the actress and playwright as whore, under the common banner of 'goods'. At the beginning of Polwhele's *The Frolicks* Rightwit tells his sister 'thou may'st make a mistress for a lord, and by thy noble trading redeem my lost estate again and make us a new fortune' (1.1.14–15). His words draw attention to the difficulties of engaging with the capitalist economy after the Civil Wars. Margaret Cavendish's *The Lotterie* (1660) and *The Sociable Companions* (1668) tackle the issue from two different perspectives.

The Lotterie (c. 1660), a short manuscript play recently attributed to Margaret Cavendish by James Fitzmaurice,[70] examines the dangers of risk in the capitalist system. It is part of a sub-genre of plays on gambling, including *She Ventures and He Wins,* where Charlotte 'ventures' on

Lovewell; Pix's *The Beau Defeated* in which Lady Bassett and Mrs Rich bet on card games; and Susanna Centlivre's *The Basset Table* and *The Gamester*, where gambling for love and for money are brought together. Unlike these plays, *The Lotterie* scrutinises the effects of risk-taking at the bottom of the social ladder. For many characters, the lottery for silver plate is a desperate attempt to escape the poverty trap. One woman has lost the rags she sells to paper mills; another has lost all the fruit she had to sell, and another her oysters and cockles. The material details lend a little sympathy to these pathetic characters. Further up the social scale, the gentlewoman who loses her daughter's christening spoons and bowls, and the sugar box she inherited from her grandmother, has enough lines to create a poignant effect. The entertainment comments critically on the lottery mounted in 1660 by Thomas Gardiner, a royalist Civil War veteran. If, as Fitzmaurice argues, *The Lotterie* was presented at court, it would have offered a salutary lesson about the undesirable consequences of such schemes for those lower down the social ladder.

The folly of banking on lotteries is seen when the winners are robbed of their silver prize while they are drunk. They are subsequently subjected to a skimmington ride, implying that Gill has forced her husband to gamble their wealth. However the text destabilises such sexist judgements; all participants recognise the lottery as an addiction. Knowing it is 'a Knavery' they cannot resist the lure of 'a prize', which 'Enters their eares, & blinds their Eyes' (p. 162). The skimmington has little educative power: Gervas announces 'I am as wise now as I was before', and it looks as though the vicious circle could repeat itself (p. 167). Cavendish's lottery players sketch out a crude but fairly accurate picture of the gambler's mentality, demonstrating the crushing power of capitalism for those who get caught up in its cycle, whether winners or losers.

Cavendish makes a more optimistic and gendered examination of the market economy in *The Sociable Companions* (1668).[71] Women's superior understanding of how to make a living in the city means that they are much more at home there than the soldiers. Cavendish implies that their experience during the Civil War, dancing tactfully through the minefield of military strategy, diplomacy and parsimony, is far more useful for urban living than the men's blunt militarism. The Colonel's satiric view of London society describes the cultural landscape of city comedies like the one they inhabit:

You had best Trade, and cozen your Customers, that is a very honest way of Living; or serve and Cozen your Master, or deceive your Mistress, that is an honest way of Living; or to Flatter some great Lord, or Lie with some Old Lady, that is an Honest way of Living, or accuse some Rich Man, to get a Morsel of his Estate for a Reward, that will be an honest Living: or Debauch a young Heir to live on his Luxuries and Riots, or Corrupt young Virgins and Married Wives with Pimping, that will be an Honest and honourable Living . . .   (p. 13)

Women's plotting is clearly more suited to the fashionable city of Restoration comedy than the men's old-fashioned code of behaviour.

The play makes much of the overlap between plotting in drama and in city life. Dorothy Turner argues that plotting could carry positive, creative connotations and that writers imagined it as 'endemic not simply to political life, but to all aspects of social interaction'.[72] Will Fullwit recognises that city life imitates the art of the theatre, but his blundering attempts to play a traditional '*Champion Knight*' drive the ladies off stage. His heroic style of drama, like the soldiers' blunt masculinity, is out of place. London is not the all-male enclave of the camp; ladies are necessary for the 'Intrigue' to work but they will not play the passive princesses to Will's St George. The men can think of no better plan than to recreate their barracks in a tavern.

The sisters of the soldiers, or 'sociable companions', are far better at plotting. They do not follow Captain Valour's advice to 'have a care and stay at home' (p. 32). Mistress Informer teaches them about the *beau monde*'s 'delightful Recreations' including cards, dancing, painting and promiscuity, advising them that women 'are as expert as the Men in those ways' (p. 25). However, the female characters reject the *beau monde*'s romantic intrigues in favour of more daring plots to win the three richest husbands the city can provide. *The Sociable Companions* reverses the usual plot of a younger brother plotting to win a rich heiress or widow. Dick highlights the inversion, telling the soldiers 'the Women's Wits may do you more service then your own; for I have heard them say their Brothers must assist them'. The brothers play supporting roles in the ensuing 'Female design' (p. 35).

The women plot to invade public, male-controlled civic institutions. Peg's design to win the hand of the usurer Get-all depends on her ability to 'outface the Court' (p. 41) and 'out-act you all' (p. 42) in a formal, public arena, with a witty performance as the wronged mother of Get-all's bastard child. Her intrigue deconstructs London's ecclesiastical judiciary with a mock 'Spiritual Court' where the soldiers are in role as its officers and Madam Informer as the midwife in the witness stand. Her rambling testimony makes a mockery of the court's insistence on circumstantial detail as a mark of authenticity, while Will's clinching medical evidence produces a totally illogical ruling from the Judge. The other sisters' plots to trick the doctor and the lawyer also succeed, the latter involving much humour from cross-dressing as the lawyer's Clark.

The men's plots to make their fortunes by marrying Lady Old Riches are pathetic by comparison. When they cannot decide which of them will be the suitor, Will points out 'we shall find it more difficult for all us men to cozen one Woman, then for one Woman to cozen all us Men' (p. 53). This line carries extra irony in that Jane, cross-dressed as the lawyer's clerk, has to help them with the plot by getting Harry to cross-dress and recommend Dick as a suitor. The play's final scene in a '*Publick Hall or Pleading Court*' gives the women the last word (p. 93). Mistress Prudence, heroine of the sub-plot, prays for women's deliverance 'from Young Mens ignorance and follies', their pride, violence, vanity, gaming, drinking, whoring, debts, diseases, bastard children and 'all such sorts of Vices and Miseries' (p. 95). The public setting and '*Publick Assembly*' who hear her judgement endow women with authority in civic institutions and legitimise their public voices.

The financial advantages of living in the capital were advertised to women in a pamphlet of *Proposals moderately offered for the full peopleing and inhabiting the city of London* (1672). It claimed that 'Wives of all sorts' could 'cheerfully induce their Husbands to come and be free Inhabitants of the City' (p. 6), because their own situation would be assured: 'if he dye without Issue, the Widdow enjoys half his Estate, and if with Children, a third part, which the Husband cannot give from her, besides what she secretly secures to her self in her Chamber &c.&.' In spite of assuring woman a place in the City, the document defines that place and woman's activities as private – or 'secret'. The city house was a much more private (in the sense of separate) place than the feudal household with vital connections to the surrounding farms, crops, livestock and the local community. As Mumford argues, it lost touch with productivity and was becoming 'exclusively a consumer's organization' (p. 383). Unlike Mary Sidney Herbert at the Pembroke estates, the mistress of a city household was not at the hub of a productive seasonal economy. Instead, she was one part of a consumer culture, a point illustrated well in *The Renowned City of London Suveyed and Illustrated*:

> Bakers, Cooks, Butchers too, with many more
> Tradesmen stand here, which I can't count, or score.
> In hope of gain here young men trace each street,
> And the grave matrons at the market meet

And mindfull of the main, how to safe keep
Their credits whole, do often break their sleep;
And to this puspose in their Morning-Gown
First in the house are up, and last, are down.[73]

In Aphra Behn's plays city dwellings frequently figure as places of confinement, particularly within enforced marriage as in *The Luckey Chance or the Alderman's Bargain* (1686). At the same time, Behn was a dramatist who was 'forced to write for bread and not ashamed to own it', so she was in a unique position to create plays which analyse the relationship between private and public dimensions of the city's economic life. Judith Peacock has commented usefully on how, for Behn and her characters, the commercial arena offers opportunities 'to enter the marketplace to perform the role of broker herself'.[74]

Behn's comedy *Sir Patient Fancy* (1678), based on Molière's *La Malade Imaginaire*, and performed at Dorset Garden Theatre on the north bank of the Thames, within the City Walls, traces the effects of being trapped in the City's market economy.[75] Appropriately, it makes more extensive use of the more confined, upper-stage area and discovery scenes than any other of Behn's plays. Derek Hughes rightly observes that Behn 'knew how to use the very structure of the stage to represent the visible and invisible walls within which most women still lived their lives'.[76] The female characters are confined to rooms, houses and walled gardens within the City. The male characters have opportunities to move outside, demonstrated most extravagantly in the scene of Sir Credulous's serenade to woo Lucretia Knowell. (Like Centlivre's *The Beau's Duel* this is another window scene in which the woman does not appear.) The spectacle includes a change of set, involving shutters and wings, from a private garden to '*the long Street, a Pageant of an Elephant coming from the farther end with* SIR CREDULOUS *on it, and several others playing on strange confused Instruments*' (3.2.331).

Sir Credulous's pageant represents the exuberant, exotic, Catholic, entertainments that are anathema to the Puritan household of Sir Patient Fancy. Sir Patient sees in it the decadence of the whole city: 'oh *London, London,* how thou aboundest in Iniquity, thy young men are debaucht, thy Virgins defloured, and thy Matrons all turn'd Bawds' (2.390). He attempts to close off his household from the social exchanges of the city marketplace. The plot implicitly defines such failure to engage with urban life as a sickness, and stages Sir Patient's cure by '*a fine City Wife*' (5.737). Lady Fancy's manipulation of people and places to pursue sexual intrigues with Wittmore eventually teaches her husband how to 'turn Spark' (5.735).

Women are instrumental in transforming Sir Patient's puritan seclusion into civic engagement. He finds his house 'besieged with impertinence' in the person of his neighbour, Lady Knowell (2.1.179). To Sir Patient, she personifies the City's extravagance, 'the most notorious fantastical Lady within the Walls' (5.92), and the threat of female wisdom in matters romantic: 'Madam *Romance,* that walking Library of Profane Books' (2.1.179–80). A common association between city wives and romantic intrigue is seen in the epilogue to Manley's *The Jealous Husband* (1696), where Miss Laetita Cross, a performer who regularly delivered smutty epilogues at Drury Lane, addresses the '*Kind hearted City Wives*' as the champions of love.[77] In Behn's play, the female characters plot the intrigues: even the seven-year-old daughter of Sir Patient plays a knowing conspiratorial role (3.2.133–6). The values held by the women are inimical to those of Sir Patient; in the play, rooms, gardens and the City beyond are contested spaces.[78]

Sir Patient Fancy's numerous bedroom scenes of dressing and undressing, illustrate what Peter Holland has called Behn's 'positively obsessive' deployment of shutters to make 'discoveries' on stage. The confinement of the undressed figures to the scene behind the proscenium was, he suggests, necessary to distinguish the character from the body of the performer.[79] The increasingly narrow 'rooms' created by shutters and wings constitute a spatial confinement contradicted by the characters' liberal attitudes to sexuality. Paradoxically, enclosure seems to intensify and unfix desire in the house and garden. In spite of the characters' declared passions, their erotic energies are easily distracted, or redirected. Lady Knowell is obviously attracted to Leander, even though she finally surrenders him to her daughter. Lodowick, who loves Isabella, also finds Lady Fancy a 'charming Woman' and is delighted when mistaken identities in the dark give him the unexpected pleasure of sex with her. At the same time, Wittmore mistakenly courts Isabella, but does not hesitate to build on this advantage afterwards, praising the 'charms of Beauty and of wit in you' (3.2.316–17).

The women are adept at manoeuvring currents of fluid desire within confined spaces. Lady Fancy's improvisations when Sir Patient and Isabella discover her in bed with Lodovick are surprising and funny. She shows similar skills when she is caught writing a letter to Wittmore and in the comic climax, when she manages to conceal her lover behind and under the bed and under her own body. This farcical tour-de-force shows that although a husband may hold the keys to the house and its rooms, a city wife can manipulate the locks and contents for her own purposes. Lady Fancy explains the appearance of Wittmore's hat and sword on her bedroom table as examples of his thrift: 'he being so soon to be Marry'd, and being straitned for time, sent these to *Maundy* to be new trimm'd with Ribbon' (4.3.117). Lady Knowell also challenges Sir Patient's exclusive authority. His refusal to sanction the marriage between his nephew Leander and Lucretia is another symptom of his refusal to engage with the city. She tells him she will marry Leander herself 'in defiance of your Inurbanity' (5.1.125) and subsequently plots to substitute Lucretia as bride. The women's triumph coincides with their release into the City. Sir Patient pairs them off to be married, (his wife accompanied by the servant Bartholemew), and retires to his sick bed and his physicians' attention. Sir Patient Fancy's mock death signifies the collapse of his household as a sanctuary from the wilder energies of the City. It releases his wife from the deceitful role of puritanical wifely modesty to embrace Wittmore openly. The resurrected Sir Patient is a changed man, 'a very pleasant old Fellow' (5.1.716) willing to accept, and even celebrate the values of the busy *beau monde*.

The limits of women's power in the City's capitalist economy is explored in *The City Heiress* (1682), Behn's most overtly Tory play.[80] Its scenes shift between indoor and outdoor settings, including public reception rooms in the households of Timothy Treat-All and Lady Galliard, the private chambers of Wilding, Diana and Lady Galliard's dressing room, and the rooms of Mrs Clacket, a Puritan bawd. In spite of their variety, all the places are contained within the City walls and all are dominated by the same capitalist forces. Expenditure and consumption, like political franchise, appear to be controlled exclusively by male Whigs and Tories. The Whig Timothy Treat-All buys food and drink to entertain his many guests but complains that his Tory nephew Wilding has spent large sums on 'Mercers, Silk-men, Exchange-men, Taylors, Shoemakers and Semstrisses; with all the rest of the unconscionable City-tribe of the long Bill' (1.1.15–17). The Tories make a more substantial contribution to the economy. Sir Anthony Meriwill, an 'old Tory Knight of Devonshire' (*dramatis personae*), approves of his nephew's expenses: 'He wears good Cloaths, why Trades-men get the more by him' (1.1.230–1).

In fact, it is the women rather than the men who hold and accumulate capital.[81] Charlot is the city heiress of the title, an identity that Diana borrows to secure a rich match herself. Lady Galliard is a widow, and thus a woman of independent means. In the first scene, she accuses Wilding of trying to seduce her like a proud conqueror who dares to 'Demand the Town without the least Conditions' (1.1.324–5). The street setting gives urban substance to the trope of woman as 'Town', and Lady Galliard's words are an accurate description of Wilding's successful speculative endeavours, both sexual and financial, in the play. The three female protagonists reflect different aspects of the City economy and, since all are regarded as prizes by the men, it is easy to read *The City Heiress* as a play in which Behn's primary political commitment is to Toryism rather than feminism.[82]

In spite of their financial independence, the women cannot produce space to their own advantage in the City. Wilding ruins the reputation of Charlot Gettall, 'the richest Jewel all *London* can afford' (3.1.35), by placing her at Mrs Clackett's lodgings. Diana must wait in her rooms, anxious that she may lose Wilding and yet conscious that his sexual relationship with her does not carry any emotional or financial weight 'how far will that go at the Exchange for Poynt? Will the Mercer take it for currant Coin?' (2.2.76–7). Lady Galliard's private chambers are invaded first by Wilding, then by Sir Charles Meriwill and his uncle. She cannot even let Wilding exit to preserve her reputation, since the back-stairs door is locked (4.427–34). In the final scene of the play, her command to 'bar up my doors' and appeal for protection from the Lord Mayor's officers (5.1.367–70), are in vain. The characters enter one by one: Wilding, Sir Anthony, Sir Timothy and Diana, Charlot and Mrs Clacket.

The unattractive hero, Wilding, embodies the fast-moving circulation of money in the City, from whose dominating influence the three female leads are powerless to escape. Behn conveys a clear feminist message about the emotional damage Wilding, and the market economy, inflicts on each of them. Lady Galliard, the most fully developed character, demonstrates the painful struggle between passion, honour and self-esteem experienced by women caught up in the marriage and money markets. From the confinement of a private chamber that has become more like Mrs Clacket's rooms, she protests:

> Ah, what malicious God,
> Sworn Enemy to feeble Womankind,
> Taught thee the Art of Conquest with thy Tongue?
> Thy false deluding Eyes were surely made
> Of Stars that rule our Sexes Destiny. . .
> Peace tempter, Peace, who artfully betrayest me . . . (4.375)

Behn rewrites the story of sin and sexual knowledge from Genesis as a perverse trap of pleasure from which women always reap pain and suffering. The inevitability of the fall into subjection is woman's unjust lot, in the city just as much as in the garden. The representation of these varied but unchanging City scenes in a theatre which was itself part of the City must have intensified the sense of claustrophobia. Dorset Garden was itself a capitalist investment:

> Where gentle *Thames* thro' stately Channels glides,
> And *England's* proud Metropolis divides,
> A lofty Fabrick does the Sight invade,
> And stretches o'er the Waves a pompous Shade . . .
> Here thrifty Rich hires Heroes by the Day,
> And keeps his Mercenary Kings in Pay . . .
> Here the lewd Punk, with Crowns and Scepters grac'd,
> Teaches her Eyes a more Majestick Cast.[83]

Kings, heroes, women, and the actors who play them are all subject to the command of commerce, personified by Mr Rich. Performed within the City walls, Behn's *City Heiress* shows that there is no world elsewhere to which women can escape. Even the fashionable arena of the Town is driven by the capitalist and sexist ideology of the City, as represented in Behn's *The Town Fop* (1676).[84] Here, the enclosure of enforced marriage is played in indoor settings: chambers in the houses of Friendlove or Lord Plotwell who control the fortunes of the romantic protagonists, Diana and Celinda. The illusion of liberty, manifested spatially in scenes outside the City like Convent Garden, is undercut by a sense that gambling and spending are substitutes to fill emotional gaps.

By using plots with high levels of risk, women dramatists opted into a dramatic form that mirrored the economic and social culture of the capital. The 1690s saw a financial revolution with the creation of the Bank of England (1694) and the New East India Company (1698). Financial speculation increased with the foundation of dozens of new corporations, some sounder than others, and an increase in stock transactions at the Royal Exchange, regulated in 1697.[85] As Perry Gauci notes, the dangers of trade 'could ruin the individual within a very short space in time, particularly in a competitive business climate'.[86] 'Gaming is an Estate to which all the World has a Pretence', Thomas Brown observed in 1705.[87] Both business and pleasure were energised by the excitement of risk. A love of gambling was a key sensibility of the age with a flourishing profusion of gaming houses and salon card games at which high stakes could be wagered.

Centlivre's *The Basset-Table* (1705) explores how gambling transforms a private dwelling into 'a public Gaming-House', a rendez-vous for a 'vast Concourse of People' (p. 205). Inconsistencies in the text introduce some confusion over who owns the house (Sir Richard or Lady Reveller). In either case, Lady Reveller's installation of the basset table opens her rooms to 'a Parade for Men of all Ranks, from the Duke to the Fidler' (p. 205). Such appropriation of the venue mirrors the shift from household theatrical to public stage: entry appears to be controlled only by finance. It is 'as a public Ordinary where every Fool with Money' including 'many Sharpers of *Covent-garden* and Mistresses of St *James's*' are admitted (p. 208).

More important than the house's disputed ownership is its location in Covent Garden. Constructed by the fourth Earl of Bedford and Inigo Jones, Covent Garden was, by 1639, a piazza fit for 'the habitations of Gentlemen and men of ability'. By 1665, it was still a residential area for the social elite, with 7.6 per cent of the householders also holding titles. Covent Garden is an ideal fashionable setting for Centlivre's dramatic exploration of the *beau monde*. After the Civil War, it became an increasingly commercial place. Its market for fruit, flowers, roots and herbs was succeeded in 1677–8 by a row of twenty-two shops for lease from the Bedford family. At the time when *The Basset Table* was first performed, further commercial expansion was underway as Bedford House was demolished and forty-eight new shops were built in the central paved area.[88]

The offstage Covent Garden setting of *The Basset-Table* is invoked in the first scene: a large hall with footmen asleep, and chairs and coaches drawing up outside (p. 203). The presence of commercial interests is figured by Mrs Sago who, in addition to the commodity signalled by her name, brings into the house 'Chocolate, Tea, *Montifiasco* Wine and fifty Rarities beside' from her husband's shop (p. 217). The city exists as the house's necessary supplement in the culture of exchange. References to social and commercial transactions 'from one End of Town to the other' (p. 203) complement the household settings as a macrocosm of the domestic processes of commodification, gaming and bargaining. Centlivre's texts explore how relationships between the three terms shift, opening or closing opportunities for female agency in the metropolitan marketplace. In *The Basset-Table* when Lady Reveller goes out to the Park, it is for company and self-display in a social market place of envy and desire. She tells her maid, 'the sweetnes of the Park is at Eleven, when the Beau Monde make their Tour there; 'tis an unpolish'd Curiosity to walk when only Birds can see one' (p. 204). Jacqueline Pearson correctly notes that *The Basset-Table* sets up parallels between gambling, forced marriage and trade to explore ideas of self-ownership and the commodification of women.[89]

The emotional instability of gambling and romance are neatly paralleled in Alpiew's account of Lady Reveller and Lord Worthy's visit to a Fair. Here, the 'Raffling-Shop' is, appropriately, the scene of a competitive romantic game in which the Lord and Lady raise the stakes by praising new favourites: 'She redoubles her commendations of the Beau – He enlarges on the Beauty of the Belle' (p. 213). The divisive nature of love as capital is figured spatially: the lovers are forced to part in order to prove their claims. Sir James Courtly and Lucy are also caught up in the competitive culture fostered by the basset table. When he tells her that he would cancel all engagements to play Picquet if her heart were the stake, she responds 'I must like the Counter-stake very well e'er I play so high' (p. 231). For Lucy, privacy is linked to emotional and financial security. She decides to keep her feelings secret so ' *'Tis out of Fortune's Power to give us Pain*' (p. 209). The play appears to endorse her condemnation of the *beau monde*, making her sympathetic and intelligent as well as critical.

Fortune's power to make or break reputations at the basset table creates a fluid social environment, spatially represented in the public household. High social status is implicitly undermined by those who 'play' in the carnival atmosphere created by Lady Reveller. The servants, Mrs Alpiew and Buckle, are self-assured characters who talk familiarly and confidently with their betters. Alpiew hopes that she may 'have a Husband one of these days' only to 'be a Widow' and achieve the same independence as her Lady (p. 206). The interchangeability of Buckle and his lord Worthy is shown when both characters are invited by Lady Reveller to perform in a pageant showing Worthy's anger (pp. 233–5). Lady Reveller's claim that she hates 'every Thing but Play' is more dangerous than it appears.

Lucy, who has a sharp understanding of finance, recognises that the *beau monde* centred on the basset table promotes an alternative, woman-centred economy that subverts the homosocial model based on trade. The culture of consumption and gift-giving involves a lively circulation of luxury goods between the women around the table. Centlivre astutely raises an appetite of expectations about the basset table on the part of spectators by postponing its presentation on stage until the final act. It is revealed in the discovery space, 'framed' by Lucy and James's introductory discussion:

L. LUCY   Cards are harmless Bits of Paper in themselves, yet through
          them, what Mischiefs have been done! What Orphans
          wrong'd? What Tradesmen ruin'd! What Coaches and
          Equipage dismiss'd for them?
SIR JAM   But then, how many fine Coaches and Equipages have they
          set up, Madam?
L. LUCY   Is it the more honourable for that? How many Misses keep
          Coaches too? Which Arrogance in my Opinion only makes
          them more eminently scandalous . . . Madam's Grandeur
          must be upheld – tho' the Baker and Butcher shut up Shop.
          (pp. 242–3)

Mrs Sago's losses at the table are expected, but more shocking is the
'discovery' of Sir James's attempt to 'possess' Lady Reveller's body in a
physical struggle, having lent her money (p. 250). The fragility of a 'feminine' economy based on leisure and luxury goods is exposed when Lord
Worthy steps in to rescue Lady Reveller and Sir James reveals that his
attempted rape was only a 'Stratagem' to further the interests of his friend
(p. 251). Pearson argues that Centlivre co-opts the rake character, with
associations from Farquhar 'for a gynocentric reformist agenda'.[90] *The
Basset-Table* certainly foregrounds an alternative subject for reform in Lady
Reveller, but its reform plot does not promote a feminist alternative to the
commodification of women. Its effect is to expose the fragility of women's
attempts to subvert the homosocial world of exchange. The alternative
feminine economy of leisure, based on consumption, gift giving and
gambling, is unsound, as the fate of Mrs Sago shows to any female spectator
wishing to speculate in the city.

Nevertheless, women's confidence on the city stages, and the city
beyond, is clear by the time Centlivre is writing. Her companion play to
The Basset-Table, The Gamester (1705), which ran for over fifty years, shows
the multiple ways in which a female dramatist could manipulate the
distinctive features of urban setting, the architecture of the stage and the
culture of London theatre.[91] Besides exploring gambling, it addresses many
of the issues already examined here: visibility and framing, women's
engagement with public space, their journeys across the city and their skills
in plotting, their struggles to write themselves as active subjects. Discussion
of *The Gamester* therefore provides an opportunity to review the prominent
features of women's drama in the city.

The heroine of Centlivre's play is named Angelica. Like her predecessor
in Behn's *The Rover Part I,* she interrogates the theatre of visibility that
threatened to dissect the female actor, just as, in literary culture, the

troubadour's blazon fragmented the person of the beloved into body fragments. Centlivre self-consciously plays with framing in *The Gamester*, opening, somewhat surprisingly, with a non-picture of the rake-hero Valere. Angelica's servant, Mrs Favourite, demands to see him, but his servant refuses to draw the shutters or curtains to the bedroom (or up-stage area) where he is asleep. As if in parody of *The Rover*, Hector asks 'would you speak with my Master in *propria Persona*, or with his Picture?' and then gives her an unflattering description of 'his Picture just as he'll appear this Morning' (p. 134). The play's opening seems to deny the gaze to women, reserving them as objects of the male eyes, as Frances Boothby's *Marcelia* had done over thirty years earlier. *The Gamester* re-engages with the problem of how women's drama operates in male-owned theatre spaces, a problem that can be traced back through Restoration drama to the entertainments of Henrietta Maria and Anna of Denmark. Their experiences of trying to produce female-centred space in venues such as Charles's and James's Banqueting Houses and palaces continued, in a different way, for early professional female dramatists learning to work within the theatre's commercial, architectural and traditional dra-matic frameworks. The dominance of a courtly gaze in theatres immedi-ately after the Restoration made the playhouse an extremely prestigious venue in which to redefine women's public roles yet threatened to reduce them to object status. However, the city context for the Duke's and King's theatres deconstructed the absolute power of the elite, male perspective, and, as this chapter has argued, a series of women's plays, beginning with Boothby's *Marcelia,* began to interrogate its commodification of women on stage. Increasingly, female dramatists and performers learnt to mark out playing spaces for themselves in the frameworks of male-dominated space.

The Gamester's plot revolves around a picture of Angelica and, at first, it appears that she will be framed, contained and packaged as an object of male desire. Valere's gaze anatomises her as he admires her 'beauteous Hand,' her 'lovely Eyes,' and 'soft forgiving lips' (p. 153). On condition that he keeps his solemn vow that he will never gamble again, Angelica promises to marry him, offering him her picture, framed with diamonds. This provisional gift of herself is not as passive or conservative a gesture as it appears. In fact, the picture tests his loyalty and love. Angelica tells him 'whilst you keep safe this Picture, my Heart is yours – but if thro' Avarice, Carelessness, or Falshood, you ever part with it, you lose me from that Moment' (p. 153).

Angelica, like her namesake in *The Rover,* the heroine Clarabell in *The Frolicks,* and women in *The City Heiress,* is a desiring subject, pained by the profligate behaviour of the rake. Her passion for him, despite her protests to the contrary, is transparent when she sees him kneeling at her sister's feet. Centlivre depicts the rivalry between Angelica and Lady Wealthy with skill. Her confidence in constructing a realistic plot line is perhaps the result of a more assured confidence in women's presence on the city stage. In many plays, assertive heroines have to work in groups. The rarer examples of closely observed female rivalry such as those in *The Rover, The Gamester,* and *The Town Fopp* show greater maturity, as do those which present ingenious combinations of co-operation and rivalry, like *Sir Patient Fancy* and Ariadne's *She Ventures and He Wins.* The city is an ideal setting and venue to explore the emotional costs of a competitive marriage market and to bring these to public attention.

Both Angelica and her sister escape the framing effect in *The Gamester.* (The sub plot presents Monsieur Le Marquis's ridiculous attempt to blazon Lady Wealthy by serenading a window, the same parodic tech-nique Centlivre used earlier in *The Beau's Duel.*) Motivated by their desire, Angelica and Lady Wealthy plot to win Valere's hand. Centlivre, like Cavendish and other female dramatists before her, contrasts the success of Angelica's intrigue with the abject failure of male characters. Hector says 'I shall never dread the Gallows for plotting' (p. 141). In *The Gamester,* as in earlier plays, the plotting woman moves into the city of London as an apparently self-determining subject, negotiating the urban geography like a maze in pursuit of her goal. To contextualise the behav-iour of Angelica and her sister, *The Gamester* presents a selection of women actively engaged in the city market. Mrs Security, the widow who enters Valere's lodging to drink wine with him, has taken over her late husband's trade of usury. Mrs Topknot, a milliner who supplies linen to Valere, bargains just as well as her male counterpart, the tailor, for the payment of her bill. Her work will provide a dowry for her daughter. The depiction of tradeswomen is infrequent in female-authored plays, al-though women's involvement in the economy as consumers is more frequent, and of course, female spectators were part of that consuming public to which the prologues and epilogues often appealed.

Angelica, like many heroines before her, cross-dresses as 'a pert young Bubble' (p. 179) – a gullible innocent type according to *The London Spy* – to travel safely through the city.[92] At the gaming table, she outplays her male rivals. Winning back her picture from Valere marks a key turning point. The love-token symbolises Angelica herself, as material object and as emotional commitment. Regaining the picture is a form of self-possession and emotional self-control: not to lose her heart to a profligate who does not return her emotions, but to choose how and when to give it to a deserving partner. Angelica's new control of symbolic and material capital puts her on a par with the play's two widows, Madam Security and Lady Wealthy, but Centlivre's play realistically shows how the two sisters' freedom is severely compromised. Lady Wealthy rejoices that 'I'm free to chuse' (p. 146), yet her desires operate within the limited competitive frame for male attention. She gambles for Valere, sending him a bill for £100 in the hope that his need of cash will be enough to win his love.

Angelica's use of her capital advantage over Valere also shows the limitations of female agency. She responds to his excuses with a rigorous attack on his attempt to commodify her: 'Is it possible thou could'st be so base to expose my Picture at a common Board, amongst a Crew of Revellers' (p. 189). However, when his father threatens him with a sword, Angelica reveals that she was the boy, and so, technically, he hasn't broken the terms of their agreement – that he shouldn't give the picture away to anyone else. It is unclear whether Valere's distress at losing the picture is because he is sorry to lose her person or her dowry, a wonderful prize to play for (and perhaps with). For Angelica, loving him is the real gamble of the play. The happy resolution, when she gives him another chance, is still a gamble. She has no guarantee that Valere will now reform or love her for herself in spite of his protestations. *The Gamester* demonstrates eloquently that material fortunes are not the only factor to be considered in the game of life. The Epilogue, spoken by Mrs Santlow, points out that marriage, no less than financial speculation, is a dangerous gamble, particularly for women:

> So I, though doubtful long which Knot to choose,
> (Whether the Hangman's or the Marriage Noose)
> Condemn'd good People, as you see, for Life,
> To play that tedious, juggling Game, a Wife . . . (p. 196)

The numerous scripts exploring arranged marriages, extra-marital affairs, and quests to find husbands, prove that for female writers, drama provided a playing space in which to explore what would probably be the biggest gamble of a woman's life.

Nancy Cotton pertinently observes that Centlivre's play 'caters to audience interest in gaming' with its scenes of card play and highly dramatic turns in the plot.[93] Gambling certainly has an erotic charge in the play whose appeal apparently 'unites men of all Ranks, the Lord and the Peasant – the haughty Dutchess and the City Dame – the Marquis and the Footman, all without Distinction play together' (p. 163). The city stages of post-Restoration London offered women the first opportunity to 'play together' with men, 'without Distinction' between the public and private arenas supposedly appropriate to their genders. Stepping out onto those city stages was a big gamble for women writers and performers, whose work had previously been confined to the private realms of home, garden, court, and convent or academy. The dangers of being objectified and abused were no less real on the stage than the traps which women had to avoid when moving through the markets and streets of the city.

What the plays show, again and again, is resilient energy in confronting the dangers of exposure, in order to chart new possibilities for women. Female playwrights who chose to set or stage their scenes in the city were no less opportunistic than the rakes of Restoration comedy. They seized on the possibilities offered by their urban environments. Working within commercial arenas meant calculating, playing to, and playing with, the changing tastes of the self-selecting public. Every production is a gamble, but for women whose recorded performance history had been in non-commercial arenas like the household, the garden, the court or the convent, moving into the professional theatre was an even bigger gamble. To perform or write for such a mercurial audience in those fluid, ludic spaces, was to place one's fortune precariously on the hazard. The plots of *The Frolicks, The Rover, Sir Patient Fancy, She Ventures and He Wins,* to name but a few, feature heroines who gamble. The heroine taking risks – placing her fortune on the hazard – is the essence of the plays' dramatic appeal. Centlivre's plays, post 1700, explicitly formalise risk-taking as part of a wider economic pattern originating in the City.

As I observed at the beginning of this book, Henri Lefebvre reads space as a gamble: 'a *stake*, the locus of projects and actions deployed as part of specific strategies, and hence also the object of *wagers* on the future – wagers which are articulated, if never completely'.[94] In the preceding five chapters, I have explored how women writers and performers transformed a range of given places into spaces of possibility where they could articulate their different experiences of the present and wager on their imagined versions of the future. Each place: home, garden, court, city, convent, and female academy, offers a mass of multiple but distinctive cultural meanings. Home, woman's place, but also the place in which she could feel abandoned and homeless, could be reconfigured through scripts that challenged the gendered demarcation of public and private arenas.

Domestic playing spaces converted house work into play, often as part of a wider pattern to restore something of the fullness of a lost *chora* or maternal home. The garden outside was an apt venue to stage women's move into a public arena. The multi-layered significance of the garden setting as a physical, social, psychological and spiritual nursery meant it readily accommodated emotional journeys into romance, conservative retreats into the past, and radical re-appropriations of the traditional associations between women and nature.

In the Court, royal and noblewomen learned to use the most powerful theatres in the kingdom to re-negotiate women's positions in a culture of spectacle and silence. Continental traditions of female performance helped the Stuart queens consort to re-invent the female courts of their Tudor predecessors within the structures of masculine absolutism. Women's convents and academies were sites of withdrawal, alternatives to mainstream society. In drama that was invariably didactic, sororal settings and venues encouraged women to foster feminist political awareness and the prioritisation of sisterly feelings. Moving into the city was an entirely new venture for women's drama. Entry into a commercial arena immersed female playwrights and actors in a marketplace of financial and cultural exchange where their increased visibility established a public presence for women.

In moving from one place to another, from inside to outside, the book has tried to open up some of the possibilities these sites offered to women when they were put into play(s) as settings or venues. Although the later chapters frequently make reference to what has gone before, it is important to recognise that they do not trace a narrative of progress. Each place offers particular opportunities for women's dramatic activities and imposes specific limitations on them. The deployment of those places as settings allows women players and playwrights to re-imagine their own cultural positioning. The emplacement of those settings within venues that carry their own meanings invariably creates new layers of significance to the performance of the scenes. What emerges is a highly complex network of energies at work (or at play) in each text. To harness those energies was, and still is, a hazardous, exciting business. Valere believes that 'a Gamester's Hand is the Philosopher's Stone, that turns all it touches into Gold' (p. 163). The early women whose fingers wrote, or whose bodies and voices brought a scene to life, were gamesters who performed a daring spatial alchemy. The crucible of drama could often be dangerous but it could also transform the dull metal of one's given place into the golden possibilities of space.

Notes

INTRODUCTION

1 Henri Lefebvre, *The Production of Space*, trans. Donald Nicholson-Smith (Oxford: Basil Blackwell, 1991), pp. 142–3.

2 Gay McAuley, *Space in Performance: Making Meaning in the Theatre* (Ann Arbor: University of Michigan Press, 1999), p. 219.

3 Michel De Certeau, *The Practice of Everyday Life*, trans. Steven Rendall (Berkeley: University of California Press, 1984), pp. 117–22.

4 A useful survey is given by J. E. Malpas, *Place and Experience: A Philosophical Topography* (Cambridge: Cambridge University Press, 1999), p. 10.

5 See Roger Chartier, 'Leisure and Sociability: Reading Aloud in Early Modern Europe', in *Urban Life in the Renaissance*, ed. Susan Zimmerman and Ronald Weismann (Newark: University of Delaware Press, 1989), pp. 103–20.

6 Lady Mary Wroth, *The Countess of Montgomerie's Urania* (London, 1621), Book 1, p. 102. Cavendish, *Playes* (1662), A3, *Sociable Letters* (London, 1664), pp. 362–3.

7 Hanna Scolnicov, *Woman's Theatrical Space* (Cambridge: Cambridge University Press, 1994), p. 1.

8 There is no sustained discussion of spatial practice in women's drama but various pieces have begun to address issues of performance, and to explore the importance of place. An interdisciplinary research project, set up in 1994, explored the performability of texts. See Alison Findlay, Stephanie Hodgson-Wright and Gweno Williams, 'The Play is ready to be Acted: Women and Dramatic Production 1570–1670', *Women's Writing* 6: 1 (1999), 129–49, a video: *Women Dramatists 1550–1670: Plays in Performance* (Lancaster: Lancaster University Television, 1999), and a book: *Women and Dramatic Production 1550–1700* (Pearson, 2000). On the importance of place see, for example, Marion Wynne-Davies, ' "My seeled chamber and dark parlour room": The English Country House and Renaissance Women Dramatists', in *Readings in Renaissance Women's Drama*, ed. S. P. Cerasano and Marion Wynne-Davies (London: Routledge, 1998), pp. 60–8.

9 Clare McManus, *Women on the Renaissance Stage: Anna of Denmark and Female Masquing at the Stuart Court* (Manchester: Manchester Univeristy Press, 2002); McManus, ed., *Women and Culture at the Courts of the Stuart*

Queens (Basingstoke: Palgrave, 2003); Derek Hughes, *The Theatre of Aprha Behn* (Basingstoke: Palgrave, 2001).

10 Katherine O. Acheson, ' "Outrage your face": Anti-Theatricality and Gender in Early Modern Closet Drama by Women', *EMLS* 6: 3 (2001), 7.1–16.

11 Karen Raber, *Dramatic Difference: Gender, Class, and Genre in the Early Modern Closet Drama* (Newark: University of Delaware Press, 2001), pp. 15, 25, 27–8.

12 Marta Straznicky, *Privacy, Playreading and Women's Closet Drama, 1550–1700* (Cambridge: Cambridge University Press, 2004).

13 See Steen Jansen, 'Le rôle de l'espace scénique dans la lecture du texte dramatique', in *Semiotics of Drama and Theatre*, ed. Herta Schmid and Aloysius ven Kesteren (Amsterdam: John Benjamins, 1984), pp. 254–79.

14 Margaret Cavendish, *Playes Written by the Thrice Noble, Illustrious and Excellent Princess, the Lady Marchioness of Newcastle* (London: 1662), A6v.

15 See, for example, Findlay, Hodgson-Wright and Williams, *Women Dramatists 1550–1670: Plays in Performance* (Lancaster: Lancaster University Television, 1999), and *Margaret Cavendish: Plays in Performance*, devised and produced by Gweno Williams (Ripon and York St John, 2004).

16 Lefebvre, *The Production of Space*, pp. 39, 41–2.

17 Ibid., p. 188.

18 Mikhail Bakhtin, 'Forms of Time and Chronotope in the Novel', in *The Dialogic Imagination*, trans. Caryl Emerson and Michael Holquist (Austin: University of Texas, 1981), pp. 84–258 (pp. 250–4).

19 Anne Ubersfeld, *Reading Theatre*, trans. Frank Collins (Toronto: University of Toronto Press, 1999), pp. 97–8.

20 McAuley, *Space in Performance*, p. 255.

21 Lefebvre, *Production of Space*, pp. 222, 116.

22 See Findlay, Hodgson-Wright with Williams, *Women and Dramatic Production*, pp. 123–50, 177–205.

1 HOMES

1 Robert Dod and John Cleaver, *A Godly Form of Household Government* (1598), p. 217.

2 Luce Irigaray, 'Sexual Difference', trans. S. Hand, in Toril Moi, *French Feminist Thought* (Oxford: Basil Blackwell, 1987), pp. 118–30 (p. 123).

3 See Marion Wynne-Davies, 'My seeled chamber and dark parlour room', in *Readings in Renaissance Women's Drama* (London: Routledge, 1998), pp. 60–8.

4 Biddy Martin and Chandra Talpade Mohanty, 'Feminist Politics: What's Home Got to Do With It?', in *Feminist Studies / Critical Studies*, ed. Teresa de Lauretis (Basingstoke: Macmillan, 1986), pp. 191–212 (p. 196).

5 *Survey of the Lands of William, First Earl of Pembroke*, ed. Charles R. Stratton, vol. 2 (London: Roxburghe Club, 1909), p. 552.

6   Joseph Hall, 'House-keeping's Dead', in *The Country House Poem*, ed. Alistair Fowler (Edinburgh University Press, 1984), pp. 39–44 (lines 30, 67–8).

7   Kari Boyd McBride, *Country House Discourse in Early Modern England* (Aldershot: Ashgate, 2001), p. 3.

8   Thomas Bilson, *The True Difference between Christian Subjection and Unchristian Rebellion* (Oxford, 1585), sig. S5, Thomas Smith, *The Commonwealth of England* (London, 1589), pp. 12–14.

9   Henri Lefebvre, *The Production of Space*, trans. Donald Nicholson-Smith (Oxford: Blackwell, 1991), p. 85.

10 Kate Mertes, *The English Noble Household 1250–1600: Good Governance and Politic Rule* (Oxford: Blackwell, 1988), p. 197.

11 Elizabeth Grosz, *Space, Time and Perversion: Essays on the Politics of Bodies* (New York and London: Routledge, 1995), chapter 7 'Women, Chora, Dwelling', pp. 111–24.

12 Ibid., p. 122.

13 Luce Irigaray, *Elemental Passions*, trans. Joanne Collie and Judith Still (London: Athlone Press, 1992), pp. 49, 36.

14 Grosz, *Space, Time, and Perversion*, p. 116.

15 See Margaret J. M. Ezell, '"To be your daughter in your pen": the social functions of literature in the writings of Lady Elizabeth Brackley and Lady Jane Cavendish', in *Readings in Renaissance Women's Drama*, ed. Cerasano and Wynne-Davies, pp. 246–58 and Marion Wynne-Davies, *Relative Values: Women Writers and Familial Discourse in the English Renaissance* (Palgrave, forthcoming).

16 The quotation is from William's advice to Elizabeth Brackley, University of Nottingham MS Portland Papers PW 25, ff. 18–19.

17 Jane Cavendish and Elizabeth Brackley, *The Concealed Fancies*, in *Renaissance Drama by Women: Texts and Documents*, ed. S. P. Cerasano and Marion Wynne-Davies (London: Routledge, 1996), pp. 131–54 (2.3.142–4). All references are to this edition.

18 Doreen Massey, *Space, Place and Gender* (Oxford: Polity Press, 1994), p. 169.

19 Henri Lefebvre, *The Production of Space*, p. 411.

20 *The Collected Works of Mary Sidney Herbert, Countess of Pembroke 1561–1621*, ed. Margaret P. Hannay, Noel J. Kinnamon and Michael G. Brennan (Oxford: Clarendon Press, 1998), vol. I, pp. 152–207. References are to line numbers in this edition.

21 The translation's depiction of a Roman invasion had particular resonance for the Countess's household just after the Armada threat. See Margaret P. Hannay, *Philip's Phoenix: Mary Sidney, Countess of Pembroke* (Oxford: Oxford University Press, 1990), pp. 143–4.

22 Suzanne Trill, 'Sixteenth Century Women's Writing: Mary Sidney's *Psalmes* and the "Femininity" of Translation', in *Writing and the English Renaissance*, ed. William Zunder and Suzanne Trill (Harlow: Longman, 1996), pp. 140–59 (p. 143).

23 See Mary Ellen Lamb, 'The Countess of Pembroke and the Art of Dying', in *Women in the Middle Ages and the Renaissance: Literary and Historical Perspectives*, ed. Mary Beth Rose (New York: Syracuse University Press, 1986) and *Gender and Authorship in the Sidney Circle* (Madison: Wisconsin University Press, 1990).

24 Katherine O. Acheson, '"Outrage your face": Anti-Theatricality and Gender in Early Modern Closet Drama by Women', *Early Modern Literary Studies*, 6: 3 (January 2001), www.shu.ac.uk/emls/06-3/acheoutr.htm.

25 Hannay, *Philip's Phoenix*, pp. 124, 120.

26 The reading took place in the Great Hall of Hoghton Tower, England, at the Lancastrian Shakespeare Conference (1999).

27 This quotation is 3r of an unlabelled gathering following I and preceding K.

28 M. E. Lamb, 'The Countess of Pembroke's Patronage', *English Literary Renaissance*, 12 (1982), 162–79, p. 177.

29 John Aubrey, *Natural History of Wiltshire*, ed. John Britton (Wiltshire Topographical Society, 1847, reprinted Newton Abbot: David and Charles Publishers, 1969), pp. 86, 89.

30 On this aspect of the play see Karen Raber, *Dramatic Difference: Gender, Class, and Genre in the Early Modern Closet Drama* (Newark: University of Delaware Press, 2001), p. 97.

31 Henri Lefebvre, *The Production of Space*, p. 248.

32 Hannay, *Philip's Phoenix*, p. 113.

33 *Women Poets of the Renaissance*, ed. Marion Wynne-Davies (London: J. M. Dent, 1987), p. 59.

34 Hannay, *Philip's Phoenix*, p. 130.

35 Lady Mary Wroth, *The Countess of Montgomeries Urania* (London, 1621), book 1, p. 102.

36 See Rosika Parker, *The Subversive Stitch: Embroidery and the Making of the Feminine* (London: Routledge, 1984), p. 6.

37 Women's production of material and literary texts is again prominent in Moffett's *The Silkewormes and their Flies* (1599), in which Mary, her daughter Anne and her gentlewomen are characterised as models of feminine industry. See especially G3–G3v.

38 Mary Sidney Herbert, *Collected Works*, vol. 2, p. 269.

39 Margaret P. Hannay, '"House-Confined Maids": The Presentation of Women's Role in the Psalmes of the Countess of Pembroke', *English Literary Renaissance*, 24 (1994), 44–71, p. 69.

40 Lamb, *Gender and Authorship*, p. 141.

41 Samuel Brandon, *The Tragicomedy of the Vertuous Octavia* (London, 1598). Samuel Daniel, *Complete Works in Verse and Prose*, ed. Alexander Grosart (New York, 1963), vol. 1, p. 117. Daniel's epistle was dedicated to the Countess of Cumberland. Brandon's letters were dedicated to Maria Thynne, Lady of Longleat, nearby to Wilton, and his play was dedicated to her mother, Lady Lucy Audeley who had encouraged the match with

Thomas Thynne. See Alison D. Wall, *Two Elizabethan Women: The Correspondence of Joan and Maria Thynne 1575–1611*, Wiltshire Record Society, vol. 38 (Devizes, 1983).

42 Lamb, *Gender and Authorship*, p. 127.

43 Marta Straznicky, ' "Profane Social Pradoxes": *The Tragedie of Mariam* and Sidnean Closet Drama', *ELR* 24 (1994), 104–34, p. 109.

44 Danielle Clark, ' "This domestic kingdome or Monarchy": Cary's *The Tragedy of Mariam* and the Resistance to Patriarchal Government', *Medieval and Renaissance Drama in England*, 10 (London: Ascociated University Presses, 1998), 179–200. Raber, *Dramatic Difference*, pp. 149–87. Rosemary Kegl, 'Theaters, Households and a "Kind of History" in Elizabeth Cary's *The Tragedy of Mariam*', in *Enacting Gender on the English Renaissance Stage*, ed. Viviana Comensoli and Anne Russell (Urbana: University of Illinois Press, 1999), pp. 135–53.

45 Stanley Vincent Longman, 'Fixed, Floating and Fluid Stages', in *Themes in Drama: The Theatrical Space*, ed. James Redmond (Cambridge University Press, 1987), pp. 151–60 (p. 158).

46 Ibid., pp. 159–60.

47 *The Solace of Sion, and Joy of Jerusalem . . . Translated in English first by Richard Robinson* (London, 1590) (c3v); James I, *The Trew Law of free Monarchies* (1597 and 1603), in *Workes*, pp. 194–5; Thomas Tymme, *A briefe description of Hierusalem . . . being verie profitable for Christians to read for the understanding of the Sacred Scriptures and Josephus His Historie* (London, 1595) (B2).

48 Elizabeth Cary, *The Tragedy of Mariam*, ed. Stephanie Hodgson-Wright (Peterborough, Canada: Broadview Press, 2000), 1.6.14, 19–20. All references are to this edition.

49 Rosemary Marangoly George, *The Politics of Home: Post-Colonial Relocations and Twentieth-Century Fiction* (Cambridge: Cambridge University Press, 1996), p. 5.

50 'The Cup of Wrath' is the headnote for Jeremiah 25 in the Geneva Bible.

51 *The Lady Falkland: Her Life* (1645), in Elizabeth Cary, *Life and Letters*, ed. Heather Wolfe, Medieval and Renaissance Texts and Studies (Cambridge, 2001), p. 106. Subsequent references are to page numbers in this edition.

52 *Victoria History of the Counties of England: Hertfordshire* (Folkestone and London: Dawsons of Pall Mall, 1971), vol. II, p. 170.

53 John Calvin, *The Institution of Christian Religion* (London, 1561), fol. 501.

54 Kegl, 'Theaters, Households and a "Kind of History"' pp. 141–9.

55 In addition to its household politics, the play may offer a subversive comment on James I's absolutism in the name of a nation state, perhaps another reason for Cary's swift attempt to recall copies of the play when it was published in 1613.

56 Amy Benson Brown, 'Writing Home: The Bible and Gloria Naylor's *Bailey's Café*', in *Homemaking: Women Writers and the Politics and Poetics of Home*,

ed. Catherine Wiley and Fiona R. Barnes, Gender and Genre in Literature (New York: Garland, 1996), pp. 23–42 (p. 23).

57 The plays of Rachel's older brother and his theatre designs are found in Mildmay Fane, *Raguaillo D'Oceano* (1640) and *Candy Restored* (1641), ed. Clifford Leech, Materials for the Study of Old English Drama (Louvain, 1638), and the British Library copy of his six plays and entertainments BL MSS Add. 34, 221. See also Gerald K. Morton, 'Mildmay Fane's Northamptonshire Theatre', in *Northamptonshire: Past and Present* (1988–9), pp. 397–408.

58 Kent Archives Office, Sackville Mss U269 F 38/3. Thanks are due to Caroline Bowden for drawing attention to this manuscript.

59 *Devon Household Accounts Part II: Henry, fifth Earl of Bath and Rachel, Countess of Bath, Tawstock and London 1637–1655*, ed. Todd Gray (Exeter: Devon and Cornwall Record Society, 1996), pp. 176, 178, 206, 239.

60 *Devon Household Accounts*, pp. xxii–xxiii.

61 All quotations from Lady Grace Mildmay's autobiography are from *With Faith and Physick: Lady Grace Mildmay 1552–1620*, ed. Linda Pollock (London: Collins and Brown, 1993), p. 24.

62 For example: 'Let wives be subject to their husbands' and 'let wives submit themselves unto their husbands as unto the lord. For the husband is the wive's head', *With Faith and Physick*, p. 44.

63 See chapter 2 for discussion of the Long Gallery.

64 Kent Archives Office, Sackville Mss U269 F38/3. The play fragment is written on both sides of a single loose leaf, quarto size.

65 James I made ten visits to Apethorpe, the last in 1624; Charles I and Henrietta Maria stayed there on a summer progress in 1631 but this was probably after the play was composed. See Emily Cole, *Apethorpe Hall, Northamptonshire: The Development of the State Suite with Reference to the Sixteenth and Seventeenth Centuries*, Historic Building and Areas Research Department, Reports and Papers 79 (English Heritage, 2003). I am grateful to Emily Cole for letting me read her report.

66 *A History of the County of Northampton*, vol. 2, Victoria Histories of the Counties of England (London: Archibald Constable and Company, 1906), p. 547.

67 Cited in Cole, *Apethorpe Hall*, p. 32. The plaque is now in Emmanuel College, Cambridge.

68 *Devon Household Accounts*, pp. xxx, xxii. Rachel's account book is reproduced, pp. 169–295.

69 Henri Lefebvre, *The Production of Space*, p. 354.

70 *With Faith and Physick*, p. 24.

71 The play is in manuscript in a large folio volume, probably prepared for presentation to William Cavendish, the authors' father, in the Bodleian Library (Bod. Rawl. MS Poet. 16). All quotations are from the modern edition in *Renaissance Drama by Women*, ed. Cerasano and Wynne-Davies (London: Routledge, 1996).

72 John Cleaver, *A Briefe explanation of the whole Booke of the Proverbs of Solomon* (London, 1615), p. 209.

73 Ibid., pp. 544–50.

74 Lorna Weatherill, 'A Possession of One's Own: Women and Consumer Behavior in England, 1660–1740', *Journal of British Studies* 25 (1986), 131–56, pp. 155–6.

75 See Lisa Hopkins, 'Play Houses: Drama at Welbeck and Bolsover', *Early Theatre* 2 (1999), 25–44.

76 William Cavendish, *Dramatic Works*, ed. Lynne Hulse, Malone Society (Oxford University Press, 1996), pp. 26–7, lines 7–14.

77 *Ben Jonson*, ed. C. H. Herford and Percy and Evelyn Simpson (Oxford: Clarendon Press, 1925–52), 7, 787–814. See Cedric C. Brown, 'Courtesies of Place and Arts of Diplomacy in Ben Jonson's Last Two Entertainments for Royalty', *The Seventeenth Century* 9 (1994), 147–71.

78 Peter Stallybrass, 'Worn worlds: clothes and identity on the Renaissance stage', in *Subject and Object in Renaissance Culture*, ed. Margreta De Grazia, Maureen Quilligan and Peter Stallybrass (Cambridge: Cambridge University Press, 1996), pp. 289–320; pp. 294, 303.

79 Bod. Rawl. MS Poet. 16, p. 23.

80 Marion Wynne-Davies notes this in *Renaissance Drama by Women*, p. 212, n. 51. *A Choice Manuall of Rare and Select Secrets in Physick and Chyrurgery* was published in 1653.

81 See, for example, Lady Grace Mildmay's *With Faith and Physick*, and Kim F. Hall, 'Culinary Spaces, Colonial Spaces: The Gendering of Sugar in the Seventeenth Century', in *Feminist Readings of Early Modern Culture*, ed. Valerie Traub, Cora Kaplan and Dympna Callaghan (Cambridge: Cambridge University Press, 1996), pp. 168–90, p. 176.

82 Gay McAuley points out the significance of passing food from the stage to the audience in *Space in Performance: Making Meaning in the Theatre* (Ann Arbor: University of Michigan Press, 1999), p. 177.

83 *The Compleat Woman, written in French by Monsieur du-Boscq, translated by N. N.* (London, 1639), p. 92.

84 Cited in Nathan Comfort Starr, 'The Concealed Fancies: A Play by Lady Jane Cavendish and Lady Elizabeth Brackley', *PMLA* 46 (1931), 802–38; p. 803.

85 P. A. Faulkner: *Bolsover Castle* (London, English Heritage, 1985), p. 42.

86 On Elizabeth's life and writings see Betty S. Travitsky, *Subordination and Authorship in Early Modern England: The Case of Elizabeth Egerton and her "Loose Papers"* (Tempe, Arizona: Medieval and Renaissance Texts and Studies, 1999).

87 See note 16.

88 Bod. Rawl. MS Poet. 16, p. 127.

89 Ben Jonson, *Ben Jonson*, 7, p. 810.

90 Bod. Rawl. MS Poet. 16, p. 141.

91 Lefebvre, *The Production of Space*, p. 98.

92 See Brown, 'Courtesies of Place', and Hopkins, 'Play Houses'.

93 Catherine Wiley and Fiona R. Barnes, eds., *Homemaking: Women Writers and the Politics and Poetics of Home*, Gender and Genre in Literature (New York: Garland, 1996), p. xv.

94 Margaret Cavendish, *Playes Written by the Thrice Noble, Illustrious and Excellent Princess, The Lady Marchioness of Newcastle* (London, 1662). All quotations from plays in the 1662 volume are to occasionally inconsistent page numbers in this volume. On their performability see Gweno Williams, 'Why may not a lady write a good play?', in *Readings in Renaissance Women's Drama*, ed. Cerasano and Wynne-Davies, pp. 95–107, and Judith Peacock, 'Writing for the Brain and Writing for the Boards: The Producibility of Margaret Cavendish's Dramatic Texts', in *A Princely Brave Woman: Essays on Margaret Cavendish, Duchess of Newcastle*, ed. Stephen Clucas (Aldershot: Ashgate, 2003), pp. 87–108.

95 Sophie Tomlinson, 'My Brain the Stage: Margaret Cavendish and The Fantasy of Female Performance', in *Women, Texts and Histories*, ed. Clare Brant and Diane Purkiss (London: Routledge, 1992), pp. 134–63.

96 Marta Straznicky, *Privacy, Playreading and Early Modern Women's Closet Drama* (Cambridge: Cambridge University Press, 2004), pp. 16–17.

97 *Sociable Letters* (1664), XXIX, p. 57, cited in Tomlinson, p. 136.

98 Marta Straznicky estimates these statistics following the figures given in *Annals of English Drama*, ed. Alfred Harbage, revised by Samuel Schoenbaum (London: Methuen, 1964). See Straznicky, 'Reading the Stage: Margaret Cavendish and Commonwealth Closet Drama', *Criticism* 37 (3), 1995, 355–390, p. 357.

99 McBride, *Country House Discourse*, p. 138.

100 See Anna Battigelli, *Margaret Cavendish and the Exiles of the Mind* (Lexington: University of Kentucky Press, 1998), p. 7.

101 Margaret Cavendish, *The Life of William Cavendish, Duke of Newcastle to which is added The True Relation of My Birth, Breeding and Life, by Margaret Cavendish, Duchess of Newcastle*, ed. C. H. Firth (London: John C. Nimmo, 1886), p. 284; Battigelli, *Margaret Cavendish and the Exiles of the Mind*, p. 20.

102 *Mercurius Rusticus*, 22 August 1642.

103 Cavendish, *The Life of William Cavendish*, pp. 290–1.

104 Gaston Bachelard, *The Poetics of Space: The Classic Look at How We Experience Intimate Spaces* (Boston: Beacon Press, 1994), pp. 14–15, 53, 56.

105 Camden, *Britain Or a Chorographicall Description of the most flourishing kingdomes England, Scotland and Ireland* (London, 1630), p. 450.

106 Max Rooses, *La Maison De Rubens* (Anvers: Imprimeries Veuve de Backer, 1888), pp. 16, 23.

107 Paule Huvenne in collaboration with Hans Nieuwdorp, *The Rubens House* (Antwerp: Credit Communal, 1992), p. 11.

108 Gweno Williams makes this observation about the title-page and the Rubenshuis archway in Findlay, Hodgson-Wright with Williams, *Women and Dramatic Production 1550–1700*, p. 106.

109 Bachelard, *The Poetics of Space*, pp. 78, 99.
110 Cavendish, *Life*, p. 277.
111 Irigaray, *Elemental Passions*, p. 49.
112 See also the depiction of Mr Underward's country house in the subplot of *The Presence* in *Plays Never Before Printed* (London, 1668), and the fate of Underward's eldest sister, Madam Impoverished (especially pp. 123–7).
113 McBride, *Country House Discourse*, p. 165.
114 Robert Dod, *A Plaine and Familier Exposition of the Thirteenth and Fourteenth Chapters of the Proverbs of Solomon* (London, 1615), pp. 77–8.
115 Hopkins, 'Play Houses', p. 44.
116 Cavendish, *A True Relation*, pp. 308–9.
117 See Anna Battigelli's *Margaret Cavendish and the Exiles of the Mind*, p. 131.
118 On self-starvation see Nancy A Gutierrez, *'Shall She Famish Then?': Female Food Refusal in Early Modern England* (Aldershot: Ashgate, 2003).

2 GARDENS

1 Henry Hawkins, *Partheneia Sacra or the Mysterious and Delicious Garden of the Sacred Parthenes, symbolically set forth* (London, 1633), A7.
2 Alison D. Wall, *Two Elizabethan Women: The Correspondance of Joan and Maria Thynne 1575–1611*, Wiltshire Record Society, vol. 38 (Devizes, 1983), p. 38.
3 Aemilia Lanyer, *Salve Deus Rex Judaeorum* (1611), reprinted in *Women's Writing of the Early Modern Period 1588–1688: An Anthology*, ed. Stephanie Hodgson-Wright (Edinburgh: Edinburgh University Press, 2002), pp. 20–77, p. 73.
4 Lanyer takes up the familiar trope of garden as paradise, but radically rewrites the tree of knowledge in a 'stately' oak under which 'many a learned book was read and scanned' (p. 76) by the women.
5 Lady Mary Wroth, *The Countess of Montgomeries Urania* (London, 1621), pp. 74–6.
6 Sir Hugh Plat, *Floraes Paradise* (London, 1608), pp. 8–9.
7 Michel Foucault, 'Of Other Spaces', *Diacritics* 16 (1986), 22–7, pp. 24–5.
8 Roy Strong, *The Renaissance Garden in England* (London: Thames and Hudson, Ltd, 1998), p. 15.
9 Scott Wilson, 'Love and the Labyrinth: Sir Philip Sidney and the Extraordinary forms of Desire', *Assays* 7 (1992), 43–69, pp. 57–8.
10 Sir Henry Wotton, *The Elements of Architecture* (London, 1624), p. 109.
11 *A Gardener's Labyrinth: Portraits of People, Plants and Places*, ed. Tessa Traeger and Patrick Kinmonth (London: Booth Clibborn Editions, 2003), p. 100.
12 Wotton, *Elements of Architecture*, pp. 109–10.
13 Simon Pugh, *Garden, Nature, Language* (Manchester: Manchester University Press, 1988).
14 *The Argument of the Pastorall of 'Florimène' with the Discription of the Scoenes and Intermedij* (London, 1635), p. 7.

15 Brian Stock, 'Reading, Community and A Sense of Place', in *Place / Culture / Representation*, ed. James Duncan and David Ley (London: Routledge, 1993), pp. 314–28 (p. 320).

16 Lady Jane Lumley's translation of Euripides' *Tragedie of Iphigenia* exists in a unique manuscript, British Library MS Royal 15. A IX Lumley. All quotations and line references are from *Three Tragedies by Renaissance Women*, ed. Diane Purkiss (Harmondsworth: Penguin, 1998), pp. 1–35.

17 Alison Findlay and Stephanie Hodgson-Wright with Gweno Williams, *Women and Dramatic Production 1550–1700* (Harlow: Pearson Education, 2000), pp. 21–2.

18 John Dent, *The Quest for Nonsuch* (Sutton: London Borough of Sutton Libraries and Arts Services, 1981), pp. 63–4. Roy Strong dates Lumley's changes to the garden to 1579–91 in *Renaissance Garden in England*, p. 64.

19 Dent, *Quest for Nonsuch*, p. 145.

20 Marion Wynne-Davies, 'The Good Lady Lumley's Desire: *Iphigenia* and the Nonsuch Banqueting House', in *Women and Drama in England and Spain 1500–1700*, ed. Rina Walthaus, Marguerite Corporaal and Helen Wilcox (Kassel: Reichenberger, forthcoming).

21 See Stephanie Hodgson-Wright, 'Jane Lumley's *Iphigenia at Aulis: multum in parvo*, or, less is more', in *Readings in Renaissance Women's Drama*, ed. S. P. Cerasano and Marion Wynne-Davies (London and New York: Routledge, 1998), pp. 129–41.

22 *The Diary of Henry Machyn* (BM Cotton MS Vitellius F. v), ed. J. G. Nichols (London: Camden Society, 1848), p. 206.

23 See James Shapiro, *Children of the Revels: the boy companies of Shakespeare's time and their plays* (New York: Columbia University Press, 1977), p. 12. Shapiro points out that as well as being a writer, John Heywood probably also assisted the company as an actor and musician (p. 11). Therefore his presence at Nonsuch as the 'master haywod' listed, does not necessarily mean he wrote the play. 'Master Phelyps' may have been the organist at St Paul's.

24 Elizabeth's speech to Parliament, 10 February 1559, in *Elizabeth I: Collected Works*, ed. Leah S. Marcus, Janel Mueller and Mary Beth Rose (Chicago and London: University of Chicago Press, 2000), pp. 56–8.

25 Roy Strong and Julia Trevelyan Oman, *Elizabeth R* (London: Secker and Warburg, Book Club Associates, 1972), p. 14.

26 Introduction to *Iphigenia at Aulis*, trans. Mary-Kay Gamel, in *Women On the Edge: Four Plays by Euripides*, ed. Ruth Blondell, Mary-Kay Gamel, Nancy Sorkin Robinowitz, Bella Zweig (New York: Routledge, 1999), pp. 305–90 (p. 309).

27 Elizabeth I, *Collected Works*, p. 57, footnote 9.

28 See Hanna Scolnicov, *Women's Theatrical Space* (Cambridge: Cambridge University Press, 1994), p. 11.

29 See Timothy Mowl, *Elizabethan and Jacobean Style* (London: Phaidon Press, 2003), p. 76.

30 Dent, *Quest for Nonsuch*, p. 60.

31 Elizabeth I, *Collected Works*, p. 57.

32 Patricia Fumerton, *Cultural Aesthetics: Renaissance Literature and the Practice of Social Ornament* (Chicago: University of Chicago Press, 1991), p. 122.

33 Ibid., p. 136.

34 *Speeches Delivered to Her Majestie This Last Progresse, at the Right Honourable Lady Russels, at Bissam, the Right Honourable the Lorde Chandos at Sudley, at the Right Honourable Lord Norris, at Ricorte* (Oxford: Joseph Barnes, 1592).

35 Catherine Nash, 'Reclaiming Vision: Looking at Landscape and the Body', *Gender Place and Culture: A Journal of Feminist Geography*, 3: 2 (1996), 149–70.

36 Thomasina Beck, *Gardening with Silk and Gold: A History of Gardens in Embroidery* (Newton Abbot: David and Charles, 1997); Strong, *The Renaissance Garden in England*, p. 42.

37 See Alexandra F. Johnston, ' "The Lady of the farme" ': The Context of Lady Russell's Entertainment of Elizabeth at Bisham, 1592', *Early Theatre* 5: 2 (2002), 70–85.

38 Mary Sidney, 'A Dialogue Between Two Shepherds: Thenot and Piers', in *The Collected Works of Mary Sidney Herbert, Countess of Pembroke*, vol. 1, ed. Margaret Patterson Hannay, Noel J. Kinammon and Michael G. Brennan (Oxford: Clarendon Press, 1998), pp. 100–1. All quotations are from this edition.

39 See Mary C. Erler, 'Davies's *Astraea* and Other Contexts of the Countess of Pembroke's "A Dialogue"', *Studies in English Literature* 30 (1990), 41–61.

40 John Aubrey, *The Natural History of Wiltshire*, ed. John Britton (Wiltshire Topographical Society, 1847, reprinted Newton Abbot: David and Charles Reprints, 1969), p. 107.

41 *Sir Philip Sidney: Selected Writings*, ed. Richard Dutton (New York: Routledge, 2002), p. 107.

42 Margaret P. Hannay, *Philip's Phoenix: Mary Sidney, Countess of Pembroke* (Oxford: Oxford University Press, 1990), p. 166.

43 Foucault, 'Of Other Spaces', p. 25.

44 Anne Ubersfeld, *Reading Theatre*, trans. Frank Collins (Toronto: University of Toronto Press, 1999), p. 110.

45 Lady Mary Wroth, *Love's Victorie: the Penshurst Manuscript*, ed. Michael G. Brennan (London: The Roxburghe Club, 1988). References are to act and line numbers in this edition. I follow the dating given by Marion Wynne-Davies, '"Here's a sport will well befit this time and place": allusion and delusion in *Love's Victory*', *Women's Writing* 6: 1 (1999), 47–64.

46 See Terry Comito, *The Idea of the Garden in the Renaissance* (Suffolk: Harvester Press, 1979), ch. 4, p. 90.

47 Sylvia Bowerbank, *Speaking for Nature: Women and Ecologies of Early Modern England* (Baltimore: Johns Hopkins University Press, 2004), p. 35.

48 John Money, *Gendermaps: Social Construction, Feminism and Sexosophical History* (New York: Continuum, 1995), p. 96.

49 Pugh, *Garden, Nature, Language*, p. 130.

50 Richard Brathwait, *The English Gentlewoman* (London, 1631), folding leaf.

51 See Naomi J. Miller, *Changing The Subject: Mary Wroth and Figurations of Gender in Early Modern England* (Kentucky: University Press of Kentucky, 1996), pp. 212–14.

52 Irene Burgess, '"The Wreck of Order" in Early Modern Women's Drama', *EMLS* 6.3 (2001), 1–24 p. 22.

53 Gary Waller's *The Sidney Family Romance, Mary Wroth, William Herbert and the Early Modern Construction of Gender* (Detroit, Wayne State University Press, 1993) offers the fullest discussion of the cousins' literary reworkings of their romance. Wynne-Davies (note 33) traces allusions to the earlier generation of Sidneys.

54 Alexandra G. Bennett, 'Playing By and With the Rules: Genre, Politics, and Perception in Mary Wroth's *Love's Victorie*', in *Women and Culture at the Courts of the Stuart Queens*, ed. Clare McManus (Houndmills: Palgrave, 2003), pp. 122–39.

55 Danielle Clarke, *The Politics of Early Modern Women's Writing* (Harlowe: Pearson Education, 2001), p. 113.

56 Barabara Lewalski, *Writing Women in Jacobean England* (Cambridge: Harvard University Press, 1993), pp. 91–5. Wynne-Davies ('Allusion and Delusion') adds Jonson's lost play, *The May Lord*, and William Browne's *Pastorals* (1616) as possible influences (p. 59).

57 The possible ownership of the Huntington Manuscript by Sir Edward Dering, whose household performed in at least one play at Surrenden, Kent, suggests a wider coterie. Michael Brennan has shown that the Plymouth Manuscript consulted by Halliwell is almost certainly HM600. It is not specifically listed in Sir Edward Dering's library catalogue, but he did not name all his manuscripts. See Michael Brennan, ed., *Love's Victory* (The Roxburghe Club, 1988), pp. 16–20, and Nati H. Krivatsy and Laetitia Yeandle, 'Books of Sir Edward Dering of Kent (1598–1644)', in *Private Libraries in Renaissance England*, ed. F. J. Fehrenbach and E. S. Leedham-Green (Medieval and Renaissance Texts and Studies, Binghamton, New York, 1992), pp. 141–2.

58 Waller, *Sidney Family Romance*, pp. 116–19 discusses Jonson's presentation in 'To Sir Robert Wroth'.

59 Miller, *Changing The Subject*, p. 86.

60 Ibid., pp. 120–1.

61 William Burgess, *A Survey of Penshurst*, by kind permission of Viscount de L'Isle from his private collection.

62 '"Your virtuous and learned Aunt": The Countess of Pembroke as Mentor of Mary Wroth', in *Reading Mary Wroth*, ed. Naomi J. Miller and Gary Waller (Knoxville: University of Tennessee Press, 1991), pp. 15–34 (p. 33).

63 Carolyn Ruth Swift, 'Feminine Self-Definition in Lady Mary Wroth's *Love's Victorie* (c. 1621)', *ELR* 19 (1989), 171–88, p. 173.

64 *Report on the Manuscripts of the Right Honourable Viscount De L'isle, VC,* vol. 6, ed. William A. Shaw and G. Dyfnallt Owen (London: HMSO, 1962), p. 549.

65 Don E. Wayne, *Penshurst: The Semiotics of Place and the Poetics of History* (London: Methuen, 1984), pp. 107–9.

66 *Manuscripts of the Right Honourable Viscount De L'Isle*, vol. 5, p. 49.

67 Henri Lefebvre, *The Production of Space* (Oxford: Basil Blackwell, 1991), pp. 164–5.

68 See John Creaser, ' "The present aid of this occasion": The setting of *Comus*', in *The Court Masque*, ed. David Lindley (Manchester: Manchester University Press, 1984), pp. 111–34, and Patsy Griffin, 'Lady Mary Egerton Herbert as Sabrina in *A Maske Presented at Ludlow Castle*', *ELN* 36: 4 (1999).

69 See Alastair Fowler, *Renaissance Realism* (Oxford: Oxford University Press, 2003), fig. 47. I am grateful to Heather Meakin for drawing my attention to Anne Drury's closet.

70 Foucault, 'Of Other Spaces', p. 24.

71 Barbara Ravelhofer, ' "Virgin wax" and "hairy men-monsters": unstable movement codes in the Stuart masque', in *The Politics of the Stuart Court Masque*, ed. David Bevington and Peter Holbrook (Cambridge: Cambridge University Press, 1998), pp. 244–72.

72 *The Poetry of Mildmay Fane, Second Earl of Westmoreland*, ed. Tom Cain (Manchester: Manchester University Press, 2001), p. 94.

73 Kent Archives Office, Sackville Mss U269 F 38/3.

74 Mowl, *Elizabethan and Jacobean Style*, p. 114.

75 Mildmay Fane, *Raguaillo D'Oceano (1640) and Candy Restored (1641)*, ed. Clifford Leech (Louvain, 1938), pp. 135–6, p. 101, p. 51.

76 See Mark Girouard, *Life in the English Country House* (New Haven: Yale University Press, 1978), p. 102.

77 The names 'Michell' and 'Burton' feature in a 1627 list of the household at Apethorpe (Kent Archives Office, Sackville Mss U69F 38/1) and both Jesper Michell and his father are listed as cast members in one of Mildmay Fane's entertainments (BL Mss Add 34221). On Dick Burton, see ch. 1, n. 57.

78 See Fane's autobiography and his poems about wine in *The Poetry of Mildmay Fane, Second Earl of Westmorland*, ed. Tom Cain (Manchester: Manchester University Press, 2001), pp. 38, 91.

79 Mildmay Fane's 'Vita Authoris' includes the tribute 'She had received a gracious first name from the Graces,' and you would think 'the choir of the Graces had descended from heaven and made its nest in that human breast' (*Poetry of Mildmay Fane*, p. 41). Much earlier, one of Rachel's schoolbooks included verses to 'Mistress Grace you loving and courteous gentlewoman', whom Rachel thanked for her hospitality and praised with the words 'If you continue in grace as you have begun, you will florish more then the roses in theire prime' (1v).

80 Penshurst Place is only ten miles from Mereworth. Sir Edward Dering of Surrenden, Kent owned one of the two manuscript copies of the play.

81 See Emily Cole, *Apethorpe Hall, Northamptonshire*, Historic Building and Areas Research Development, Reports and Papers 79 (English Heritage, 2003), p. 39.

82 *Devon Household Accounts Part II: Henry, fifth Earl of Bath and Rachel, Countess of Bath, Tawstock and London 1637–1655*, ed. Todd Gray (Exeter: Devon and Cornwall Record Society, 1996), pp. xxii–xxiii.

83 See May Woods, *Visions of Arcadia: European Gardens from Renaissance to Rococo* (London: Aurum Press, 1996), ch. 2, and Roy Strong, *The Renaissance Garden*, chs. 4–6.

84 'Poems, songs a Pastorall and a Play', Bodleian Library Rawlinson MS Poet 16, a folio manuscript probably prepared as a presentation volume for their father William (see ch. 1). All references are to ms page numbers. A second, apparently earlier copy of the manuscript containing the pastoral and poems and a poem probably by John Egerton, is in the Beinecke Library, Yale University (Osborn MS b.233).

85 Records of demolition of the medieval 'old Wall' in 1612–13 date the beginning of the reconstruction work, while the fountain dates from after 1628, since it is decorated with an earl's coronet. The gardens would have been finished in time for Charles I and Henrietta Maria's visit to Bolsover in 1633. See Lucy Worsley, *Bolsover Castle* (English Heritage, 2000), p. 27.

86 Ibid., pp. 24–6.

87 *Dramatic Works by William Cavendish*, ed. Lynne Hulse, Malone Society Reprints 158 (Oxford: Oxford University Press, 1996), p. 46.

88 William Cavendish, 'Parte off a Pastorall' MSPwv24, fols. 16a–18a, in *Dramatic Works*, pp. 47–54.

89 Lynne Hulse, 'Apollo's Whirligig: William Cavendish, the Duke of Newcastle and his Music Collection', *The Seventeenth Century* 9 (1994), 213–46.

90 Margaret Cavendish, *The Life of William Cavendish, Duke of Newcastle, to which is added the True Relation of my Birth, Breeding and Life*, ed. C. H. Firth (London: John C. Nimmo, 1886), p. 84.

91 See my 'Sisterly Feelings in Cavendish and Brackley's Drama', in *Thicker Than Water: Sibling Relations in Early Modern Europe*, ed. Naomi Miller and Naomi Yavneh (Ashgate, 2006), pp. 195–205.

92 Cavendish, *The Life of William Cavendish*, p. 141.

93 John Milton, 'A Mask Presented at Ludlow Castle', in *John Milton*, ed. Stephen Orgel and Jonathan Goldberg (Oxford: Oxford University Press, 1990), pp. 44–71, lines 425–6.

3 COURTS

1 *Proceedings in the Parliaments of Elizabeth I*, ed. T. E. Hartley, vol. II, 1584–9 (London: Leicester University Press, 1995), p. 251.

2 *The Works of Ben Jonson*, ed. C. H. Herford, Percy and Evelyn Simpson, 11 vols. (Oxford: Clarendon Press, 1925–52), vol. X, p. 457.

3 Jacques Du Bosc, *The Compleat Woman*, trans. N. N. (London, 1639), A3.

4 Walter Montague, *Miscellanea Spiritualia, or Devout Exercises* (London, 1648), pp. 88–9.

5 Jean Baudrillard, *Selected Writings*, ed. Mark Poster (Polity Press, 1988), p. 170.

6 Richard Brathwait, *The English Gentlewoman* (London, 1631), pp. 70–1.

7 Margaret Cavendish, *Plays never before Printed* (London, 1668), p. 38.

8 See Sarah Carpenter, 'Performing Diplomacies: the 1560s Court Entertainments of Mary Queen of Scots', *Scottish Historical Review*, (2003), 82, 194–225, p. 203.

9 Michael Lynch, 'Queen Mary's Triumph: the Baptismal Ceremonies at Stirling in December 1566', *Scottish Historical Review* 69: 1 (1990), 1–21.

10 Ibid., p. 12.

11 'Dramatic Records from the Lansdowne Manuscripts', ed. E. K. Chambers and W. W. Greg, *Malone Society Collections II* (Oxford: Malone Society, 1908), pp. 144–8 (pp. 144–5). References are to page numbers in this edition.

12 Bodleian MS e Museo 55, reproduced in *Renaissance Drama by Women: Texts and Documents*, ed. S. P. Cerasano and Marion Wynne-Davies (London: Routledge, 1996), pp. 6–12. Elizabeth translates the third Chorus speech, starting from line 600. See *Seneca in Nine Volumes*, IX, *Tragedies II* (London: Heinemann, 1968), pp. 235–41. Latin quotations and English translations are from this edition.

13 Elizabeth I, *Collected Works*, ed. Leah S. Marchs, Janel Mueller and Mary Beth Rose (Chicago: University of Chicago Press, 2000), p. 320.

14 A reference to Rome (line 50) with no source in Seneca suggests that, in Elizabeth's translation, the greedy usurper's unquenchable thirst for territory carries echoes of the Counter-Reformation mission (thus implying a date after 1581).

15 *Proceedings in the Parliaments of Elizabeth I*, II, p. 250.

16 See Zillah Dovey, *An Elizabethan Progress* (Frome: Alan Sutton Publishing, 1996).

17 Michael Leslie, ' "Something Nasty in the Wilderness": Entertaining Queen Elizabeth on Her Progresses', *Medieval and Renaissance Drama in English* 10 (1998), 47–72, p. 54.

18 Sir Philip Sidney, *The Lady of May*, in *Renaissance Drama*, ed. Arthur F. Kinney (Oxford: Blackwell, 1999), pp. 35–44.

19 Jean Wilson, ed., *Entertainments for Elizabeth I* (Woodbridge: D. S. Brewer, 1990), pp. 96–118, pp. 105, 106, 110, 112. Further references are to pages in this edition.

20 *The speeches and honorable entertainment giuen to the Queenes Maiestie in progresse, at Cowdrey in Sussex, by the right honorable the Lord Montacute* (London, 1591), p. 2. Further references are to pages in this edition.

21 Arbella Stuart, *The Letters of Lady Arbella Stuart*, ed. Sara Jayne Steen (New York and Oxford: Oxford University Press, 1994), p. 193. Subsequent references are to page numbers in this edition.

22 See Helen Margaret Payne, 'Aristocratic Women and the Jacobean Court, 1603–1625', PhD thesis, Royal Holloway and Bedford New College, University

of London, 2001. Worcester's comment is cited on p. 45; Fowler's complaint on p. 82.

23 Payne, 'Aristocratic Women', p. 16. *The Diary of Anne Clifford 1616–1619*, ed. Katherine O. Acheson (New York: Garland Publishing, 1995), pp. 62, 66–8, 94.

24 See Leeds Barroll, *Anna of Denmark, Queen of England, A Cultural Biography* (Philadelphia: University of Pennsylvania Press, 2001), p. 139. On Campion's *Somerset Masque*, and the marriage controversy, see David Lindley, *The Trials of Frances Howard: Fact and Fiction at the Court of King James* (Routledge, 1993), pp. 137–44.

25 Samuel Daniel, *Hymen's Triumph* (1614), in *Works*, ed. Alexander B. Grosart (New York: Russell and Russell, 1963), III, pp. 325–98, p. 331.

26 Barroll, *Anna of Denmark*, pp. 139, 141.

27 On Daniel and the Queen's subversive masquing see Barbara Lewalski, *Writing Women in Jacobean England* (Cambridge: Harvard University Press, 1993), pp. 15–44.

28 Barroll, *Anna of Denmark*, p. 34.

29 See James Knowles, ' "To Enlight the Darksome Night, Pale Cinthia Doth Arise" ': Anna of Denmark, Elizabeth I and Images of Royalty', in *Women and Culture at the Courts of the Stuart Queens*, ed. Clare McManus (Basingstoke: Palgrave, 2003), pp. 21–48 (p. 34).

30 Marion Wynne-Davies, 'The Queen's Masque: Renaissance Women and the Seventeenth-Century Court Masque', in *Gloriana's Face: Women, Public and Private in the English Renaissance* (New York: Harvester1992), pp. 79–104 (p. 82).

31 *Ben Jonson*, ed. Herford and Simpson, X, p. 457.

32 See Clare McManus, *Women on the Renaissance Stage: Anna of Denmark and Female Masquing in the Stuart Court 1590–1619* (Manchester: Manchester University Press, 2002), p. 103.

33 Meg Twycross and Sarah Carpenter, *Masks and Masking in Medieval and Early Tudor England* (Aldershot: Ashgate, 2002), pp. 164–8, 179–83, and Barroll, *Anna of Denmark*, pp. 81–7.

34 Samuel Daniel, *The Vision of the Twelve Goddesses*, in *Works*, III, pp. 301–24. All references are to line numbers in this edition.

35 McManus, *Women on the Renaissance Stage*, p. 109.

36 *Dudley Carleton to John Chamblerlain 1603–: Jacobean Letters*, ed. Maurice Lee Jr (New Brunswick: Rutgers University Press, 1972), p. 56.

37 John H. Astington, *English Court Theatre 1558–1642* (Cambridge: Cambridge University Press, 1999), pp. 136, 139–41.

38 McManus, *Women on the Renaissance Stage*, p. 104.

39 On the significance of these courtiers see Barroll, *Anna of Denmark*, pp. 95–6.

40 *Dudley Carleton to John Chamberlain*, p. 56.

41 *Ben Jonson*, ed. Herford and Simpson, vol. X, p. 445.

42 Ben Jonson, *The Masque of Blackness*, in *Court Masques: Jacobean and Caroline Entertainments 1605–1640*, ed. David Lindley (Oxford: Oxford University Press, 1995), pp. 1–9 (20–1). Line references are to this edition.

43 See Kenneth Robert Olwig, *Landscape, Nature and the Body Politic: From Britain's Renaissance to America's New World* (Madison: University of Wisconsin Press, 2002), p. 40.

44 *Ben Jonson*, ed. Herford and Simpson, vol. X, pp. 446, 449.

45 See Mara R. Wade, 'The Queen's Courts: Anna of Denmark and Her Royal Sisters', in *Women and Culture*, ed. McManus, pp. 49–80 (pp. 61–2).

46 *Ben Jonson*, ed. Herford and Simpson, vol. VII, pp. 181–94. The delay in presenting the Daughters' return is discussed by Boreas and Januarius.

47 Olwig, *Landscape, Nature and the Body Politic*, pp. 89–90.

48 Ibid., pp. 92–3.

49 *Ben Jonson*, ed. Herford and Simpson, vol. X, p. 457.

50 James J. Joab, 'Architecture as Virtue: The Luminous Palace From Homeric Dream to Stuart Propaganda', *Studies in Philology* 75: 4 (1975), 403–31.

51 Astington, *English Court Theatre*, p. 114.

52 Gary Waller, *The Sidney Family Romance* (Detroit: Wayne State University Press, 1993), pp. 234–5.

53 Lady Mary Wroth, *The Countess of Montgomerie's Urania* (London, 1622), p. 322.

54 Ben Jonson, *The Masque of Queens*, in *Court Masques*, ed. Lindley, pp. 35–53. Line references are to this edition.

55 Peter Holbrook, 'Jacobean Masques and the Jacobean Peace', in *The Politics of the Stuart Court Masque*, ed. David Bevington and Peter Holbrook (Cambridge: Cambridge University Press, 1998), pp. 67–87 (p. 79).

56 McManus, *Women on the Renaissance Stage*, p. 117.

57 Lewalski, *Writing Women*, pp. 37–8.

58 Stephen Orgel and Roy Strong, eds., *Inigo Jones: The Theatre of the Stuart Court* (London: Sotheby Parke Bernet, 1973), nos. 19 and 16, pp. 140 and 143.

59 Samuel Daniel, *Tethys Festival*, in *Court Masques*, ed. Lindley, pp. 54–65. Line references are to this edition.

60 Margaret Cavendish, *The Presence*, in *Playes Never Before Printed* (London, 1668), pp. 124–5.

61 C. E. McGee, ' "The Visit of the Nine Goddesses": A Masque at Sir John Crofts's House', *English Literary Renaissance* 21 (1991), 371–84, p. 378. References are to this transcription.

62 Erica Veevers, *Images of Love and Religion: Queen Henrietta Maria and Court Entertainments* (Cambridge: Cambridge University Press, 1989), pp. 14–47 gives an excellent analysis of the culture of Henrietta Maria's court.

63 Walter Montague, *The Shepherds Paradise*, ed. Sarah Poynting (Oxford: Malone Society Reprints, 1997). All line numbers are to this edition.

64 See Anna Battigelli, *Margaret Cavendish and the Exiles of the Mind* (Lexington: University Press of Kentucky, 1998), p. 37 on the play's satiric dimension.

65 Rudyard to Nethersole 18/12/1625, *CSP* Charles I 16/12/4 and Report from Rossi to Doge, *CSPV 1625–6*, p. 680, cited in Charles Carlton, *Charles I: The Personal Monarch* (London: Ark, 1984), p. 87.

66 See Henry Carrington Lancaster, *French Dramatic Literature in the Seventeenth Century*, vol. 1 (Baltimore: Johns Hopkins Press, 1929, reprinted 1966), pp. 162–7.

67 Honorat de Bueil Racan, *Poesies: Les Bergeries*, ed. Louis Arnould (Paris: E. Droz, 1937), pp. 962–4. All further quotations are to line numbers in this edition.

68 John Orrell, *The Theatres of Inigo Jones and John Webb* (Cambridge: Cambridge University Press, 1985), p. 81.

69 Orgel and Strong, eds., *Inigo Jones*, p. 384.

70 'A true Relation of that which passed betwixt the King's Officers, And the ffrench Embassaders followers by Occasion of Apprehending Englishe Subjects Papists', *Catholic Record Society Publications*, 1, Miscellanea, v, pp. 92–5. All quotations are from this letter, probably by Sir Thomas Wilson.

71 Ben Jonson, *Chloridia*, in *Court Masques*, ed. Lindley, pp. 147–54. References are to line numbers in this edition.

72 Racan, *Poesies*, ed. Arnould, p. 39.

73 Aurelian Townshend, *Tempe Restored*, in *Court Masques*, ed. Lindley, pp. 155–65, line 268.

74 Melinda J. Gough, '"Not as Myself": The Queen's Voice in *Tempe Restored*', *Modern Philology* 101 (2003), 48–68, p. 61.

75 For the continuation of this tradition and court culture of the Netherlands see Nadine N. W. Akkerman and Paul R. Seilin, 'A Stuart Masque in Holland: *Ballet de La Carmesse de La Haye* (1655)', *Ben Jonson Journal* 11 (2004), 207–58, and *Princely Display: The Court of Frederik Heinrich of Orange and Amalia Van Solms*, ed. Marika Keblusek and Jori Zijlmans (Zwolle: Waanders, 1997).

76 Suzanne Gossett, ' "Man-maid begone": Women in Masques', *English Literary Renaissance* 18 (1988), 96–113, and Sophie Tomlinson, 'Theatrical Vibrancy on the Caroline Court Stage: *Tempe Restored* and *The Shepherds' Paradise*', in McManus, ed. *Women and Culture*, pp. 186–203 (p. 191).

77 Montague, *The Shepherds Paradise*, p. viii.

78 Orgel and Strong, *Inigo Jones*, no. 250.

79 541 lines is the estimated length from the Tixall manuscript using lineation in Sarah Poynting's edition of the play.

80 Sarah Poynting, ' "In the Name of all the Sisters": Henrietta Maria's Notorious Whores', in *Women and Culture*, ed. McManus, pp. 163–85.

81 Orgel and Strong, *Inigo Jones*, no. 507.

82 Montague, *The Shepherds Paradise*, ed. Poynting, p. x.

83 Orrell, *Theatres of Inigo Jones*, p. 123.

84 Ibid.

85 Orgel and Strong, *Inigo Jones*, p. 505.

86 Ibid., p. 125.

87 See Olwig, *Landscape, Nature and the Body Politic*, p. 58.

4 SORORITIES

1 Thomas Becon, *The Catechism* (1559), cited in David Cressy, ed. *Education in Tudor and Stuart England* (London: Edward Arnold, 1975), p. 108.

2 Mary Astell, *A Serious Proposal to the Ladies for the advancement of their True and Great Interest In Two Parts* (London, 1697), pp. 36 and 45.

3 Mikhail Bakhtin, 'Forms of Time and of the Chronotope in the Novel', in *The Dialogic Imagination: Four Essays*, ed. Michael Holquist, trans. Caryl Emerson and Michael Holquist (Austin: University of Texas Press, 1981), pp. 246 and 250. See also Tess Cosslett, 'Feminism, Materialism and the "House of Women" in Contemporary Women's Fiction', *Journal of Gender Studies* 5 (1996), 7–18.

4 Jo MacNamara, *Sisters in Arms: Catholic Nuns Through Two Millenia* (Cambridge, Mass.: Harvard University Press, 1996), p. 6.

5 Barry Collett, ed., *Female Monastic Life in Early Tudor England with an edition of Richard Fox's Translation of the Benedictine Rule for Women, 1517* (Aldershot: Ashgate, 2002), p. 95. All quotations from Fox are referenced by page numbers to this edition.

6 See Sarah Foote, *Veiled Women II: Female Religious Communities in England, 871–1066* (Aldershot: Ashgate, 2000), pp. 243–52.

7 Alexia Gray, *The Rule of the Most Blissid Saint Benedict* (1632), p. 15.

8 Valerie Traub, *The Renaissance of Lesbianism* (Cambridge: Cambridge University Press, 2002), pp. 182–3.

9 N. N. [Laurence Anderton], *The English Nvnne* (St Omer, 1642), H5, IV.

10 PRO SP Flanders: 77/9, fol. 119, cited in Claire Walker, *Gender and Politics in Early Modern Europe: English Convents in France and the Low Countries* (Basingstoke: Palgrave Macmillan, 2003), p. 36.

11 Margaret Cavendish, *The Convent of Pleasure* (1688), in *Women's Writing of the Early Modern Period 1588–1688*, ed. Stephanie Hodgson-Wright (Edinburgh: Edinburgh University Press, 2002), pp. 257–86 (p. 260). All quotations and references are to page numbers in this edition.

12 See Karl Young, *The Drama of the Medieval Church*, 2 vols. (Oxford: Clarendon Press, 1933).

13 Dunbar H. Ogden, *The Staging of Drama in the Medieval Church* (Newark: University of Delaware Press, 2002), p. 145.

14 Ibid., p. 145.

15 Susan K. Rankin, 'A New English Source of the *Visitatio Sepulchri*', *Journal of the Plainsong Medieval Music Society* 4 (1981), 1–11, lines 1–3. All subsequent quotations are from Rankin's transcription.

16 Maggie Kast, 'Dancing in Sacred Space: Some Reflections on Liturgy and Performance', *Religion & The Arts* 4 (June 2000), 217–31, p. 223.

17 Quotations from the *Depositio Crucis* and *Elevatio Hostiae*, and *Visitatio Sepulchri*, produced under Katherine of Sutton's direction as Abbess, are taken from Young, *The Drama of the Medieval Church*, vol. 1, pp. 164–6 and 381–4 (p. 165). Subsequent references are to page numbers in this edition.

18 Jocelyn Wogan-Browne, *Saints' Lives and Women's Literary Culture c. 1150–1300: Virginity and its Authorizations* (Oxford: Oxford University Press, 2001), p. 197.

19 *The Ordinale and Customary of the Benedictine Nuns of Barking Abbey*, ed. J. B. L. Tolhurst. Henry Bradshaw Society, 65 and 66 (London, 1927–8), p. 359.

20 Alfred W. Clapham, 'The Benedictine Abbey of Barking: A Sketch of its Architectural History and an Account of Recent Excavations on its Site', *Essex Archeological Transactions* 12 (1913), 69–87, pp. 79–80

21 Thomas Barrie, *Spiritual Path, Sacred Place: Myth, Ritual and Meaning in Architecture* (Boston and London: Shambhala Press, 1996), p. 11.

22 Pamela Sheingorn, *The Easter Sepulchre in England* (Kalamazoo: Medieval Institute, 1987), p. 34.

23 For feminine associations with the north side of cruciform churches see Roberta Gilchrist, *Gender and Material Culture: The Archeology of Religious Women* (London: Routledge, 1994), pp. 139–45.

24 See Marvin L. Colker, 'Texts of Jocelyn of Canterbury which Relate to the History of Barking Abbey', *Studia Monastica* 7 (1965), 398–417.

25 Tolhurst, ed., *The Ordinale*, p. 99.

26 Young, *Drama of the Medieval Church*, p. 65.

27 Ogden, *Staging of Drama*, pp. 82 and 226, note 12.

28 Susan Haskins, *Mary Magdalen, Myth and Metaphor* (New York: Harcourt Brace, 1994), p. 94.

29 Ibid., p. 169.

30 Margaret Pappano, 'Sister Acts: Conventual Performance and the Visitatio Sepulchri in England and France', in *Medieval Construction in Gender and Identity: Essays in Honor of Joan M. Ferrante*, ed. Teodolinda Barolini (forthcoming, Medieval and Renaissance Texts and Studies).

31 Clapham, 'Barking Abbey', p. 80.

32 Ibid.

33 Haskins, *Mary Magdalen*, p. 134. Paul Lee, *Nunneries, Learning and Spirituality in Late Medieval English Society* (Woodbridge: York Medieval Press, 2001), pp. 139, 143, 146.

34 Elissa B. Weaver, *Convent Theatre in Early Modern Italy: Spiritual Fun and Learning for Women* (Cambridge: Cambridge University Press, 2002) and 'Antonia Tanini (1452–1501), Playwright, and Wife of Bernado Pulci (1438–88)', in *Essays in Honor of Marga Cottino-Jones*, ed. Laura Sanguineti White, Andrea Baldi and Kristin Phillips (Florence: Edizioni Cadmo, 2003), pp. 23–37.

35 Antonia Pulci, *Florentine Drama for Convent and Festival*, annotated and translated by James Wyatt Cook and Barbara Collier Cook (Chicago: University of Chicago Press, 1996); *Saint Domitilla* is pp. 75–101, *Saint Guglielma* is pp. 103–33. Quotations and line references are to this English translation.

36 Weaver, 'Antonia Tanini', pp. 29 and *Convent Theatre*, p. 99.

37 Bakhtin, *The Dialogic Imagination*, p. 252.

38 Lines 263–4. The Italian for line 264 is 'il quanda ti manda il tuo sposa de Cielo', translated by Elissa Weaver.
39 See Weaver, *Convent Theatre*, p. 101.
40 Saundra Weddle, 'Women's Place in the Family and the Convent: A Reconsideration of Public and Private in Renaissance Florence', *Journal of Architectural Education* 55: 2 (2001), 64–72, p. 67.
41 Weaver, *Convent Theatre* pp. 87–91.
42 Maria Costanza Ulbaldini, ms in Achivio Buonarroti 94, fols. 202–76. Weaver gives a different discussion, *Convent Theatre*, p. 195.
43 Ibid.
44 An English translation, *House of Desires*, by Catherine Boyle (London: Oberon Books, 2004), opened in a lively RSC production at the Swan Theatre, 30 June 2004.
45 A. C. F. Beales, *Education under Penalty: English Catholic Education from the Reformation to the Fall of James II 1547–1689* (London: Athlone Press, 1963), pp. 203–4. On Mary Ward and other female teaching communities see McNamara, *Sisters in Arms*, pp. 460–5.
46 Walker, *Gender and Politics in Early Modern Europe*, pp. 38–42.
47 *The Life of the Reverend Fa: Angel of Joyeuse* (Douai, 1623), sig. 5, cited in Walker, *Gender and Politics*, p. 118.
48 Robert White, *Cupid's Banishment*, in *Renaissance Drama by Women: Texts and Documents*, ed. S. P. Cerasano and Marion Wynne-Davies (London: Routledge, 1996), pp. 76–89. References are to line numbers in this edition.
49 Paula Henderson, 'Secret Houses and Garden Lodges: The Queen's House, Greenwich, in context', *Apollo* (1997), 29–35.
50 *Calender of State Papers, Venetian, 1615–17* (London: HMSO, 1908), XIV, p. 412.
51 Clare McManus, 'Memorialising Anna of Denmark's Court: *Cupid's Banishment* at Greenwich Palace', in *Women and Culture at the Court of the Stuart Queens*, ed. Clare McManus (Houndmills: Palgrave, 2003), pp. 81–99.
52 Edmund Bolton, father of one of the performers, offered Catholic sponsorship for a college planned in 1617, and apparently still open in 1620 when Sir Richard Newdigate sent his daughter Lettice there. See Beales, *Education under Penalty*, p. 194, and Kenneth Charlton, *Women, Religion and Education in Early Modern England* (London: Routledge, 1999), p. 137.
53 *A Brief Relation of the Order and Institute of English Religious Women at Liège* (Liege, 1652), p. 54.
54 Traub, *The Renaissance of Lesbianism*, pp. 253–8, 265–9.
55 Jacques Du Bosc, *The Compleat Woman*, trans. Walter Montague (London, 1655), p. 54.
56 Thomas Birch, *The Court and Times of Charles the First*, 2 vols. (London: Henry Coburn, 1848), vol. 2, p. 316.
57 Margaret Cavendish, *The Presence*, in *Playes Never Before Printed* (London, 1668), pp. 14–15.

58 Erica Veevers, *Images of Love and Religion: Queen Henrietta Maria and Court Entertainments* (Cambridge: Cambridge University Press, 1989).

59 Alice E. Wood, 'Mary's Role as Co-Redemptrix in the Drama of the Trinity', *Maria* 2: 2 (2002), 42–79, p. 74.

60 Birch, *Court and Times of Charles the First*, vol. 2, pp. 308–9.

61 Sir William Davenant, *Dramatic Works* (New York: Russell and Russell, 1964), vol. 1, pp. 286–316 (p. 286).

62 The women's costume colour perhaps recalled the convent of Minoresses (a branch of the Poor Clares constituted under the 'Isabella Rule'), which stood outside Aldgate until 1539. *Victoria County History of London*, vol. 1 (London, 1909), pp. 516–19.

63 Winefred Thimelby professed at Louvain in the Low Countries in 1635. See below for further discussion. She or her elder sister, Katherine Thimelby, who married Lord Aston in 1639, could have been the dancer in the masque.

64 Veevers, *Images of Love and Religion*, p. 155.

65 Birch, *Court and Times of Charles I*, vol. 2, p. 308.

66 Veevers, *Images of Love and Religion*, p. 142.

67 Sir William D'Avenant, *Luminalia, or The festivall of light Personated in a masque at court, by the Queenes Majestie, and her ladies* (London, 1638). Quotations and references are to this edition.

68 John Orrell, *The Theatres of Inigo Jones and John Webb* (Cambridge: Cambridge University Press, 1985), p. 150.

69 *Mercurius Britannicus*, no. 101 (13–20 October 1645, BL Thomason Tracts E305, cited Orrell p. 17).

70 James J. Yoch, 'Architecture as Virtue: The Luminous Palace from Homeric Dream to Stuart Propaganda', *Studies in Philology* 75 (1978), 403–31, p. 426.

71 Birch, *Court and Times of Charles I*, vol. 2, pp. 323–8.

72 Frances Lenton, *Great Britains Beauties, or The Female Glory* (London, 1638).

73 Orrell, p. 154. See Orgel and Strong, *Inigo Jones*, vol. 2 for details of sets.

74 *Miscellanea 9* (London: CRS 14, 1914), pp. 34–5; *Franciscana: The English Franciscan Nuns 1619–1821*, ed. R. Trappes-Lomax (London: CRS 24, 1922), p. 23; Abbess Neville's 'Annals of Five Communities of English Benedictine Nuns in Flanders 1598–1687', ed. M. J. Rumsey, *Miscellanea V* (London: CRS 6, 1909), p. 31.

75 See my 'Sisterly Feelings in Cavendish and Brackley's Drama', in *Thicker Than Water: Sibling Relations in the Early Modern World*, eds. Naomi J. Miller and Naomi Yavneh (Ashgate, 2006), pp. 195–205.

76 Lucy Worsley, ' "An Habitation Not So Magnificent as Useful": Life at Welbeck Abbey in the 17th Century', *Transactions of the Thoroton Society of Nottinghamshire* 108 (2004), 123–43. See also Robert Thoroton, *Antiquities of Nottinghamshire* (London, 1677), pp. 452–3.

77 Katie Whitaker, *Mad Madge: Margaret Cavendish, Duchess of Newcastle, Royalist, Writer and Romantic* (London: Chatto and Windus, 2003), pp. 291, 306.

78 Margaret Cavendish, *Youths Glory and Death's Banquet*, in *Playes* (London, 1662), pp. 121–80.

79 Annette Kramer, ' "Thus by the Musick of a Ladyes Tongue": Margaret Cavendish's dramatic innovations in women's education', *Women's History Review* 2 (1993), 57–79, p. 58.

80 Daphne Spavin, *Gendered Spaces* (Chapel Hill and London: University of North Carolina Press, 1992), p. 3.

81 Susanna Centlivre, *The Basset-Table,* in *The Works of the Celebrated Mrs. Centlivre* (London: John Pearson, 1872), vol. I, pp. 199–258, p. 218.

82 See Walker, *Gender and Politics,* p. 35.

83 Judith Peacock, 'Writing for the Brain and Writing for the Boards: the Producibility of Margaret Cavendish's Dramatic Texts', in *A Princely Brave Woman: Essays on Margaret Cavendish, Duchess of Newcastle,* ed. Stephen Clucas (Aldershot: Ashgate, 2003), pp. 87–108 (p. 94).

84 Traub, *Renaissance of Lesbianism,* ch. 6.

85 See Kate Chegdzoy, ' "For Virgin Buildings Oft Brought Forth": Fantasies of Convent Sexuality', in *Female Communities,* ed. Rebecca D'Monte and Nicole Pohl (Houndmills: Macmillan, 2000), pp. 53–75, and Theodora A. Jankowski, 'Good Enough to Eat: The Domestic Economy of Woman–Woman Eroticism in Margaret Cavendish and Andrew Marvell', in *Privacy, Domesticity and Women in Early Modern England,* ed. Corinne S. Abate (Alderhot: Ashgate, 2003), pp. 83–110.

86 *The Poems of Andrew Marvell,* ed. Nigel Smith (London: Longman, 2003), p. 223, lines 258–66.

87 Patsy Griffin, ' "Twas no Religious House till now": Marvell's "Upon Appelton House"', *SEL* 28 (1988), 61–77.

88 John Ogilby, *The Relation of His Majestie's Entertainment Passing Through the City of London* (London, 1661), p. 17.

89 Arthur Clifford, ed., *Tixall Poetry* (Edinburgh: Ballantyne, 1813), pp. 166–8, 371.

90 Walker, *Gender and Politics,* p. 36, citing BL Add Ms 36452, fol. 70 Winefrid Thimelby to Herbert Aston *c.* 1657. On the women's writing see Julie Sanders, 'Tixall Revisted: The Coterie Writings of the Astons and the Thimelbys in Seventeenth-Century Staffordshire', *Meridian* 18: 1 (2001), 47–57, and on Winefred Thimelby's letters see Claire Walker, ' "Doe not suppose me a well mortified Nun dead to the world", Letter-Writing in Early Modern English Convents', in James Daybell, ed. *Early Modern Women's Letter Writing 1450–1700* (Basingstoke: Palgrave, 2001), pp. 159–76.

91 Arthur Clifford, ed., *Tixall Letters,* 2 vols. (Edinburgh: Ballantyne), II L, pp. 30–1.

92 Traub, *Renaissance of Lesbianism,* p. 184.

5 CITIES

1 L. Mumford, *The City in History* (London: Secker and Warburg, 1961), p. 5.

2 Donatella Mazzoleni, 'The City and the Imaginary', trans. John Koumantarakis, in *Space and Place: Theories of Identity and Location,* ed. Erica Carter,

James Donald and Judith Squires (London: Lawrence and Wishart, 1993), pp. 285–302. Subsequent references are to page numbers in the text.

3 Robert Burton, *Historical Remarques and Obvervations of the Ancient and Present State of London* (London, 1681), pp. 1, 5.

4 Michel de Certeau, *The Practice of Everyday Life* (Berkeley: University of California Press, 1984), p. 93.

5 Ibid., p. 94.

6 Elizabeth Polwhele, *The Frolicks or The Lawyer Cheated*, ed. Judith Milhous and Robert D. Hume (Ithaca and London: Cornell University Press, 1977), Act 1, lines 45–50. All subsequent references are to this edition.

7 Margaret Cavendish, *The Unnatural Tragedy*, in *Playes never Before Printed* (London, 1668), pp. 323–66 (p. 357).

8 See Katie Whitaker, *Mad Madge: Margaret Cavendish, Duchess of Newcastle, Royalist, Writer and Romantic* (London: Chatto and Windus, 2003), p. 306.

9 T[homas] P[arker], *A Wittie Combat* (London, 1663). On the Carleton narratives see Hero Chalmers, ' "The person I am or what they made me to be": The Construction of the Feminine Subject in the Autobiographies of Mary Carleton', in *Women, Texts and Histories 1575–1760*, ed. Clare Brant and Diane Purkiss (London, Routledge, 1992), pp. 164–94.

10 John Evelyn, *A Character of England, As it Was Lately Presented to a Noble Man of France* (London, 1659), pp. 26–7, 41–3.

11 See Paula R. Backscheider, *Spectacular Politics: Theatrical Power and Mass Culture in Early Modern England* (Baltimore: Johns Hopkins University Press, 1993), pp. 1–31.

12 Burton, *Historical Remarques*, pp. 5, 116.

13 Sir William Davenant, *Salmacida Spolia*, in *Court Masques*, ed. David Lindley (Oxford: Oxford University Press, 1995), pp. 200–13, lines 409–13.

14 David Thomas, ed., *Theatre in Europe: A Documentary History, Restoration and Georgian England 1660–1788*, pp. 10–12, and p. 60. For details of the theatres and model reconstructions see also Robert D. Hume, ed. *The London Theatre World 1660–1800* (Carbondale and Edwardsville, 1980).

15 Robert Slack, 'The Consumer's World: Place as Context', *Annals of the Association of American Geographers* 78: 4 (1988), p. 661.

16 Gerard Langbaine [and Charles Gildon], *The Lives and Characters of the English Dramatick Poets* (London, 1699), p. 111.

17 See William Van Lennep, ed., *The London Stage: Part I 1660–1700* (Carbondale: Southern Illinois University Press, 1965), pp. 128–9. Philips's translation of *Pompey* was performed at Smock Alley, Dublin, in 1663. According to Gildon's *Lives of the Dramatick Poets*, it was revived by the Duke's Company in 1678 (p. 111). For discussion of Philips, see Alison Findlay and Stephanie Hodgson-Wright with Gweno Williams, *Women and Dramatic Production 1550–1700* (Harlow: Pearson, 2000), pp. 124–30.

18 Cynthia Wall, *The Literary and Cultural Spaces of Restoration London* (Cambridge University Press, 1998), p. 35.

19 Ibid., pp. 44–53.

20 For discussion see Richard Wilson, 'The Management of Mirth: Shakespeare via Bourdieu', in *Region, Religion and Patronage: Lancastrian Shakespeare*, ed. Richard Dutton, Alison Findlay and Richard Wilson (Manchester: Manchester University Press, 2003), pp. 50–67, p. 54.

21 Robert Hume, 'The Economics of Literary Culture in London 1660–1740', paper given at *Leviathan to Licensing Act (1650–1737)*, University of Loughborough, 15–16 September 2004.

22 Elizabeth Polwhele, *The Faithfull Virgins*, Bodleian MS Rawl. Poet. 195, pp. 49–78. See *Reading Early Modern Women: An Anthology of Texts in Manuscript and Print 1550–1700*, ed. Helen Ostovich and Elizabeth Sauer (New York: Routledge, 2004), pp. 439–43.

23 Cynthia Lowenthal, 'Sticks and Bags, Bodies and Brocade: Essentializing Discourses and the Restoration Playhouse', in *Broken Boundaries: Women and Feminism in Restoration Drama*, ed. Katherine M. Quinsey (Lexington: University of Kentucky Press, 1996), pp. 219–34 (p. 229).

24 Susanna Centlivre, *The Basset-Table*, in *Works* (London: John Pearson, 1872), vol. I, pp. 199–258 (p. 211). Subsequent references are to page numbers in this edition.

25 Wall, *Literary and Cultural Spaces*, p. 129.

26 *The Petition of the Ladies of the Court Intended to be Presented to The House of Lords against The Pride and Luxury of the City Dames* (London, 1692), p. 1.

27 Susanna Centlivre, *The Beau's Duel or A Soldier for the Ladies*, in *Works*, vol. I, pp. 59–129, p. 82.

28 Mary Pix, *The Beau Defeated*, in *Female Playwrights of the Restoration: Five Comedies*, ed. Paddy Lyons and Fidelis Morgan (London: J. M. Dent, 1991), pp. 161–234. All references are to page numbers in this edition.

29 *Petition of the Ladies*, p. 1.

30 Johannes Adamus Transylvanus, *Londinium heroico carmine perlustratum The Renowned City of London Surveyed and Illustrated*, trans. W. F. (London, 1670), p. 15.

31 See Judith Milhous, *Thomas Betterton and the Management of Lincoln's Inn Fields* (Carbondale and Edwardsville: Southern Illinois University Press, 1979), pp. 141–4.

32 Judith A. Garber, ' "Not Named or Identified": Politics and the Search for Anonymity in the City', in *Gendering the City*, ed. Kristine B. Miranne and Alma H. Young (Janham, Maryland: Rowman and Littlefield Publishers, 2000), pp. 19–39 (pp. 20, 24).

33 Juliet Blair, 'Private Parts in Public Places: The Case of Actresses', in *Women and Space: Ground Rules and Social Maps*, ed. Shirley Ardener (Oxford: Berg, 1993), pp. 200–21 (pp. 200–2).

34 Henri Lefebvre, *The Production of Space*, translated by Donald Nicholson-Smith (Oxford: Basil Blackwell, 1991), p. 310.

35 'Ariadne', *She Ventures and He Wins*, in *Female Playwrights of the Restoration*, pp. 103–60 (p. 107). Subsequent references are to pages in this edition.

36 Cited in Thomas, *Theatre in Europe*, p. 66.

37 Ibid., pp. 69, 95–100.
38 Edward S. Casey, *The Fate of Place: A Philosophical History* (Berkeley: University of California Press, 1997), pp. 135–6.
39 Collin Visser, 'An Anatomy of the Early Restoration Stage: *The Adventures of Five Hours* and John Dryden's 'Spanish' Comedies', *Theatre Notebook* 29 (1975), 56–69.
40 Marta Straznicky, 'Restoration Women Playwrights and the Limits of Professionalism', *ELH* 64 (1997), 703–26, p. 713.
41 Francis Boothby, *Marcelia; or The Treacherous Friend* (London, 1670).
42 *The Forc'd Marriage*, in *The Works of Aphra Behn*, ed. Janet Todd (London: Pickering, 1996), vol. 5, pp. 1–82, lines 43–6.
43 Catherine Gallagher, ' "Who Was that Masked Woman?": The Prostitute and the Playwright in the Comedies of Aphra Behn', in *Aphra Behn: Contemporary Critical Essays*, ed. Janet Todd (Basingstoke: Macmillan, 1999), pp. 12–31; p. 15.
44 See, for example, Elin Diamond, '*Gestus* and Signature in Aphra Behn's *The Rover*', *English Literary History* 56 (1989), 519–41.
45 All references to *The Rover* are to the text in *The Works of Aphra Behn*, ed. Janet Todd, vol. 5, pp. 445–521 (2.289).
46 *The London Theatre World*, ed. Hume, p. 42.
47 Barbara Freedman, 'Frame-Up: Feminism, Psychoanalysis, Theatre', in *Feminist Theatre and Theory*, ed. Helene Keyssar (Basingstoke: Macmillan, 1996), pp. 78–108.
48 Milhous, *Thomas Betterton*, p. 119.
49 See my discussion in 'Daughters of Ben', in *Jonsonians: A Living Tradition*, ed. Brian Woolland (Ashgate, 2003), pp. 107–20, p. 112.
50 Barry O'Connor, 'Late Seventeenth-Century Royal Portraiture and Restoration Staging', *Theatre Notebook* 49: 3 (1995), 152–64.
51 Spiro Kostof, *The City Assembled: The Elements of Urban Form Through History* (Boston: Bulfinch Press, 1992), p. 194.
52 Lorenzo Magalotti, *The Travels of Cosmo The Third, Grand Duke of Tuscany Through England During the Reign of King Charles II, 1669*, ed. J. Mawman (London, 1821), pp. 315, 399.
53 Elizabeth Wilson, *The Sphinx in the City: Urban Life, the Control of Disorder and Women* (London: Virago, 1991), pp. 9, 14.
54 De Certeau, *The Practice of Everyday Life*, pp. 103, 125.
55 There is no record of the performance of the play, but Polwhele's dedication to Prince Rupert, who was a good friend of Killigrew and whose mistress Margaret Hughes had been a member of the King's Company, suggests that this is the performance destination she imagined when composing it.
56 Elizabeth Howe, *The First English Actresses* (Cambridge: Cambridge University Press, 1992), p. 20.
57 Ibid., p. 59. For further argument that the role was probably written for Gwyn see Findlay *et al.*, *Women and Dramatic Production*, pp. 139–43.

58 Jacqueline Pearson, *The Prostituted Muse: Images of Woman and Women Dramatists 1642–1737* (Hemel Hempstead: Harvester Press, 1988), pp. 100–19 (p. 100).

59 Wilson, *Sphinx in the City*, p. 3.

60 See Anne Marie Stewart, 'Rape, Patriarchy and the Libertine Ethos: The Function of Sexual Violence in Aphra Behn's "The Golden Age" and *The Rover Part I*', *Restoration and Eighteenth Century Theatre Research* 12: 2 (1997), 26–39.

61 Ibid., p. 31.

62 Derek Hughes, *The Theatre of Aphra Behn* (Basingstoke: Palgrave Macmillan 2001), p. 81.

63 *Works of Aphra Behn*, vol. 6, pp. 223–298.

64 Milhous, *Thomas Betterton*, p. 101.

65 Magalotti, *Travels of Cosmo The Third*, p. 168.

66 *The Poems of John Wilmot, Earl of Rochester*, ed. Keith Walker (Oxford: Basil Blackwell, 1984), pp. 64–8, lines 25–32.

67 Michael McKeon, *The Origins of the English Novel 1660–1740* (Baltimore: Johns Hopkins University Press, 1987), p. 169.

68 Wall, *Literary and Cultural Spaces*, p. 27.

69 Theophilus Philalethes, *Great Britains glory, or A brief description of the present state, splendor and magnificence of the Royal Exchange* (London, 1672).

70 James Fitzmaurice, 'English Lotteries and "The Lotterie", A Manuscript Play Probably by Margaret Cavendish', *Huntington Library Quarterly* 65: 4 (2004), 155–67. Page numbers are to this transcription.

71 Cavendish, *Plays Never Before Printed* (1668), pp. 1–95. All references are to page numbers in this text.

72 Dorothy Turner, 'Restoration Drama in the Public Sphere', *Restoration and Eighteenth Century Theatre Research* 12: 1 (1997), 18–39, p. 24.

73 Johannes Adamus Transylvanus, *Londinium heroico carmine perlustratum, The Renowned City of London Surveyed and Illustrated*, trans. W. F. (London, 1670), p. 28.

74 Judith Peacock, 'Writing for the Brain, Writing for the Boards: The Producibility of Margaret Cavendish's Dramatic Texts', in *A Princely Brave Woman, Essays on Margaret Cavendish, Duchess of Newcastle*, ed. Stephen Clucas (Aldershot: Ashgate 2003), 87–108.

75 *Works of Aphra Behn*, vol. 6, pp. 1–81.

76 Hughes, *Theatre of Aphra Behn*, p. 13.

77 Mrs Manley, *The Lost Lover, or, The Jealous Husband* (London, 1696), BIV; On Laetitia Cross, see Milhous, *Thomas Betterton*, p. 93.

78 Hughes, *Theatre of Aphra Behn*, pp. 96–108, gives a good reading of the play's spatial practices.

79 Peter Holland, *The Ornament of Action* (Cambridge: Cambridge University Press, 1979), pp. 41–2.

80 *Works of Aphra Behn*, vol. 7, pp. 1–77.

81 Mark Lussier, ' "The Vile Merchandize of Fortune": Women, Economy and Desire in Aphra Behn', *Women's Studies* 18 (1991), 379–93, p. 384.

82 Susan J. Owen notes that political ideology dominates Behn's plays at the height of the Exclusion crisis in ' "Suspect my loyalty when I lose my virtue": Sexual Politics and Party in Aphra Behn's Plays of the Exclusion Crisis', *Restoration* 18 (1994), 37–47.

83 Emmett L. Avery, 'A Poem on Dorset Garden Theatre', *Theatre Notebook* 18 (1964), 121–4 (p. 122).

84 *Works of Aphra Behn*, vol. 5, pp. 317–85.

85 Gary Stuart De Krey, *A Fractured Society: The Politics of London in the First Age of Party 1688–1715* (Oxford: Clarendon Press, 1985), pp. 121–2.

86 Perry Gauci, *The Politics of Trade* (Oxford: Oxford University Press, 2001), p. 57.

87 *The Works of Mr Thomas Brown* (1705), cited in John Ashton, *Social Life in the Reign of Queen Anne, Taken from Original Sources* (London: Chatto and Windus, 1883), pp. 82–8.

88 Robert Thorne, *Covent Garden Market: Its History and Restoration* (London: The Architectural Press, 1980), pp. 7–9.

89 Jacqueline Pearson, 'Textual Variants and Inconsistencies in Susanna Centlivre's *The Basset-Table*' (1705), *Restoration and Eighteenth Century Theatre Research* 15: 2 (2000), 40–59, p. 42.

90 Ibid, p. 49. Pearson argues that the character of Sir James is modelled on the rake Sir Harry in Farquhar's plays *The Constant Couple* and its sequel *Sir Harry Wildair*, played by Robert Wilks, who also played Sir James (pp. 45–6). The appearance of the names of 'Sir Harry' for James and 'Firebrand' for the Captain are inconsistencies in the text that show evidence of revision by Centlivre, possibly to avoid charges of plagiarism.

91 Susanna Centlivre, *The Gamester*, in *Dramatic Works*, I, pp. 131–87. References are to page numbers in this edition.

92 Ashton, *Social Life in the Reign of Queen Anne*, p. 83.

93 Nancy Cotton, *Women Playwrights in England c. 1363–1750* (Lewisburg: Bucknell University Press; London: Associated University Presses, 1980), p. 131.

94 Lefebvre, *Production of Space*, pp. 142–3.

Index

Lightning Source UK Ltd.
Milton Keynes UK
UKOW02f0824200915

258924UK00001B/85/P